Praise for *There's Always Help;*
There's Always Hope

"Eve Wood's book is an excellent resource to assist on your journey to healing. Don't struggle unnecessarily and lose your way. Read the wisdom contained here and find the way to your desired destination."

— **Bernie S. Siegel, M.D.,** the author of *Love, Medicine &*
Miracles and *Prescriptions for Living*

"This book is awesome—a wonderful addition to this world. It offers welcome relief, hope and healing to all who suffer from ADD, depression, anxiety, addictive illness or even general malaise."

— **Edward M. Hallowell, M.D.,** instructor, Harvard Medical School;
author of *Driven to Distraction* and *Human Moments*

"Eve Wood is one of those much-needed voices building the long-awaited bridge between psychology and the realm of the sacred. . . .This is an important book that should not be missed."

— **Rabbi Marc Gafni,** the author of *The Mystery of Love* and *Soul Prints*

"This is a heartfelt book by a clinician of uncommon skill and empathy. It is a unique combination of deep caring born of the desire to relieve suffering and of practical advice. It expresses how care-giving in this age of modern medicine can still attend to the complete human being in all his glorious aspects."

— **Gregory Fricchione, M.D.,** associate professor of psychiatry, Harvard Medical School

"You only get wisdom this good from your grandmother at the kitchen table. Dr. Wood offers us a road map for our own psycho-spiritual evolution."

— **Rabbi Lawrence Kushner,** the Emanu-El scholar, Congregation
Emanu-El, San Francisco; the author of *Invisible Lines of Connection*

"This is a book with a real soul...I would recommend this sensitive rendering of a psychiatrist's work to all stakeholders in mental health, including students, patients, family members and healers."

— **Edward F. Foulks, M.D., Ph.D.,** Sellars-Polchow professor of psychiatry
and associate dean for Graduate Medical Education, Tulane
University Health Sciences Center School of Medicine

"This book is a must, not only for patients, but for all of us who care for others as well as ourselves. I definitely recommend this book not only to practicing physicians and healthcare providers, but also to medical students and residents as essential to their training as physicians."

— **Christina M. Puchalski, M.D., FACP,** associate professor of medicine, The George
Washington University School of Medicine and Health Services; director,
The George Washington Institute for Spirituality and Health

There's Always Help; There's Always Hope

There's Always Help; There's Always Hope

AN AWARD-WINNING PSYCHIATRIST SHOWS YOU HOW TO HEAL YOUR BODY, MIND, AND SPIRIT

Eve A. Wood, M.D.

HAY HOUSE, INC.
Carlsbad, California
London • Sydney • Johannesburg
Vancouver • Hong Kong • Mumbai

Published and distributed in the United States by: Hay House, Inc.: www.hayhouse.com •
Published and distributed in Australia by: Hay House Australia Pty. Ltd.:
www.hayhouse.com.au • **Published and distributed in the United Kingdom by:** Hay House
UK, Ltd.: www.hayhouse.co.uk • **Published and distributed in the Republic of South Africa
by:** Hay House SA (Pty), Ltd.: orders@psdprom.co.za • **Distributed in Canada by:** Raincoast:
www.raincoast.com • **Published in India by:** Hay House Publications (India) Pvt. Ltd.:
www.hayhouseindia.co.in • **Distributed in India by:** Media Star: booksdivision@mediastar.co.in

The author of this book does not dispense medical advice or prescribe the use of any technique as a form of treatment for physical, emotional, or medical problems without the advice
of a physician, either directly or indirectly. The intent of the author is only to offer information
of a general nature to help you in your quest for emotional and spiritual well-being. In the
event you use any of the information in this book for yourself, which is your constitutional
right, the author and the publisher assume no responsibility for your actions.

In One™ is a trademark of Eve A. Wood, M.D. It symbolizes the imperative to treat body, mind,
and spirit in one, as well as the affirmation that the Divine resides within each one of us. In
One represents Dr. Wood's perspective and approach to healing.

Originally published under the title *Medicine, Mind, and Meaning* by In One Press, Tucson,
AZ: ISBN: 0-9741083-0-8

Library of Congress Cataloging-in-Publication Data

Wood, Eve A.
  [Medicine, mind, and meaning]
  There's always help, there's always hope : an award-winning psychiatrist show you how to
heal your body, mind, and spirit / Eve. A. Wood.
     p. cm.
  Includes bibliographical references and index.
  ISBN-13: 978-1-4019-1119-5 (tradepaper)
  ISBN-10: 1-4019-1119-6 (tradepaper)
  1. Mental illness—Treatment—Popular works. 2. Self-help techniques. 3. Mind and body.
4. Healing. I. Title.
  RC460.W66 2006
  616.89'1—dc22   2005026696

ISBN 13: 978-1-4019-1119-5
ISBN 10: 1-4019-1119-6

09 08 07 06   4 3 2 1
1st printing, April 2006

Printed in the United States of America

In memory of my dearly departed Grandmother, Shirley Weiner, who worshiped God, loved me unconditionally, and left this earthly life having always given more than she ever asked for in return.

May the words of my mouth and the blessings of my heart serve to honor her memory for all time.

A NOTE TO THE READER

I wrote this book out of my concern for the millions of people who are looking to heal and who are getting stuck, discouraged, or giving up along the way. Because our systems of care are broken, many people are getting lost, overwhelmed, or are falling between the cracks, but *there's always help; there's always hope*. My patients have taught me that no problem is so big that it can't be solved somehow. We just need to be open-minded, creative, and willing to do whatever it takes. In order to show you what I mean, I've chosen to share my patients' tales of challenge and triumph in a book.

This book contains real-life stories. At my request, many of my patients allowed me to share their own miraculous journeys with you. In order to assure their privacy, I instituted a rigorous approval and review process. Each patient participated in choosing their own pseudonym and has read and approved my rendition of their story prior to publication; some patients chose to share their stories in their own words and have authored portions of this book. I thank my patients for their willingness to participate in this effort to reach out to others in need. I have altered some minor identifying pieces of information to protect their identities. Beyond this, their stories are completely accurate.

Today, psychiatric illnesses are among the greatest causes of morbidity and mortality in the world. In fact, data from the massive Global Burden of Disease study just conducted by the World Health Organization, the World Bank, and Harvard University reveals that mental illness, including suicide, accounts for over 15 percent of the burden of disease in established world markets.

Additionally, hoping to take charge of their emotional lives, 43.8 million Americans will seek therapy in a given year. As the statistics indicate, every one of us is either immediately affected, or at most, one step removed from someone who is affected by one of these common illnesses. Hence, in some way, this book is everyone's story.

This book is meant to empower you in your healing journey. However, you can use this book in many ways: read it to become a better friend, parent, child, co-worker, teacher, student, doctor, spouse, or therapist. Read it for inspiration, insight, or guidance. Let this book help you evaluate your own growth journey and/or the models of care you have been exposed to or have been involved with in the past. However you use it will be healing, for whenever we share in the experience of pain and redemption, we are transformed for good.

Of course a book such as this could never replace the care that trained professionals can offer you; this book is meant to be one piece in a larger puzzle.

Please do not hesitate to get whatever help you need to grow and heal your amazing self. *There's always help; there's always hope.* You deserve to live a life of fulfillment and internal peace.

My hopes and prayers go with you.

— Eve A. Wood, M.D.

ACKNOWLEDGMENTS

No person is an island, separate and alone. We are interdependent creatures who need one another. Anyone who has touched me, directly or indirectly, has affected my growth as a human being and a healer. Each one has enriched me somehow. To all of you, I am infinitely grateful.

Special thanks must be given to my parents, Glory Ann Wood and Leonard Wood, may they rest in peace, for the immeasurable gift of life. Thanks also to all my foremothers and forefathers for the same. Thank you to all of my patients, my best teachers, for sharing your worlds with me. I am particularly grateful to those of you who have allowed me to tell your stories in this book. You all know who you are even though I cannot print your names on this page.

I am filled with gratitude for the support and encouragement of many people who played a role in the actual birth of this book. You are Leonard Wood; Rabbi Alan LaPayover; Russell Force; Dan Gottleib; Susan Kendrick, my gifted literary agent; Jessica Papin; my talented cover design team at Lightbourne; my partners at Greenleaf Book Group; my intellectual property attorneys, David E. Rogers and Michael Lechter; and my master publicist and dear friend, Cate Cummings.

I also thank my numerous esteemed colleagues who, without knowing me, took the time to read my prepress manuscript and offer support. You are Edward Foulks, Gregory Fricchione, Mordechai Gafni, Ned Hallowell, Harold Koenig, C. Everett Koop, Lawrence Kushner, Stephen Post, Christina Puchalski, and Bernie Siegel. You have all empowered me beyond belief. Thank you for your loving words and moving comments. You have all become angels in my world.

I must also thank my children, Benjamin, Gabriel, Shira, and Glory, for being your blessed selves. Your joy, enthusiasm, and boundless interest in my work helps keep me writing and spreading the word. You four are among the greatest lights in my life.

To my best critic, strongest support, dearest friend, wondrous keyboarder, husband, and soul mate, Rick Isenberg, I say *thank you* from the deepest recesses of my being. Without your faith in my dreams to change the world, I would never have been able to complete or share this work. Your love continues to illuminate the path. I cannot thank you enough for being there.

Since the birth of this book as *Medicine, Mind, and Meaning* in June 2004, more angels have entered my world. While I cannot possibly name you all here, you have all become stars in the firmament of my life.

I offer special thanks to Cynthia Frank and her staff at Cypress House, to Robin Bartlett, Jan Nathan and Terri Nathan at PMA, to Marilyn McGuire, to Amy Weintraub for inviting me into the world of yoga, and to dear friends Victoria Maizes, Amy Brantz, Carol Karsch, Patty Vallance, and Larry Siegel. I am also grateful for my literary agent and friend Ned Leavitt, for my attorney and friend Jonathan Kirsh, and for cantors Ivor Lichterman and Janece Cohen, and all my choir buddies for bringing great music, distraction, joy, humor, and love into my world. I thank heavens for all my giving, compassionate, and visionary colleagues and friends at the Program in Integrative Medicine for sharing themselves with me as we journey together to promote whole-person healing. I feel blessed to have my wonderful new "family" at Hay House, including Reid Tracy, Stacey Smith, Jill Kramer, Christy Salinas, Jacqui Clark, Angela Torrez, Nancy Levin, and Summer McStravick in my life.

And, finally, with awe, gratitude, and love of God for the gifts I have been given, I thank you, my readers, for inviting me into your lives.

Contents

Foreword

I first met Eve Wood at a Spirituality & Crisis Conference in 2003, sponsored by Johns Hopkins Medicine Institute. For over fifty years Johns Hopkins Medicine has been hosting an annual spirituality and medicine conference dedicated to the discussion of ministering to both the physical and spiritual needs of patients. The conference includes clergy, physicians, surgeons, psychologists, psychiatrists, nurses, social workers, as well as many others who deal with the physical, mental, and spiritual well-being of our culture.

I gave two talks at that conference. The first was a professional perspective on Spirituality and Crisis, and the second was a personal perspective on the same topic.

Eve Wood approached me after my first lecture. I was seated at a table with other keynote speakers, meeting and greeting the attendees. After waiting some time to speak to me, she approached to tell me how much she had connected to what I had been saying during my talk. She explained that her clinical work was about the integration of traditional psychiatric practices, as well as more avant-garde spiritual ideas, and that my lecture had resonated with her own experience. We spoke for a little while, and then she asked if I would be willing to read something she was working on, and if it was at all possible for me to give her some feedback on it.

I explained to Eve that, although I was flattered, I tended not to do that. I find it rather difficult to accommodate all the requests I receive, and have made a practice of declining those where I have not personally been involved in the work or manuscript itself. Eve, ever gracious, said she understood this entirely.

Nonetheless, we continued to talk, touching upon a number of different topics, including our respective ideas about medicine and healing. Apparently, one of the experiences I had shared in my lecture had reminded her of one of the patients she had been treating in her clinical practice.

The story I had shared was about an infant, but a few days old, whom I had treated thirty years before while I was Surgeon-in-Chief of the Children's Hospital of Philadelphia. The parents had brought the baby to me in what seemed like a last-ditch effort to save their child's life. The little boy suffered from multiple congenital abnormalities, several of them incompatible with life, and his parents had been told by four other surgeons that it was absolutely impossible to save him. Indeed, the parents were advised to let their child pass away peacefully in the corner of the hospital nursery. They were clearly distraught and devastated by the news, but still found the resolve to continue looking for a surgeon who was at least willing to try. They asked me if I would be willing to operate on their baby, and if it was possible to save his life.

I examined the infant, and realized that this was a serious undertaking. While any one of these anomalies was repairable, there were so many of them that it did seem unlikely that the child could be saved. And yet, I wondered why it wouldn't be possible to treat the child step-by-step, operating on the most threatening issues first, and slowly but surely correcting all of the abnormalities over a lengthy period of time. I explained the risks involved in such an endeavor, and how I would have to bring in other doctors to do procedures that were outside of my expertise. The parents decided to proceed.

It took over fifty operations, spanning the course of many years, but the child lived. In fact, that child went on, after college, to graduate as a minister from Westminster Theological Seminary. I have followed his education closely. I contacted as many of the surgeons who had helped me in this process as I could find. I wanted them to know the wonderful turn of events and recognize the role they had played in saving the life of that little boy.

For Eve, this story reminded her of her patient, Gillie. As you read this book, you will likely see the similarities as well. Like the little boy I treated, it seemed that few of Gillie's therapists had actually tried to cure her. Instead, they seemed to accept that her biology and circumstances were her destiny, and while surely trying to make her life more comfortable, they continued to treat her for years without believing there would ever be an end to her suffering.

As Eve told me about her experiences with Gillie—the many challenges, as well as the many rewards—I realized that she and I were very similar creatures. Neither of us was afraid to risk our reputations if it meant helping a patient; nor did we take our task as physicians lightly. Both of us tend to look past the diagnoses and illness, in order to see and realize the potential for a healthy, happy life. We do not choose to become mired in the challenges of a task, but rather look for intuitive, creative ways to find solutions, regardless of how daunting that task might be. Finally, Eve and I share the sense that there is something larger than ourselves involved in the healing process; and that faith belongs in the doctor's bag as much as a scalpel, a stethoscope, or a prescription pad.

In short, Eve had convinced me that this was a book worth looking at.

I have seldom been so moved by a book. You simply won't find one like this very often. It is written by a physician who loves her patients and has come to see that life depends not on the hand you are dealt, but on how you choose to live it. As Eve says throughout, the path to fulfillment is simple; it just isn't always that easy to achieve. Part of that responsibility rests with our cultural approach to medicine. But, there is a science for the soul as well. And if we are each body, mind, and spirit, how can we be healed if we don't treat all three together? With [this book], however, we have finally been given a model that integrates the treatment of the body, mind, and spirit. To my way of thinking, it is the only model of healing that makes sense, and I have learned more from this book than I have elsewhere in a very long time.

It has been my privilege to meet Eve Wood and let her get into my mind. Indeed, we have become good friends. Throughout our correspondence, I have consistently urged her to get her message out to the public. I am pleased that, with the publication of this important and inspiring book, she has finally done just that.

I'm not given to hyperbole, but I do feel that this book will strike a chord for a generation that sees itself in a poor light, and all too often finds itself lost and confused. I believe this text should be part of a curriculum for any student preparing for a career as a healthcare professional—and I would especially like it to be compulsory reading for all psychotherapists. But whether you are a healthcare provider or a fellow seeker, this book stands out like a lighthouse in stormy weather.

C. Everett Koop, M.D. ScD,
former U.S. Surgeon General;
McInerny Professor of Surgery, Dartmouth Medical School

THE BLIND MEN AND THE ELEPHANT

by John Godfrey Saxe

(1816–1887)

It was six men of Indostan
To learning much inclined,
Who went to see the Elephant
(Though all of them were blind),
That each by observation
Might satisfy his mind

The First approached the Elephant,
And happening to fall
Against his broad and sturdy side,
At once began to bawl:
"God bless me! but the Elephant
Is very like a wall!"

The Second, feeling of the tusk,
Cried, "Ho! what have we here
So very round and smooth and sharp?
To me 'tis mighty clear
This wonder of an Elephant
Is very like a spear!"

The Third approached the animal,
And happening to take
The squirming trunk within his hands,
Thus boldly up and spake:
"I see," quoth he, "the Elephant
Is very like a snake!"

The Fourth reached out an eager hand,
And felt about the knee.
"What most this wondrous beast is like

Is mighty plain," quoth he;
'Tis clear enough the Elephant
Is very like a tree!"

The Fifth, who chanced to touch the ear,
Said: "E'en the blindest man
Can tell what this resembles most;
Deny the fact who can
This marvel of an Elephant
Is very like a fan!

The Sixth no sooner had begun
About the beast to grope,
Than, seizing on the swinging tail
That fell within his scope,
"I see," quoth he, "the Elephant
Is very like a rope!"

And so these men of Indostan
Disputed loud and long,
Each in his own opinion
Exceeding stiff and strong,
Though each was partly in the right,
And all were in the wrong!

Moral:
So oft in theologic wars,
The disputants, I ween,
Rail on in utter ignorance
Of what each other mean,
And prate about an Elephant
Not one of them has seen!

Bringing Meaning and Medicine Together

AN INTEGRATIVE MODEL OF HEALING

To See or Not to See—*That* Is the Question

It was 7:30 A.M. on a weekday and a blind woman, dressed for work, was walking in center-city Philadelphia with her Seeing Eye dog at her right side. As I crossed the street, walking toward her, I noticed that the dog had stopped dead in his tracks, refusing to lead the woman any farther down the sidewalk toward Walnut Street. The woman, with a distressed look on her face, called out to the universe: "Is there something in front of me?"

By then, I was close enough to respond to her, "No ma'am. There is only the sidewalk in front of you."

She was confused and clearly distressed. "He won't go, and he keeps behaving as if there is something blocking my way." I looked down at her dog and, as if on command, he dropped something from his mouth. I bent down to pick it up and realized immediately that it was the blind woman's earring—she must have dropped it—for there, on her other earlobe, hung its mate.

"Your dog had your earring in his mouth and just dropped it in front of me," I told her. "You are only wearing one earring. Perhaps he was waiting for someone to help him give this one back to you?"

She seemed relieved. "Perhaps he was," she smiled. After asking me if she was heading in the right direction, she and her guide continued on their way.

But as I continued on my way, tears came to my eyes; and except for my blurry vision, I could see where I was going. As I made my way to work, I felt intensely grateful for the gift of sight and for having had the opportunity to share in the loving support of a Seeing Eye dog for its master.

• • •

While many of us are blessed with the gift of sight, we all have psychic blind spots that we must negotiate, and each of us could use a "Seeing Eye dog" on occasion. More often than not, we operate from our limited vantage points, which—if they go unchallenged—become roadblocks on our paths to self-actualization. Our biggest blind spots tend to encompass how we choose to look at things, what we choose to tell ourselves, or what we opt to believe. Like the blind woman on Walnut Street, we usually see the roadblocks as external. We suffer a job loss, or the death of a dream, and allow these experiences to become the *cause* of our misery. As a result, we are unable to productively move along the life-path. We allow ourselves to be done in or victimized by our pain. We permit our grief to overtake us, robbing us of the joy and fulfillment we are due. We are all, to some extent, tripped up by our own blind spots.

We can all learn a valuable lesson from the blind woman, though. She deduced that there was something blocking her way, but she was also willing to challenge her assumption. She called out to the universe for help. In doing so, not only did she learn that her path was clear, she learned that what was blocking her continued passage was in fact a gift of love. Upon receiving the gift, she was able to continue along her path with increased faith and trust in the support available to her and in her ability to make good use of it. If only we could all be as visionary and courageous as that blind woman en route to work.

• • •

Each of us has probably heard the expression "There is none so blind, as he who *will* not see." As the following anecdote illustrates, to see is a *choice*.

Many years ago, I was at a two-day review course in preparation for the National Board examination in psychiatry. One part of the examination involves having the candidate sit before two or three psychiatrist examiners, while a patient, unknown to the candidate, is brought into the room. The candidate is given fifteen or twenty minutes to observe and interview the patient. Once the patient has left the room, the candidate must discuss, in psychiatric terms, the relevant observations, diagnostic possibilities, and treatment ideas generated by the interview.

One of the teachers at this review course, whom I will call Dr. Z, had been a National Board examiner for years. He told us a powerful story about the *choice* to see—and this story has stayed with me ever since.

As is often the case, examiners such as Dr. Z have the opportunity of observing the same patient interviewed by five or six different candidates in the course of a day. One such patient seen by Dr. Z was a schizophrenic who had a neuro-muscular movement disorder called "tardive dyskinesia." Tardive dyskinesia is a common problem resulting from the long-term use of some of the medicines used to treat schizo-phrenia, involving abnormal and involuntary movements of the tongue and other muscle groups. Typically, a clinician will look for the condition by observing a patient at rest, as well as by asking the patient to perform a series of maneuvers, such as sticking his or her tongue out, or holding his or her hands palm-up. During these exercises, the clinician watches for the muscle twitching, indicating tardive dyskinesia.

Of all the candidates that Dr. Z observed that day, the only candidate who picked up on this patient's obvious physical abnormality was the one who was legally blind. All of the other candidates with full ocular vision missed it. None of them ever asked the patient to do the simple maneuvers necessary to detect the disorder. The blind candidate, however, was unable to see the muscles of the patient seated before him, and so he asked all the right questions, including, "Are you aware of having any abnormal tongue, hand, or arm movements?" This candi-date was rewarded with a full and honest disclosure by the patient, who volunteered having the disorder.

I am sure it will come as no surprise to hear that the

blind candidate was the only one of the six candidates to pass the National Board exam that day.

• • •

What do we choose to see? How do we choose to view ourselves and our experiences in the universe? What questions do we allow ourselves to ask? What assumptions or fixed beliefs do we carry with us wherever we go? What ideas do we allow ourselves to challenge? How much do we allow ourselves to grow?

We live in an imperfect and painful world. To live this earthly life is to experience fear, disappointment, abandonment, failure, loss, loneliness, death, grief, and even despair. "Happily-ever-after" is rather rare on this planet. Life can be brutal and unrelenting. There are no guarantees. Just when we think we can't possibly handle any more pain, the rug is ripped right out from under us again, and we find ourselves even further down than before.

So how are we to handle this monumental and overwhelming task of living—and still keep a song in our heart? As we sit with our rumps on the floor, knocked for yet another loop, how are we to find any solace? How can we find meaning in the pain, growth in the loss, and hope in a place of despair?

In my experience of over 28,000 one-on-one intimate hours with troubled human beings from all walks of life, I can tell you what I have learned about these questions. I have come to understand, beyond a shadow of a doubt, that how well you live is ultimately a reflection of how you choose to look at life in all its complexity. It is a function of whether you choose to look for lessons in loss, connection in loneliness, and opportunity in failure. It is a function of whether you choose to accept those things you cannot change, and work like the blazes to change the things you can. It is a function of whether you choose to forgive yourself and others for limitations, and look to develop yourself into the best person you can be. It is a function of whether you allow yourself to be grateful for the gifts you have been given and look for opportunities to nurture and share them. It is a function of whether you choose to look at yourself as an individual endowed with some innate value worthy of encouragement. It is a function of how hard you work to support and grow the unique, wonderful, gifted individual that you are.

As a child, I attended Hebrew day school and learned a very important lesson from Mishna Sanhedrin: "If a person saves one life, it is as if he has saved the entire world. And if a person destroys one life, it is as if he has destroyed the entire world." This sentiment, embodying all that really matters in the universe, continues to be my touchstone. With its simple eloquence, this lesson reminds us that every life is of infinite value and deserves to be nurtured. It advises us to respect the internal world of the self, as that is where much of real consequence in this world resides. It extols the virtue of self-love and love of others. It instructs us on how to find meaning and fulfillment in life: save yourself and save others, love yourself and love others, grow yourself and help others do the same. When any life ends we grieve, but at the same time, we must remember the value that all lives bring to the world.

In my work as a psychiatrist, I have had the privilege to be welcomed into the most intimate aspects of people's lives. This opportunity to share in both the pain and joy of many brave souls remains a great honor. I have seen myself reflected in each one of my patients, just as each one of my patients reflects a piece of me. In this process, I have learned a great deal about myself and about the art of healing. While we are all unique and special individuals, we are far more alike than we are different. Each one of us has a story that is its own beautiful tale, and we can learn a great deal when we choose to share our stories with one another.

Because of this, I have chosen to share my patients' stories and experiences in this book. I have learned that without focusing upon the *human* element of the healing endeavor, theoretical concepts are useless. Whether you are a practicing physician, a patient, or someone simply looking for guidance, you, too, can learn as you identify with my patients. You will see parts of yourself in their stories; and as you empathize with them, you will be supported in your own journey toward health.

When I decided to write this book, I knew I had to share the most powerful, moving, intense, long-term, and amazing story of healing that I have personally experienced. It is the story of Gillie, who became my patient fourteen years ago. When Gillie and I met, she was one of the most shattered people I had ever seen—and yet, as time went on, Gillie proved to be far more emotionally distressed than I had previously imagined. She had been diagnosed with multiple personality disorder, or dissociative identity disorder. Those of you who know the books *The Three Faces of Eve* and *Sybil* can appreciate what this diagnosis involves. After decades of psychiatric treatment and multiple psychiatric hospitalizations for serious suicide attempts, suffering from a pervasive inability to stay present in her own skin, and an absolute aversion to sharing her internal world with anyone, Gillie asked me to help her.

The story has a powerful lesson: the determination to heal can pay off. Gillie now enjoys sound emotional and mental health. She no longer has dissociative identity disorder, and she is one of the most impressive people I have ever known.

Within Gillie's story there is another tale to tell. It is my story; I want to share that with you as well, to show you how my relationship with Gillie taught me profound lessons about the art of psychiatry and the wonder of healing. Gillie and I began our relationship at the same time as I began my psychiatric practice, and I learned from her just as she was able to learn from me. This remarkable woman forced me to reach down to the bottom of my soul to find a way to help her. In doing so, she taught me to be resolute in the face of amazing challenges, patient and hopeful in the face of continued despair, and dogged in my belief that, if she would let me into the deepest recesses of her internal world and allow me to guide her, I would be able to help her. I couldn't just *hope* that I would be able to help Gillie; I had to *believe* I could. I had to trust that I could help her move from a place of obsession with self-destruction and distrust, to a place of fulfillment, joy, and love.

Gillie's story is the ultimate demonstration of the power of faith in healing. For although I took advantage of every medical teaching and therapeutic technique I had ever learned in my attempt to help her heal, her cure would have been impossible had I left love, unity, empathy, and hope out of her treatment.

My work with Gillie led me to trust what *feels* natural. I had to quiet the rational side of myself, and draw on my inner-wisdom, capacity for empathy, ability to love, and faith that I would be given answers. I needed to become Gillie's guide through the labyrinth, and be her model of a happy, integrated, and reliable woman.

Through my work with Gillie, I learned to integrate medicine, mindset, and the spiritual realm. I came to trust in the unconventional in my clinical work. I now know that in order to help my patients heal themselves, I must go beyond my medical training. I employ a body-mind-spirit approach that I have chosen to represent with the three-legged stool in this book. My goal in the coming pages is to show you that when it comes to healing broken psyches, we cannot separate body, mind, and spirit from one another. These elements depend upon one another just as the tides depend upon the moon, and the earth depends upon the sun.

The Three-Legged Stool

Perhaps you recognized the allusion to Hamlet's soliloquy in the previous section's title. "To See or Not to See," of course, refers to the line "To be or not to be," in Shakespeare's *Hamlet*. Hamlet used those words to ponder life and death. For us, the choice is not only *if* we want to live, but how *fully* we want to live; and fulfillment involves adopting an approach that integrates the body, mind, and spirit in one seamless, cohesive model.

Visualize in your mind's eye a three-legged stool: any size, shape, or material will do. The three-legged stool is a symbolic representation of my approach to life, wellness, and healing. Each one of the legs stands for an equally crucial piece of the whole. The legs are the body, mind, and spirit. Without one of its legs, the stool falls down. Without attention to each of these aspects of life, the human being will likely remain ill. This three-legged stool approach is fundamental to my work; it informs everything I do with patients, and I have come to regard it as a necessity.

The notion that body, mind, and spirit are fundamental aspects of human wellness is surely not new. In fact, its endurance over time leads me to wonder why the three legs of the stool are not routinely considered in the Western model of healing. Unfortunately, we Westerners are like the blind men and the elephant. We are all experts in discrete aspects of the elephant, but forgetful that the parts do not represent the whole. We are cardiologists, gastroenterologists, psychiatrists, or neurologists. We are occupational therapists, physical therapists, or massage therapists. We are personal trainers, herbalists, mystics, or spiritual leaders.

In medical school I learned a scientific, disease-based model. The focus was on how organ systems worked, what could go wrong within them, and what treatments could be used to fix them. By and large, body parts or organ systems were viewed as separate from one another. Patients were examples of diseases or organ systems gone awry rather than people who had particular illnesses. Even though the will to live has been recognized as crucial in physical healing for hundreds of years, body and mind were further split from one another. Mental health was not viewed as something related to the body; and the realm of spirituality or religion was never even mentioned at all. If a patient brought spirituality or religion up, the hospital chaplain was called in. Doctors did not deal with matters of the soul.

I was terribly depressed during my early years of medical school. I kept looking for the humanism that I naively expected to characterize medicine. I was disappointed again and again. While I knew that there was value in the scientific approach and intervention model, I was struck by the absence of what seemed to matter the most.

People had the diseases, but *people* did not seem to matter very much at all. Their feelings, thoughts, and beliefs were disregarded. Even their physical pain was often under-treated. My deep disillusionment with this approach led me to search for alternative models. I began to augment my medical school coursework with the study of Chinese medicine taught by alternative healers.

In my Chinese medicine courses, I learned about Chi energy and its pathways or meridians. I came to understand a model of wellness/illness that made far more sense to me. Chi energy is what we Westerners might call spirit, soul, or life force. The Chinese see the body as composed of a series of energy pathways called meridians, which need to be in balance for well-being. When the Chi energy is out of balance, a person may feel ill. In my courses, I learned to evaluate these energy pathways by taking a series of pulses. I learned how to promote healing by rebalancing the energy flow. I discovered that in Chinese medicine, body, mind, and spirit are insepa-rable. In the Chinese model, healers are also spiritual leaders.

I do not mean to present a treatise on Eastern medicine, nor do I use these Eastern diagnostic techniques in my work today. I share the model only as a counterpoint to the Western medical model of healing; and more specifically, because the ancient Chinese understood the importance of what I have symbolically called the three-legged stool. In fact, they have their own wellness and healing model that is very similar to it. We Westerners, on the other hand, seem to have thrown the baby out with the bathwater. We have neglected to integrate all of the necessary parts. Unfortunately, like the blind men and the elephant, we continue to think that the trunk is the entire elephant!

• • •

It is important to pause here and clarify what I mean when I say I cannot imagine doing healing work without using a body, mind, and spirit model. What exactly are the body, mind, and spirit legs anyway? How do I conceptualize them, and how do I actually work with this model?

First, the *body leg* of the stool encompasses your biology, genetics, inborn personality characteristics, feelings, particular vulnerabilities, and diagnosable medical conditions. We might think of it as the "who" question: "Who am I?" It is the stuff you came with. It is the wonder and the challenge of you. It is what needs to be nurtured and what needs to be worked with. It might be a passion to sing or dance, a love of numbers, or an aversion to organic chemistry. It might be a learning disability, a major depression, or a fear of public speaking. It is your constitution, your genetic fingerprint, and your medical conditions.

The *body leg* is the one modern medicine tends to be most comfortable with; it is the leg that I learned the most about in medical school.

The *mind* or *mindset leg* of the stool encompasses your thoughts about yourself and others. It is dramatically affected by the models you are exposed to or taught, especially during your childhood or formative years. We might think of it as the "what" question: "What do I think?" It is the growth-enhancing stuff you learned that needs to be promoted and the harmful stuff you learned that needs to be unlearned. The *mindset leg* might involve knowing: I am a gifted musician, a talented mathematician, or a spatially challenged individual. It would include thoughts such as: I am a failure, there is no way I can succeed, or I am not so pretty, and I wish I were skinnier. It includes your perfectionism, judgmental nature, self-concept, and body image. It is the negative internal voice that criticizes your every move, as well as the encouraging internal cheerleader who says: *Go for it! You can do it!*

The *mindset leg* is the one most therapists are comfortable with; these therapists could be psychoanalysts, cognitive therapists, behaviorists, or just about any others who are not predominantly psychopharmacologists. It is the leg that I learned the most about in my psychiatric residency training. It is the leg that is represented in self-help literature and on the covers of most popular magazines.

The *spirit leg* concerns the meaningfulness and purpose of existence. It includes notions of a higher calling, one's sense of connection to something bigger and grander than the self, and the belief that we are here to share our gifts to help and enrich one another. We might think of it as the "why" question: "Why am I here?" It is the realm of religion, mysticism, and meditation. It is both the seed and the tree of hope. It is the root of life, and the source of the infinite within each one of us. It is the experience of connection and oneness that unites all creatures. It is the *creative healing force* that reverberates between two or more people who share a mutual, almost karmic connection to each other; and it is that very same connection between a single soul and the universe-at-large. This *creative healing force* can be felt in that astonishing moment when it seems that the wisdom of the world has been revealed to us. It is the whole, which is infinitely greater than the sum of its parts. It is the miraculous in the mundane.

This is the leg that I learned the most about in Hebrew day school as a child; and the ideas I contemplated during spiritual retreats and in solitude as I walked through the forests near my family's home. It is the leg most spoken of by spiritual leaders and their followers, and the leg least visited by most physicians.

As you think about my descriptions of the three legs, you will begin to realize that the separation of body, mind, and spirit is somewhat arbitrary. Each leg is, in some way, isolated. Yet, in many other ways, the legs blend into one another and continuously affect one another. While we can often pick out and identify which leg is prominent in a given expression of the self, we cannot separate that leg from its context. It is a fundamental part of one and only one human being. I like to think of this concept as the "separate-but-one principle." For purposes of diagnosis, treatment, and healing, it is necessary to tease apart or describe the characteristics of each of the legs individually; however, we also must recognize their interdependent natures.

Let's look at an example of the separate-but-one principle in action. I will use an example from my psychiatric practice to demonstrate the point. Although I will be focusing on psychiatric illness, keep in mind that the principles apply to all aspects of being.

If you think back to my description of the *body leg*, you will recognize that the diagnosis of major depression belongs in this category. Major depression is a common, serious medical illness with a high degree of morbidity and mortality. It is the result of a chemical or neurotransmitter imbalance in the brain. Its symptoms often remit when antidepressant medicines are taken, and they often return when the medications are stopped.

Major depression is diagnosed when someone experiences a persistent depressed mood or a loss of interest or pleasure in usual activities for at least two weeks. It involves symptoms of significant weight loss or gain, insomnia or excessive sleeping, physical agitation or slowing of motion, excessive fatigue or loss of energy, feelings of worthlessness or guilt, impaired concentration and recurrent thoughts of death. It is a medical condition often treated by psychiatrists, and other primary-care doctors, with medicines. It is the focus of much drug development by pharmaceutical companies and the subject of many symposia and educational programs offered to physicians.

All told, major depression is a biological, or *body leg* illness, plain and simple, right? Many doctors would say so. They would look to make the diagnosis, start the patient on medicine, and ask the patient to return for a follow-up medication check some weeks hence. Many of their patients would improve from this intervention.

And yet, the symptoms of major depression also include thoughts about the self and the universe. Doesn't that mean the *mind* and *spirit legs* are involved as well? A depressed woman's feeling of guilt reflects her belief that she is doing, or not doing, something she should be doing. A depressed man's recurrent thoughts of death reflect his experience of hopelessness in the universe. These ideas may stem from his belief that the world would be better off without him or that he deserves to suffer. Excessive guilt and recurrent thoughts of death bring the diagnosis of major depression into the realm of mind and spirit. It is not purely a *body leg* illness at all.

In fact, some cognitive therapists would tell you that negative thoughts *cause* depression. They would say that a series of negative distortions of life experience, like pessimism or self-criticism, are learned and lead to a depressed mood. They would approach the treatment of major depression quite differently from the typical physician.

Rather than prescribe medications, they would work with their patients to identify and modify the negative thoughts involved in the genesis and perpetuation of their particular depressions. They would encourage a sharing of the self-defeating thoughts and then develop an active behavior modification program. They would instruct their patients to substitute specific positive thoughts for their particular negative ones. This mindset view and form of treatment tends to be extremely effective for some depressed patients.

So, if medication or *body leg* treatment works, and cognitive therapy or *mind leg* treatment works, what about the *spirit leg* in major depression?

It turns out that in reviewing some eighty studies that have been published during the last one hundred years, McCullough and Larson found that religious/spiritual factors were often tied to decreased rates of clinical depression.* Religious commitment reduces the risk of developing major depression. Furthermore, several studies have shown that people whose religious faith is a central motivating factor in their lives recover more quickly from depression than those who are not religious. Finally, therapy with religious content that draws on the patient's spiritual resources, hastens recovery whether or not the therapist is religious. Major depression is clearly a *spirit leg* illness too.

So major depression is a *body leg* illness, a *mind leg* illness, and a *spirit leg* illness; the disorder is an illustration of the "separate-but-one principle" mentioned previously. Each leg is in some ways discrete, and yet the legs come together to support and affect one another.

---

* "The Patient's Spiritual/Religious Dimension: A Forgotten Factor in Mental Health" in *Directions in Psychiatry* by David B. Larson, MD, MSPH, Susan S. Larson, MAT and Harold G. Koenig, MD, MHSc—volume 21, lesson 21, November 2001 (a publication of the International Center for the Integration of Health and Spirituality; website www.ICIHS.org).

Unfortunately, many doctors and therapists treat patients with major depression as if one leg were the whole stool. They prescribe medication or institute psychotherapy. At times, they even recommend a combination of the two. However, it is extremely rare for them to include a spiritual approach in their treatment of depressed patients. A fully integrated model has not yet found its way into clinical training or practice. Even though it has been shown that religious commitment reduces the risk of developing major depression and helps in its recovery, this aspect of wellness remains somewhat taboo.

This is where I differ. I simply do not know how to separate body, mind, and spirit from one another. Truthfully, this is because I became a doctor for religious reasons; the Mishna lesson from my youth, *to save one life is to save the entire world*, has been the greatest driving force of my life. As a child I thought: what could possibly be more spiritually correct than entering the profession of lifesavers?

That said, I am a *medical* doctor who is particularly committed to making all appropriate medical diagnoses in my patients. I am grateful to be able to offer the best that modern medicine can provide to them. But, my treatment approach involves integrating all three dimensions, not focusing upon one leg to the exclusion of the other two. So, while I often prescribe medications to my patients suffering from major depressive episodes, I seem to be incapable of seeing anyone for "medication management" alone; I involve all of my patients in psychotherapy concurrently. I work with them to identify their particular vulnerabilities and the precipitants involved in the onset of their depressions. My goal is to help them develop life strategies and coping mechanisms that will minimize the likelihood that they will suffer recurrent episodes.

Each time I sit with a patient, I am awed by the sanctity and majesty of the life before me. I am inspired by the human being who is brave enough to seek counsel during such personal, and often times, devastating periods. I can't help but identify with the pain and hopelessness each of my patients grapples with. Given this, I am routinely moved to share my own spiritual outlook with them. I don't speak in terms of the spirit, soul, or God, but rather share my spiritual beliefs as they relate to my patients' struggles. I believe there is a piece of the divine within all of us and that we are meant to experience fulfillment. I share my sense of hope in order to show my patients that they can, will, and are meant to recover. I tell them that they have unique and wonderful gifts that are meant to be discovered, nurtured, and shared with the world—and they are gladdened to hear that part of our work together will enable them to achieve just that. It follows that patients who stay in treatment long enough to arrive at a place of personal fulfillment often leave my care far more spiritually connected or religious (in their own religious heritage) than they were when we met.

Putting the Theory into Action

Now that you understand the three-legged stool concept, you probably want to know how to incorporate it into your own healing journey. What is involved in the process, and how do you go about doing it?

While each of the legs is equally crucial to your healing process, I recommend addressing them in a specific order and manner. The first step is the *body leg*; the second step is the *mind leg*; the third step is the *spirit leg*; and the final step is what I call *process*. This book is organized to walk you through each of these steps in a sequential manner. But remember, while the legs blend together and affect each other, you first need to tease them apart in order to define your healing path.

The first step of your personal growth journey involves identifying and working with the biological pieces you possess. It includes, but is in no way limited to, the importance of establishing proper diagnoses to enable you to move on. It also involves identifying and accepting inborn vulnerabilities, strengths, feelings, gifts, and limitations. Many individuals end up stuck in their attempts to heal because some of these necessary givens have not been appropriately addressed. When we get to Step One, I will show you how to identify and work with the biological issues that you need to confront in order to heal.

The second step of your journey to health involves identifying and working with your mindset and attitudes— your thoughts about yourself and others. This leg of the stool is often dramatically affected by models you were exposed to in childhood. As such, addressing it may involve working to identify and resolve family issues. We will discuss how to identify and work on your mindset challenges at length.

The third step involves the spiritual dimension: your sense of purpose, value, and connection to something greater than yourself. In spite of the fact that spirituality is the cornerstone of emotional health, people tend to find that active involvement in spiritual pursuits is difficult for them in the earliest stages of healing. Step Three will not only show you how to identify your spiritual needs, but how to pursue a spiritual path that can further your recovery.

The fourth step of your journey involves learning to appreciate the nature of the healing process as a whole. Even though there are a series of steps to follow, the road to recovery can be anything but straight. Steps One through Three often need to be revisited. When we reach Step Four, or the chapter I have titled "Putting It All Together," we will discuss how to stay the course in spite of the bumps you encounter along the way.

I want to help you put the stool legs together for your own healing journey. Perhaps you have been looking to heal for some time, but sense that you are going around in circles. Or, perhaps you have experienced some benefit from a series of approaches and activities but don't know how to put them all together. Maybe you can't even seem to get started because you do not know what to do or where to go first. You may be stuck in your attempts to heal as a result of:

* Lacking a diagnosis
* Carrying the wrong diagnosis
* Inadequate attention to family-of-origin issues
* Skipping over a key step in the healing journey
* Lacking a comprehensive model of healing

But take heart; no matter what issues you face, they can be resolved. And while this book is not intended to be a substitute for professional help, it can be your "Seeing Eye dog." Allow it to empower and guide you through the healing process. It is my belief that you can become the best steward of your own healing path if you are given the proper tools and guidance.

• • •

Before we move on, consider where you feel yourself to be in your healing journey and what you most hope to learn from this book. If you are feeling particularly hopeless and need a tale of inspiration to help you gain perspective, read Gillie's story and its lessons first. If you think you would do better by diving right into the step-by-step approach to healing, read those chapters before Gillie's tale. While it is important that you follow the steps in the order they are given, feel free to go back and forth between the steps and the stories this book has to offer

Now let's turn to "Gillie's Story: Where There's a Will, There's a Way," to see the three-legged stool and the "separate-but-one" principles in action. As you read, look for the *body*, *mind*, and *spirit legs* in Gillie's story. Ask yourself: What is the role of each leg in Gillie's illness and her healing? If you challenge yourself to look for the theory in action, you will be amazed—not merely by what you will see, but how much you can learn from her powerful and inspiring journey.

Gillie's Story: Where There's a Will, There's a Way

A DRAMATIC EXAMPLE OF THE HEALING MODEL IN ACTION

Travel back in time with me to the late spring of 1988. I was nearing the close of my psychiatric residency and had decided not to take a job, but rather start my own private practice. While my fellow residents had been thinking, planning, talking, and worrying about what direction they were going to go in, those months leading up to my graduation were largely consumed with other issues.

On January 31, 1988, I had given birth to my first child, a long-awaited but colicky baby boy. Suddenly getting enough sleep, learning how to nurse a baby, and figuring out how to be a mom without losing myself in the process was the major focus of my spring.

It wasn't until May of 1988 that I began to grow anxious. Somewhere between signing a lease for an office on the grounds of a psychiatric hospital, paying my malpractice insurance for the first time, and ordering business cards and stationery, I began to think: *What if no one comes to see me for treatment? How will I cover the expenses? What if no one sends me patients? Am I kidding myself thinking that I can make this work?*

Spending time with my fellow psychiatry residents, who were equally anxious, only seemed to fuel my self-doubts. I needed to create space between my colleagues and myself and find other means of support—otherwise I feared I would self-destruct.

I spoke to some of my senior colleagues about my worries. They kindly confessed that they had felt panicky before taking the plunge as well. They reassured me that I would thrive, told me that I was a talented doctor, and said they would refer patients to me. This certainly helped, but I still woke up in the middle of the night filled with worry. Luckily, my husband was there to comfort me, telling me I could do it and that it would all work out. I chose to believe all of these people, and went forward with my plans.

I bought a beeper and sent notices to all of my senior colleagues announcing that I was opening a private psychiatric practice. I was sure to let them know that I would be around and easily reachable all summer to provide coverage for any of their patients in need during their vacations. Soon after my notices went out, a call came in.

"Eve, Jason Glick here. Got your notice about the coverage availability, and I have someone I'd like you to cover. She is a woman with multiple personality disorder. She has been my patient for ten years. Her father was the perpetrator. She has been in treatment since adolescence and hospitalized many times for serious suicide attempts. She is a forty-two-year-old widow, with three children ages twelve, fourteen, and sixteen years. I haven't had anyone cover her before, but I think she would do better to be seen this time. She had a tough August last year. . . . Are you available to do that?"

I answered without hesitation.

• • •

On July 26, at the appointed hour, I knocked on Jason Glick's office door to meet his patient, Gillie, as we had previously arranged. He opened the door and returned to his seat. On his office floor sat a somewhat heavyset woman in blue jeans and a long-sleeved shirt. Her short brown hair was cropped around her face, which remained expressionless. She stared at the wall, refusing to make eye contact with anyone, and said nothing. I introduced myself to her and explained that in her doctor's absence I was planning to see her for coverage visits during the month of August. I let her know when I would be able to meet with her for the first time. I asked her if that time suited her and whether she had any questions she wanted to ask me. Without looking at me or uttering more than one word, she nodded her head to let me know that the time was fine, and she shook her head to indicate that she had no questions. I placed an appointment card containing my office address and phone number beside Gillie on the floor, said my good-byes, and left.

Outside, I began to think about the enormity of what

had just occurred. I had just taken on the responsibility for the care and well-being of a woman who would neither look at nor speak to me. Would she even show up for her first appointment? What if she didn't? What would I do then? I was responsible for her even if she didn't come. I decided to get the contact information from Jason; just in case, I needed to know how I could track her down, and how I could get in touch with him if the need arose.

Several days later, grateful that I knew how to reach Jason if necessary, I sat in my office wondering if Gillie would appear. At several minutes past two o'clock, I decided to look for her in the hallway. I spied her pacing back and forth, and it was clear that she was extremely agitated. Gently, I invited her into my office. After some hesitation, she followed me into the room.

Gillie was surrounded by chairs but would not sit down. In fact, she struggled with my suggestion that she have a seat and—after what seemed like hours, although it was just a few minutes—she sat down on the floor. This was the first act of what I have come to think of as the *chair dance*.

• • •

Bear with me as we step from the treatment room for a moment, in order to address how we might think about beginnings and givens. I frequently find myself saying that *life happens in the details*. Everything we do, say, and feel is a significant reflection of who we are. There is a reason for everything and often times, the things we want and need to know about one another and ourselves can be ascertained if we pay careful attention to the details of life and how we feel about them.

So, what are some of the givens, or *body leg* details, that I knew and was thinking about in regard to Gillie's situation? I knew that although Gillie had a very serious psychiatric illness, she was still able to care for three dependent children. She was able to keep track of time and space well enough to be where she needed to be when she was supposed to be there. I knew that she wanted to be helped. She was willing to come to see me whenever I told her to do so. I also knew that she was sitting on a psychic fence: a piece of her was functioning relatively well in the universe, while an equally substantial piece of her existed in a primitive, magical, and somewhat crazy world. The healthier part of her came for psychiatric treatment appointments, was available to her children, participated in the PTA, made cookies for bake sales, and drove carpools. The unhealthier part of her sat on the floor and refused to talk to her psychiatrist.

From Jason's cryptic history, I knew that Gillie had been repeatedly overwhelmed and abused by her father during childhood. She had experienced enough consistent trauma from an early age that, in order to survive, she had developed multiple personality disorder—a primitive psychological coping structure, and fundamentally a disorder of memory.

Multiple personality disorder (MPD) and dissociative identity disorder (DID) are different names for the same disorder. Unless one of us has suffered a genetic or in-utero brain trauma, such as oxygen deprivation, alcohol exposure, or infection, we are all born with the capacity to remember the bulk of what happens to us from our preschool years on. We are also endowed with the capacity to forget or block from our conscious memory experiences that have been overly traumatic or too upsetting to recall. However, if we suffer enough persistent trauma beginning in the early years of our development, we may not be able to forget or bury all our pain. In situations like these, we need to come up with another way to prevent the trauma from overwhelming our minds so we do not lose all capacity to function. The development of separate personality states, or identities, is one of the brilliant psychic mechanisms that fills this need; each identity experiences and stores some information which it keeps somewhat hidden from the other personality states. While all the different identities co-exist within the same human being, that individual has minimal, if any awareness of the separate identities, and would surely never experience them as a part of him or herself. In DID patients, this mechanism is what enables the self to function.

I will try to clarify the concept by way of an example. Let's look at a span of several hours in the life of Lisa, a six-year-old girl with multiple personality disorder.

During the course of an intense episode of abuse at the hand of her father, one identity is present and in control of the child's behavior. This identity stores the memory of that abuse. Several hours later a different identity takes control so as to allow Lisa to go to school and participate in first-grade activities. This identity stores the memory of the school day. In fact, it may be the identity that always goes to school. At the end of the school day, in anticipation of returning home to the site of an episode of abuse earlier in the day, a third protective identity—with no memory of the abuse—takes control. This enables Lisa to return home. The process goes on and on. All sorts of creative memory functions in the form of different identities will come into play to allow Lisa a modicum of continued function.

Having looked at Lisa's story as an example of MPD function, let's now look at the way the disorder is described in psychiatric terms. In the *DSM IV*, the *Diagnostic and Statistical Manual of Mental Disorders IV*, the features of dissociative identity disorder are described as follows:

> The essential feature of Dissociative Identity Disorder is the presence of two or more distinct identities or personality states (Criterion A) that recurrently take control of behavior (Criterion B). There is an inability to recall important personal information, the extent of which is too great to be explained by ordinary forgetfulness (Criterion C). The disturbance is not due to the direct physiological effects of a substance or a general medical condition (Criterion D). In children, the symptoms cannot be attributed to imaginary playmates or other fantasy play.

> Dissociative Identity Disorder reflects a failure to integrate various aspects of identity, memory, and consciousness. Each personality state may be experienced as if it has a distinct personal history, self-image, and identity, including a separate name. Usually there is a primary identity that carries the individual's given name and is passive, dependent, guilty, and depressed. The alternate identities frequently have different names and characteristics that contrast with the primary identity (e.g., are hostile, controlling, and self-destructive). Particular identities may emerge in specific circumstances and may differ in reported age and gender, vocabulary, general knowledge, or predominant affect. Alternate identities are experienced as taking control in sequence, one at the expense of the other, and may deny knowledge of one another, be critical of

one another, or appear to be in open conflict. Occasionally, one or more powerful identities allocate time to the others. Aggressive or hostile identities may at times interrupt activities or place the others in uncomfortable situations.

Individuals with this disorder experience frequent gaps in memory for personal history, both remote and recent. The amnesia is frequently asymmetrical. The more passive identities tend to have more constricted memories, whereas the more hostile, controlling, or "protector" identities have more complete memories. An identity that is not in control may nonetheless gain access to consciousness by producing auditory or visual hallucinations (e.g., a voice giving instructions). Evidence of amnesia may be uncovered by reports from others who have witnessed behavior that is disavowed by the individual or by the individual's own discoveries (e.g., finding items of clothing at home that the individual cannot remember having bought). There may be loss of memory not only for recurrent periods of time, but also an overall loss of biographical memory for some extended period of childhood. Transitions among identities are often triggered by psychological stress. The time required to switch from one identity to another is usually a matter of seconds, but less frequently, may be gradual. The number of identities reported ranges from 2 to more than 100. Half of reported cases include individuals with 10 or fewer identities.*

* Reprinted with permission from the *Diagnostic and Statistical Manual of Mental Disorders, Fourth Edition.* Copyright 1994 American Psychiatric Association.

You now have a pretty good sense of the significant *body leg* details of Gillie's story as I myself knew them at the time. Yet, while I knew that Gillie had DID and that much of the diagnostic description above applied to her, how much of that diagnostic description, and in what fashion it applied, was still unclear. And because *life happens in the details*, what was transpiring between Gillie and me during those initial, seemingly minor moments was in fact of monumental importance. As we played out the first act of the *chair dance,* I was asking myself: *Will Gillie engage with me or not? Will she talk to me or keep me in the dark? Will she be able to partner with me?* As we return to the treatment room, keep these questions in mind; they reflect massive issues that were to play out through a series of microscopic moments.

• • •

I had remained standing when Gillie seated herself on the floor; and admittedly, I felt quite anxious. If I was going to be able to help this woman survive the month of August, I couldn't begin this session with a replay of that July 26th scene in Jason Glick's office. I also realized that I couldn't support the unhealthy side of this tortured woman, or she would become progressively worse over the month. Even if Gillie was unaware of her strength and health, and even if she felt unable to nurture and grow that healthier side of her person, *that* was the side I had to ally myself with in order to assist her. I resolved to do whatever I could think of to get Gillie to sit up and talk to me about her struggles, knowing that the only way I could help her was to get her to partner with me. If I could encourage her to do that, perhaps then she would let me into her internal world so I could come to know her where she *lived*.

And so, standing in the treatment room, I said, "Gillie, you need to sit in the chair. Please do not sit on the floor." Somewhat stunned and rattled, she looked at me and then quickly turned away. As I continued standing—for what seemed like an eternity—she slowly lifted herself into the closest chair. She perched herself on its very edge, as if she dared not put too much of herself into the thing; and yet, with this simple action, I realized she was making an effort to work with me the best she could.

To my astonishment, Gillie went on to conduct herself in a most mature and reasonable fashion throughout our first treatment session. She answered most of my questions and began to tell me about herself. She told me that, as of late, all of her children had been sleeping on her bedroom floor because she had the only room with a decent air conditioner. She let me know that her lack of privacy was an issue, but she did not begin to convey the magnitude and significance of that fact until the next time we met. She did however share something extremely intimate with me; she told me that she had known about the presence of the "other people," referring to the various identities of her MPD, for many years before she had been willing to tell her psychiatrist about them.

At the close of that first session, I sensed there was a thread of connection between the two of us; and yet, I was extremely anxious about letting more than twenty-four hours pass before seeing her again. I scheduled a second visit for her the next day, and reminded her of how she could reach me before that time, if need be.

• • •

When Gillie arrived for her appointment the next day, she came into my office but stood frozen with fear inside the doorway. She looked as if she were about to jump out of her skin and run away. The *chair dance* had resumed. I stood waiting, as I had the day before, and encouraged her to take a seat. Again, time seemed to stand still as I watched her. Finally, she perched herself on the edge of the same chair that she had chosen the day before.

Although she seemed to be far more unsettled at the start of this second appointment as compared to the first, she communicated more openly with me. She told me that she couldn't remember much of anything about Dr. Glick, including what he looked like. She showed me a series of severe burns on her left forearm—the result of many consecutive days of self-destructive behavior. She told me that she used a hot iron to burn herself each day and that hiding this ritual from her children, since they were now sleeping in her room, was a challenge. After telling me that she was excessively anxious, that she had thoughts of killing herself, and that she used the burning ritual to help her "stay in control," she asked me if she was sick or normal. I adamantly, but patiently, explained to her that her level of anxiety, her difficulty remembering her psychiatrist of ten years, her self-destructive behavior, and suicidal thoughts were all reflections of a very serious illness. Gillie was truly ill, and in need of much help.

She left with an appointment scheduled for forty-eight hours hence, but called me before that time. She wanted to "apologize" for the things she had said during the prior session and let me know that I didn't "need to see her anymore." I reassured her that she had done nothing wrong, and that I was planning to see her the next day.

On August 6, Gillie appeared, but there was another identity in control. She spoke with the voice of a young child called Finny, an eleven-year-old girl. She sat down on the floor, appearing quite frightened, and asked me where Gillie was. I told her I was wondering the same thing. Together we tried to sort out what had happened. I asked her what the first thing she remembered was. She told me that she had found herself in the hall outside my office, but had no idea how she had gotten there. She didn't know who had brought her or why. She told me a lot about her fear of finding herself alone in unfamiliar situations. She wondered who I was. I explained, "I am a psychiatrist covering for Dr. Glick in caring for Gillie. I was waiting for Gillie to come for her appointment when I found you in the hall instead." As we continued to talk, I became aware of how frequently "Finny" found herself dropped into situations that confused her. Then, after about twenty minutes, she abruptly gave over control and Gillie appeared.

Gillie seemed to be confused about how *she* had gotten into my office. Again, I encouraged her to sit in the chair, and she did as I suggested. She then asked me if Finny had been there. I said yes and then asked her, "What is the last thing you remember?" She told me that she had been in the hallway outside my office and had suddenly become frightened when a man walked past her. She could not remember anything further. I explained to Gillie that she must have turned over control to another personality when she became frightened, and I shared what Finny had told me about *her* experience of appearing at just the moment Gillie had described as her last memory. I told her that I would call this phenomenon "switching," and explained to her that Finny was a part of her that she "switched" into when she was too traumatized to stay present as Gillie. The concept of switching was extremely disturbing to Gillie; and she made it clear to me that she did not see Finny as a part of herself. However, she did go on to let me know that she was struggling with a great deal of anxiety and was thinking about coming into the hospital if it continued.

When Gillie arrived for her next scheduled appointment on August 10, 1988, she sat in her chosen chair, and told me that she was "afraid of losing control and breaking into little pieces." She went on to say that while she felt compelled to burn herself in order to "stay in control," she did not want to be doing it. "It hurts," she said, "but I cannot stop."

She also shared that she had "bought a rope" ten days before and was obsessed with the thought of hanging herself. She described a recurring image of one end of the rope attached to a high crossbeam in her cathedral ceiling bedroom, and the other end of the rope tied into a noose. She envisioned herself climbing onto a chair, putting the noose around her neck, and kicking the chair out from beneath her.

Just when I was about to insist that she stay in the hospital, she told me, "Meeting with you helps." We made an appointment for the next day, and agreed that she would bring her insurance information along so that arrangements could be made for her to stay in the hospital if necessary. She also agreed to bring me the rope.

I continued to see Gillie for frequent sessions throughout the month of August. As the month progressed, she seemed to become increasingly anxious, depressed, and self-destructive. She began to come to the hospital grounds earlier and earlier in the morning just to be near the office. She would sit in her car in the parking lot for hours waiting for her appointment. Even though she felt "bad" and undeserving of care, she felt safer there than at home. At Gillie's request, she was hospitalized for three days at the end of the month.

Lest you get the impression that I was comfortable in this situation for even one day of that month, let me disabuse you of that notion now. Although Gillie had begun to connect with me, and even wondered all weekend preceding our August 15th appointment why she trusted me, her ability to communicate was limited, tortured, and extremely inconsistent. She was silent for long periods of time during most of our sessions. She required a tremendous amount of probing and support to share what she did tell me. Gillie's other identities took control on a number of occasions, and when Gillie was present, she frequently thought that I was angry with her and did not want to see her.

Of course, I was never angry or disinterested in seeing her, but it would be dishonest not to say that I found the responsibility for her well-being overwhelming. I had never met such an ill person before, never mind taken responsibility for keeping such a tortured soul *alive.*

As the month drew to a close, I found myself anxiously anticipating Jason Glick's return and the day I would be relieved of this responsibility. I couldn't help but think to myself, *I am just learning how to be a mother, a co-parent, and a private-practitioner; and surely I am not seasoned enough to know how to ensure the safety of this woman, much less* heal *her.* Unbeknownst to me, Gillie and the universe had other designs for me.

● ● ●

On August 25, Gillie told me that she found me "one hundred times less scary to talk to than Glick." While she was willing and committed to resume meeting with Dr. G upon his return, she desperately wanted to continue our meetings as well. As the days progressed from there, she struggled to make me aware of just how much she needed to continue meeting with me. She confessed that she had never been able to be open with Dr. G about the extent and severity of her self-destructive behavior. As if that didn't worry me enough, Gillie went on to share that she had taken a near fatal overdose while he was away the summer before, and hadn't told Dr. G or anyone else about it.

I told her that I would have to discuss her request with Dr. G when he returned, but I found myself struggling inside. How could I abandon this woman who was hanging on to life by a thread? What would happen to her if I reeled in my spool? Yet, how could I continue to treat her when I felt so fearful and distressed by the degree of responsibility her well-being required?

I found myself visiting my spiritual beliefs a great deal. *To participate in the saving of one life is to participate in the saving of the whole world, and to have a hand in the loss of one life is to participate in the destruction of the whole world.* If Jason was amenable to a partnership, I would have to agree to it as well. I could not possibly live with myself if I did otherwise.

It will probably not come as a surprise to you that upon his return, Jason was thrilled by Gillie's suggestion. He could see only benefit in the collaborative arrangement, and urged me to continue meeting with her.

And so I did. I met with Gillie once or twice a week for the next several months. I gave her low doses of anti-anxiety medications to use when she got panicky, pictures of me to take home so she would remember me when we were apart, and a great deal of encouragement to call my office and listen to my voice on the answering machine whenever she felt the need to hear it.

Toward the end of October, she began to withdraw in a progressive manner. Although she was coming for her regular therapy appointments, she had increasing difficulty getting herself to sit in the chair. Once seated, she was quieter and more agitated than I had ever seen her. She began to allude to a suicide plan, but would not discuss it further. By the end of the month, I had made arrangements with the hospital to admit her at the drop of a hat. When she came for her October 31, 1988 appointment, I let her know that unless she could assure me that she would be safe until our next scheduled visit, she needed to be admitted to the hospital right then. Gillie told me that she had some things to take care of first, including her regular appointment with Dr. Glick, but she would come back later in the day to be admitted to the hospital. Again, I stressed that she could leave only if she would commit to staying safe until her return. She vacillated a great deal, but finally gave me a commitment not to engage in any self-destructive behavior without calling me to talk about it first. I chose to believe her.

· · ·

Before I go on, I want to explain why I chose to believe Gillie when she made her safety commitment to me.

One of my senior colleagues once told me, never lie to a patient because all you really have between you and the patient is the relationship. I took this advice to mean: if there is no trust, there is no sharing. If there is no sharing, there is no healing. If there is no healing, there is no point.

Honesty is the cornerstone of a successful therapeutic relationship. Dishonesty on either side will ultimately undermine any therapeutic effort.

Each one of us has our own private and unique internal world. We cannot read one another's mind, nor can we ever stand in one another's shoes. We can only know each other if we are honest and earnest in our sharing of ourselves. Thus, in the therapeutic relationship, the patient must be able to let the psychiatrist into her internal world by sharing her thoughts, feelings, and plans honestly. The psychiatrist must be able to believe her patient and deal honestly and respectfully in response. If psychiatrist and patient cannot unite in this way, no healing can ever occur.

Given Gillie's chronic self-destructive impulses and suicidal ideation, I was unable to know when she was at the greatest risk of self-destruction; I had to be able to rely on her to tell me how she was doing, or I could not help her at all. I had to choose to believe her at all times, or abandon my work with her altogether. Although I was constantly anxious about her safety, I had to trust her to tell me when she needed greater protective measures. And so on October 31, 1988, when Gillie told me that she would be safe until she returned to be admitted into the hospital later that day, I took her at her word, arranged an admission time for several hours hence, and sent her on her way.

• • •

But Gillie did not appear at the appointed time. I went into the hallway to look for her and discovered her slumped over in a chair outside my office. At first she seemed to be asleep, but I was horrified to discover I couldn't rouse her. She was breathing but unconscious. There was no obvious sign of bodily injury, and I surmised that she had probably taken an overdose of some medicine—or medicines. My head was buzzing with questions. What had she taken? When did she take it? How much did she take? How much of it has been absorbed into her body already? Will she survive or die? If she survives, will she be left with irreparable damage to her vital organs? *What should I do?*

If Gillie were going to survive, I needed to act quickly and decisively; and as my office was on the grounds of a psychiatric hospital without full medical facilities, I called 911. The paramedics transported her to the nearest emergency room for immediate assessment and medical intervention.

I called Dr. Glick as well. He confirmed that Gillie had kept her appointment, but another identity had been in control. Further, she had not told him anything at all about her suicidal intentions. As we discussed our respective experiences with Gillie that day, we realized that she was splitting the treatment team apart whether she knew it or not.

• • •

I drove home from my office that evening filled with both intense anger and paralyzing fear. I hoped and prayed that Gillie would survive, but I was angry at her dishonesty and for selling herself so short. I was also overwhelmed by fear that she would die by her own hands. I was barely able to move, never mind focus on my husband or child. I sat very still and waited for word of Gillie's fate.

During our conversation earlier in the day, I had told Jason that I was extremely angry with Gillie for lying to me, so much so that I felt unable to continue working with her.

I explained to him that I felt betrayed, and that her dishonesty made a therapeutic relationship with me impossible. If she survived this attempt on her life, I would need to step out of any role in her treatment henceforth. Since this team approach was not working, he would need to resume full responsibility for her care. He understood and agreed.

Thankfully, the emergency room physician called within a few hours to let me know that Gillie would survive her overdose unscathed. Measures had been taken to minimize her bodily absorption of the medication she had taken, and while the medication remaining in her system was extremely sedating, it was not toxic. He expected her to be medically clear and ready for psychiatric hospital admission later that night or the next morning. I informed him of the arrangements that had been made for her transfer, hung up the phone, and felt a massive weight lift from my body.

I went to bed that night believing that my work with Gillie had come to a close; I had done my part to keep her alive for four months, but would no longer play a role in the unfolding drama of her life. But once again, Gillie, Dr. G, and the universe had other designs for me.

• • •

With Gillie admitted to the psychiatric hospital under Dr. G's care, I was free to focus on my other patients and to let the universe begin to work its strange healing magic. Every week or so, Jason would call me. "Gillie really wants to start meeting with you again. She is devastated that you won't see her. Would you at least be willing to talk to her?"

Slowly, but surely, my anger diminished to the point where I agreed. "No promises," I said to him. "She has a lot of convincing to do, but I am willing to talk to her."

On December 15, 1988, Gillie reentered my life. She begged me to take her on as a patient again; and in turn, I shared my concerns and reluctance to do so. When I explained to Gillie that she had established a pattern of splitting the therapists, and as a result had undermined her treatment, she looked confused. A review of the events of October 31st was in order. I described what had happened: "Being suicidal, you agreed to be admitted into the hospital later that day. Then, after giving me a safety commitment so that you could go to your appointment with Dr. G, you kept your danger a secret from him. Upon returning to my office to be admitted, you took an overdose of medication before seeing me."

Gillie listened intently as I spoke. Her eyes seemed to swallow my words as she tried to grasp what I was saying. I went on. "This type of splitting and dishonesty is incompatible with treatment. You will need to convince me that you will not split or lie to me again before I can begin to consider resuming your care."

Although she seemed anxious and motivated to satisfy my requirements, she was clearly baffled. Gillie then shared *her* experience of the situation with me. She told me that she had not been at Dr. G's office on October 31st, and named another identity that had gone in her place. Furthermore, she had not kept a secret from Dr. G because, in her mind, she hadn't been there. Even though she now realized that she had taken over one hundred sedative pills, enough to render herself unconscious, she insisted that she had taken the medicine to keep herself from *feeling* anything.

"I know you don't believe me," she said, "but I really wasn't trying to kill myself."

In a strange sort of way, I understood her experience.

Given her dissociative disorder diagnosis, I knew that she had developed a very complex internal system of memory holding. Gillie did not experience all of her identities as parts of herself; she was not consciously aware of turning over control to another identity and forfeiting knowledge of her actions as a result. Of course, over the course of her treatment, I had also seen how she used many different forms of self-destructive behavior to keep her anxiety in check; and that when she was so overwrought, she had little capacity to consider the danger involved in those behaviors.

I knew that I was asking a great deal of Gillie by holding her to healthier standards of being—but I also knew that if I did not set the bar high enough, she would not heal. So I told her: "Gillie, I know that you do not think you were at Glick's office, and that you do not believe you were being deceptive. However, all of those identities are parts of *you*. You can no longer allow them to take over with the belief that you are not responsible for their actions. I also hear that you were not trying to kill yourself. However, you engaged in behavior that was deadly. You can no longer allow yourself to engage in life-threatening activities. That means that if you make a safety commitment, you have to make sure you keep it. You have to commit to sharing your struggles rather than allowing yourself to check out. You may not allow yourself to lie ever again. No one can help you heal if you are withholding or dishonest in your communication."

We ended the session with the understanding that I was still unconvinced that I would be able to take on her care. I asked Gillie to think about what we discussed, and stressed that she needed to figure out whether or not she was able and willing to agree to the terms that I had laid out. We would see each other again on December 21st.

Gillie left my office and I found myself full of mixed emotions. I wanted to help her, but I was unsure I could. Would she be able to meet my terms? Would I be able to trust her again? Was I asking too much of her? Was I kidding myself to think that I could help this forty-two-year-old woman who was still this massively impaired after twenty-five years of intensive treatment?

Again, it was my spiritual belief system that answered these questions for me: "If she will choose to be saved, you have to try to save her. You are obligated to do so. There must be an approach that can work. Trust that you will discover the path. You will find it."

Gillie, of course, had her own struggles to deal with between our meetings; and when we met on December 21st, she shared them with me. Should she choose life or should she choose death? Should she take on and commit to what she knew would be a challenging treatment process? Could she do it? She realized that in choosing to work with me she would have to revisit and share her abuse history. Would she be able to do that without the option of suicide if it got to be too much? She was truly overwhelmed by the whole prospect and left that session without making a decision.

When she returned on December 26th, she told me that she was afraid of losing our relationship. I was the only woman she had ever trusted. While she was not sure she could commit to the terms just yet, she would continue to think about it. I let her know that she would need to bring me a list of the goals she had for treatment when she came to see me the next time. If we were going to be able to work together, we would need to agree on the goals, as well as her treatment terms.

When she came for her January 3rd appointment, Gillie

gave me the following list and description of her goals. We were making headway.

1. Deal with fear of being alone, of being abandoned. Think break apart, disappear, go crazy if alone. Reality changes when not connected to anybody. Anxious so much of the time that going to lose control, be sent away, left. Scared of too much—occupies so much time trying to avoid all situations feel anxious in.

2. Handling compulsion to hurt myself. Doing for 38 years. Do so can feel in control, not be overwhelmed, be real, punished so no guilt. Rely on so I don't have to feel any fear, anger. Been controlling behavior since hospital but not desire to do. Trouble with handling impulsiveness.

3. Learn some control over mood swings. No consistency in emotions; all over the place. Change rapidly and too intense. Particularly impossible to control before period.

4. Learn to handle anxiety when around people. Think staring, laughing—so self-conscious trouble functioning. Feel stupid when talk. Go behind eyeholes, inside too much, super sensitive to criticism.

5. Get rid of images. Determine emotional responses. There almost all of the time. Rule me. Go back to being little so fast, scared. React like six—feels like that is where I actually am. Repeat his yelling.

6. Develop trust in adults. See men as unpredictable, taking advantage, hurting you, powerful, volatile, smarter, rejecting you because bad, teasing and laughing, more important. Women as stupid, weak, phonies, liars, abandoning you. Lot of trouble

trusting not going to be hurt by either. Learn to relate better so not have to always feel different, alone.

7. Handle anger—can't express well or deal with others' anger toward me without feeling going to collapse. Don't know what to do with rage feel except deny or direct at self.

8. Deal with stuff with Dad because haven't been able to get away from. Possesses me—think about it every day, lot of dreams. Still real, flashes of scenes all the time. Feel scared, guilty, dirty, angry.

9. Identify with being female. Don't want to be vulnerable. Clothes for comfort; sexual protection; make you stronger, nothing hurt, asexual; awkward in skirts, imposter, wrong parts.

10. Difficulty in keeping depression away for more than a day or two at a time. Feelings of worthlessness, failure, hopelessness. Separate feelings and thoughts. Feel empty, unreal.

* Stay connected/not allow self to drift, go inside
* Weight
* Finish decorating started two years ago
* See people more, not so much hiding in house
* Get back to sewing
* House jobs, shopping
* Part-time work or training in fall or before
* More interacting with kids

Over the course of the next month, Gillie and I continued to meet weekly. We discussed her list of goals and her past history. We worked to identify and challenge our respective reluctance to re-engage in a therapy relationship. By the end of January we had worked out our reservations enough to make a commitment to resume the treatment relationship. Although Gillie harbored grave doubts about her ability to share her internal world with me, and had no idea how she would refrain from self-injurious behavior, she agreed to both conditions. I had no idea what I would need to do to help her heal, but I assured her that if she pushed herself to open up to me and committed herself to doing the homework I prescribed, I could and would help her find her way to a better place.

• • •

In the Jewish tradition there is a story told of a simple man who goes to the wise Rebbe (a Hebrew word meaning "my Teacher") of the village asking to be taught the lessons of the Bible while he stands (briefly) on one foot. Rather than waste a teaching opportunity, the wise Rebbe tells him: "Love thy neighbor as thyself. This is all you really need to know."

What does it mean to love your neighbor as yourself, and why do I digress to share this ancient wisdom in the midst of Gillie's story? Well, for me, to try and summarize Gillie's lifetime of trauma, pain, and redemption in one chapter of a book is as unreasonable a task as the Rebbe was confronted with when asked to convey the message of the Bible in one minute. Yet, the Rebbe decided to take the complex and ineffable and make it immediate. He chose to take the intricate web of richness in the Bible and reduce it to the most fundamental lesson. He focused on the value of self-love and love of others as the ultimate pathway to redemption.

So, now, like the Rebbe, I am going to attempt to distill the essence of the rich and complex tale of how I managed to help Gillie move from a place of despair to a place of fulfillment and joy. Gillie's transformation was anything but easy; each moment of that intense and challenging journey was pregnant with possibility in the face of massive pain. I cannot possibly share the full extent or nature of the four-teen-year, many thousand-hour journey we took together, but what I can do is give you a sense of the horror and magnificence of the tale. The journey was horrific for its pain, trauma, and suffering; and magnificent for its mounting slivers of hope, progressive steps of growth, and the ultimate realization of pure joy.

• • •

Over the course of our first year of work together, Gillie made a progressive transition from seeing me once a week and Dr. G three times a week, to seeing me four times per week and Dr. G not at all. Although the whole thing was self-motivated, Gillie was extremely anxious at the time. In April of 1989, as she described feeling "bad" because she was leaving Dr. G, she had a lot of trouble staying off the floor, or avoiding an old primitive behavior. She worked hard to sit in a chair during our sessions. She described feeling more hopeful when meeting with me, but she was more fearful about my ability to keep her alive than she was when she met with Dr G. Although I too felt anxious about my ability to keep her alive, I maintained hope, faith, and resolve. I reassured her that if she continued to share her internal world with me, we would find our way together.

Over the course of the next six months, I encouraged her to audiotape our psychotherapy sessions and to listen to the tapes between visits. I wanted her to begin to see how she "switched" within the sessions whenever she was over-whelmed by something. I also wanted to help her keep our therapy relationship and the conversations we had together as "real" as possible; hopefully listening to the tapes would provide her with a way to drown out the negative internal voices of her critical personalities. I prescribed anti-anxiety medications, gave her lists of coping skills, and urged her to call me between sessions whenever she was feeling over-whelmed or self-destructive. Each time she called, I would reassure her. Sometimes I would need to tell her that what she was reliving was in the past and that she was safe now. At other times, I would need to remind her that I *did* want to see her; and that I cared deeply about her. Often, I would explain that she had done nothing wrong. I would always say, "hang in there," and remind her of when we would next meet. Finally, I would tell her that she was welcome to call me again if she needed to reach me before our next visit. She was not alone.

By the end of September 1989, Gillie had made enough of a connection to me to stop seeing Dr. G for regular appointments. I sensed that she felt unable to deal with two sets of messages and approaches; she needed to choose one set of expectations. I think Gillie chose to become my patient because I expected her to heal.

Throughout those early years of work together, I regularly collected Gillie's ropes, pills, and knives. I gave her stuffed animals and plants to replace them. I taught her a Step Two mindset lesson: when she focused on self-harm she repeated the abuse of her childhood and kept herself mired in the past. She had to stop reliving that trauma or she would never heal. I also explained that Gillie and I had to build on and grow *our* relationship, as the solutions we were seeking would be found in our connection to one another. Since it was often hard for Gillie to connect, I urged her to bring me notes of her thoughts and feelings as springboards for conversation. When she seemed unable to utter a single word, I encouraged her to talk about anything she could think of no matter how insignificant it seemed. "As long as we maintain some sort of connection, even if what we discuss seems silly, we are accomplishing something," I would say, "Just talk to me." Eventually, she began to do that.

I routinely reassured Gillie that the voices she heard, as well as the people she saw, were only in her mind. No one was in the treatment room with us. She was safe, and I was not going to let anyone hurt her. I explained that she could talk back to those negative internal voices, and she could even tell them to be quiet. Frequently, the voices of her other identities would tell her not to listen to me; and when she handed over a knife or made a safety commitment to me, they would go so far as to threaten to hurt her.

Part of Gillie's treatment involved teaching her about her illness; she needed to learn that these "protective" personality states had come into being to defend her against the abusive episodes she experienced as a child. While crucial then, they were no longer necessary or beneficial to her now. She didn't need to fear them or relinquish control to them; in fact, given the rules we had established in our therapy contract, the rules of her old internal system were no longer valid. She could not and no longer needed to turn over control to the other identities. Instead, I would be there to help her learn how to take care of herself. And as I explained all of this to her, she slowly began to recognize how these "protective" messages from other identities were now actively destructive. She began to challenge them.

After about a year and a half of work with me, Gillie began bringing me cookies and small gifts for my son. I was becoming more and more real to her. She began to wonder aloud why she found herself able to talk to me. Then, in the spring of 1990 she informed me that she hadn't cut or burned herself at all for a *full year*. She said, "The urges are decreasing a lot. I thought it was impossible to stop after thirty-nine years of activity. But, I am beginning to see that you are right. Maybe I can really do this after all." Her accomplishment and growing sense of hope were surely milestones in our work together. I quietly began to celebrate our success.

However, although we had made substantial headway, we still had miles to go on our journey. Gillie was still switching between identities, both in and out of session. Each time she switched and I was confronted with a different identity, I would learn more about her history. Once that identity returned control to Gillie, I would share what I had learned with her. This practice allowed Gillie to reclaim the splintered pieces of her personal history, most of which she had no conscious knowledge of at all.

The best way to illustrate these phenomena is by example. For the first two years of our work together, Gillie was afraid to use the public bathrooms in my office building. She couldn't explain her fear, but she was nonetheless crippled by it. I was at a loss to help her. Then in June of 1990, a young child identity came to the session. She described frequent episodes of sexual abuse that occurred whenever her father came upon her in the household bathroom. "I hate bathrooms," she told me, before returning control to Gillie. When Gillie was present again, I explained why she feared public restrooms, and I assured her that the restrooms in my office were safe. I taught her how to lock all the doors so that no one could walk in on her when she was in the restroom. I even let her know that I was ready and able to stand guard outside the door if she wanted. She asked me to do that once or twice; thereafter, the explanation and assistance enabled her to begin using certain public restrooms without excessive fear.

Within a few months of that particular breakthrough, Gillie began to remember more of her abuse history. As she began to own more of her experiences and self, she became extremely concerned that I would somehow abandon her. She clearly knew she could not withstand the challenge of her growing integration alone. So, I continued to provide her with lots of reassurance, and she continued to persevere. Slowly but surely, Gillie reclaimed more and more of her own life story.

Three years into our therapeutic work together, Gillie felt that she would be able to maintain a greater sense of hope and connection to me if she were making something for one of my children. With my blessing, she began to make quilts for my then two children. As in our therapeutic work together, each completed square of the quilt was the result of hours of work. At times, Gillie would include me in the quilting process by letting me pick patterns and fabrics from the selections she brought to our appointments. I supported her in her gift, and admired her ability to create something beautiful from teeny, tiny bits of material. Simultaneously, I supported her in her ability to create a beautiful, integrated, and joyful life from the splintered bits of her self. As she presented me with one beautiful creation after another, she nurtured her growing sense of connection to another soul, as well as her own personal integration.

As time went on, Gillie found herself switching less and

less. These episodes were replaced by frequent, vivid flashbacks. Gillie would relive experiences of abuse as if they were actually happening to her in the present. Without switching to another identity, she would feel as if her father were actually there, abusing her. She would see, hear, and physically feel him. She would be overcome with panic.

By May of 1991, she began having flashbacks in my office. My ability to talk her through them grew progressively; I encouraged her to stay with me in the present, and not to give in to the pull of reliving the past. I would say, "Can you hear me, Gillie? Can you look at me instead of at what you are reliving? Can you stay with me?"

Gillie often felt the need to move closer to me, and I encouraged that, especially when she found herself overwhelmed. Slowly, she would move to a closer chair. And although she frequently wanted to sit on the floor at my feet, I would not allow her to bow to that primitive urge. While repeating the regression of our first meeting in Dr. G's office was out of the question, I was willing to do almost anything else to help her.

By allowing me to guide her through her flashbacks, Gillie was able to stay connected to me and combat overwhelming trauma. As she learned to stay in the present, she felt less of a need to resort to switching identities or hurting herself. Over time, she became increasingly adept at staying in her own skin while in my office.

• • •

Our hard work was paying off and so I raised my expectations. I encouraged her to use the strategies she was learning in her sessions to help her through the flashbacks she was experiencing at home. "Think of me and try to stay connected to me," I would say. In June of 1991, she told me that over the previous weekend she had imagined herself as a "tiny" person, existing safely "inside of [me]." Another cause for celebration! Gillie was beginning to integrate a healing force into her life; and even when I was not physically with her, she was learning to experience the safety and security our sessions represented to her. She was truly getting better.

As Gillie continued to improve, her other identities began to lose control in a progressive way. For example, she had an aggressive male identity who was her most vigilant protector. Early on in my work with Gillie, an identity who called himself the Boy would come to some sessions and demand that I give him back the knives Gillie had turned over to me. He would insist that they were his and if I did not return them, he would hurt Gillie. I would, of course, refuse to do so, and in anger, he would eventually turn control back over to Gillie.

By November 1991, the Boy had lost considerable power. On November 11, 1991 he came to the session to let me know when and why he had come into being. It was the first time he was not hostile to me. He had emerged when Gillie was about eighteen years old to protect her from her father, who was beating her up. I reassured him that I was able to help Gillie care for herself now, and that he needn't continue to exert control over her. That November 11th session was one of the last times I saw the Boy. Although he reappeared a number of times over the ensuing years, and surely caused Gillie an excessive amount of pain and trauma, he was becoming integrated.

Lest you think otherwise, Gillie was neither happy nor comfortable in her own skin as all this growth was occurring. At times she could see her progress, but she was still very depressed, anxious, and suicidal. I used every medication I could think of as I attempted to regulate her mood and anxiety states. I gave her new pictures of me and notes of hope to take home. I continued to encourage her to listen to the tapes of our sessions and to call me for extra support if she needed it. We were engaged in a very bumpy ride.

In 1996, when all of her children left home for college and post-graduate life, she began to have increased difficulty at home. She began switching personalities incessantly and hallucinating. She literally felt that the walls of her house were closing in on her, and that the world was coming to an apocalyptic end. She felt alone and isolated in her big, empty house, and was unable to leave it except to come for appointments with me.

I began to talk to her about the destructiveness of her isolation, and urged her to consider moving to a communal living space. We discussed how her current living situation was replicating the loneliness and abandonment she had experienced in her childhood; and how she needed to be surrounded by caring people if she were to stay out of old emotional responses. She needed to create a different structure around herself if she was going to experience a different result. Her current isolation was feeding her anxiety and depression. Connection would fuel her emotional growth. While Gillie was at first reluctant to consider a move, ultimately she decided to follow my advice.

She asked an older, maternal woman whom she had known since her young adulthood to share a home with her. Mrs. P was unwilling to leave her parish and the neighborhood where her children and grandchildren lived, so Gillie decided that she would move there. She offered to sell her big house and buy a new one in the community where Mrs. P lived, so that they could live together. By moving into Mrs. P's highly developed support community, Gillie was making a monumental decision to restructure her life. On April 17, 1996, she put an offer on a house in Mrs. P's neighborhood and initiated the sale of her old one. By July of that year she was installed in her new home with Mrs. P as her house-mate. I began a quiet internal celebration for reasons I will go on to explain.

In the Jewish tradition, it is often said that it takes a village to raise a child. I have found that this wisdom applies to my healing work with patients as well. I need partners in my attempts to grow and heal the people who come to me for help. Just like the parent who needs the support of the village in order to raise a child, I need the support of a community in my efforts to transform lives.

In my attempts to foster their healing, I push all of my patients to reach out for every bit of village-like support they can get. I urge them to read books that offer new perspectives. I encourage them to make new friends who will assist them in challenging their circumstances, engage in new activities, and make life-altering moves. I push and cajole, convince and support, press and urge, challenge and *expect* them to grow themselves in these ways. I do it because I have to: they need the extra support, and in my efforts to help them heal, I need all the help I can get.

When Gillie's children left home, she began to regress and she lost a tremendous amount of ground. The isolation was so damaging that we needed a whole village worth of support to recover what she had already reclaimed as her own. I needed to push her out of her hole and into a commu-nity. I had to convince her to move in with Mrs. P no matter what it took. I worked hard at it, but no matter how arduous the process was, Gillie's desire to heal was what enabled her to accept the challenge in the end. Through a series of fits and starts, *Gillie* made the move.

• • •

In the ensuing years, Gillie grew immensely. Although not a Catholic, she started singing in the Catholic church choir. Mrs. P suggested the idea, partly to build up the little singing group at her church, but also to help Gillie make connections. Gillie began to make friends with the other choir members, and to her great surprise, found that she even *enjoyed* singing! She began looking forward to choir practices and performances. Her joy and success led her to take on more. She started voice and piano lessons, and while she found both activities challenging and was periodically highly critical of her skill, she took great pleasure in her practice.

But the growing didn't stop there. She began to watch and talk about her reactions to the Oprah Winfrey show. Oprah's focus on matters of spirituality, body care, financial life management, and relationships was the springboard of many of our discussions, so much so, that *I* began to feel the healing effects of Oprah and her many guests. The more Gillie brought in concepts from the show that resonated with my years of work with her, the more I began to appreciate Oprah for her willingness to use her celebrity and media presence for such good. One day Gillie said, "I really like that show," and I quietly thanked God for Oprah Winfrey.

Meanwhile, Gillie's quilting became more and more a source of joy. She began to see the beauty of the quilts she created. She no longer hated what she produced, but was increasingly satisfied with her work. As she continued to make quilts for my growing family, her work became increasingly more exquisite. She used fewer patterns and began to create her own designs. As she grew emotionally, the quality of her work grew—it became more intricate, more inspired. As she became increasingly more integrated, her quilting work began to approach museum quality.

With the help of the village-at-large, Gillie was also able to address long-ignored matters of her physical body. When Mrs. P and one of her daughters decided to enroll in Weight Watchers, Gillie decided to take on her own significant weight problem. She moved from her historic position of disowning her physical body, to a place where she would try to heal it. She went to Weight Watchers with her friends, established a goal for herself, followed the food plan, engaged in regular exercise, and with amazing will and consistency, she was ultimately able to lose one hundred pounds!

By August of 1999, the spiritual influences of the Catholic church where she sang coalesced with the messages of hope, faith, and love that she had been hearing from me for years. She was increasingly drawn to religious questions and pursuits in a novel way. Gillie had always felt that God had abandoned her because she was "bad," but now she began to talk about her evolving concept of a loving God. I encouraged her to pursue religious questions, and in January of 2000, she began taking the Christianity classes necessary to become a Catholic. As she studied, she began to use her therapy sessions to address spiritual and religious questions in a new way. In revisiting her history, she began to challenge her self-concept and worldview. She worked diligently to integrate her growing religious viewpoint. Eventually, she came to think of herself as a child of God.

She was ready to become a practicing Catholic. She took on her new religion in a ceremony the following Easter. She had finally found a spiritual home.

During this incredible four-year period of consolidation and growth, the frequency of our visits diminished dramatically. Every few years, we were able to cut down by one more weekly visit. Over time, she was increasingly able to keep herself together—*literally*. I remained real to her between visits. She found herself less dependent on the tapes of our sessions. She began switching less and less often, until at some point, she stopped switching altogether. By the time she became a Catholic, she had become an active member of her village. She had achieved integration, and she and I were meeting only once a week. We were almost finished with our journey.

• • •

Gillie and I continued to meet weekly through the spring of 2002. Our sessions routinely focused on the challenges of day-to-day life, as opposed to past trauma. We worked on issues of healthcare, relationships, parenting, finances, expectations of self and others, personal fulfillment, and spiritual wellness: here-and-now problems. We had moved from an intensive therapeutic relationship centered on her past, to a proactive, present-day partnership; Gillie and I were now talking about how to make life *work*.

On April 24, 2002, Gillie told me that she had never been as consistently happy as she was now. "I don't do anything I don't want to do in my life, and I enjoy everything that I do!" In reviewing our history together, she realized that she had accomplished all of the treatment goals she had presented to me on January 3, 1989.

In the following session, I told Gillie that I was writing a book about how life is all about how you choose to look at it, and she gave me a knowing smile. Upon my request, she willingly agreed to let me share her story of healing. She was anxious to help others confront the tragedies, challenges, and issues they faced in order to grow beyond them. She understood that her journey was a true miracle, and by sharing her story, she could offer hope to others who found themselves in despair. She knew the healing power of its message.

As I write this, Gillie and I are meeting every other week. She is able to do quite well from session to session. She continues to experience joy and fulfillment on a regular basis. She feels blessed to have arrived at this place of peace, and I feel similarly blessed to have had a hand in her redemptive journey. We learned an amazing lesson together. While its actualization is complex, the message is very simple: where there is the will to transform a life, there is *always* a way to do it.

Lessons of Inspiration: How Gillie's Tale Relates to You

THE HEALING MODEL EFFECTS CURE IN EVEN THE MOST SEVERE OF CASES

How does Gillie's story relate to you? What can you learn from her journey? At its core, Gillie's inspirational story illustrates exactly what this book is about: by paying attention to our bodies, our minds, and our spirits, miracles can occur. If you stay the course and pursue your healing according to a reasonable plan of growth, you can achieve a state of wellness and inner peace—just as Gillie did.

Let's return to our three-legged stool—our symbolic representation of the body, mind, and spirit. This model is universally applicable; it crosses all diagnostic categories, all lifestyle challenges, and all spiritual persuasions. It can help the sickest among us, as well as the healthiest. It is a model for personal empowerment regardless of the trials you face in your life.

In this chapter, I want to review the elements of each stool leg, and show you how I worked with them to assist in Gillie's cure. Remember that while the legs are each somewhat discrete, they blend together and affect one another. For the purposes of diagnosis, treatment, and healing, it is necessary to tease apart and name the legs; it is equally important, however, to recognize their interdependent nature within the individual as a whole. While this chapter is meant to expand your understanding of the concepts and model, it is not designed to teach you how to apply them. The step-by-step chapters to follow will serve that purpose.

Identifying Body Leg Elements in Gillie's Tale

The *body leg* of the stool encompasses biology, genetics, inborn personality characteristics, feelings, particular vulnerabilities, and diagnosable medical conditions. It is the *who* part of the question, "Who am I?"

If we are to apply these notions to Gillie's story, what do we find? Who is she anyway? What did she come with? What vulnerabilities and gifts were included in the package of her being? What bits of her needed to be nurtured, and what bits needed to be challenged? What was her unique place in the universe? What was she created to express?

Gillie was born a shy, fearful child who was, at the same time, extremely anxious to please. Unlike her more aggressive sister who fought off her father's advances at an early age, and ultimately engaged her mother in protecting her, Gillie felt herself powerless in the face of her father's continued violations. Fearful of conflict and eager to placate her father, Gillie found a way to cooperate with his abuse. However, she was unable to withstand the extreme trauma of his abuse and still continue to function as one integrated human being; as a result, she developed the complex system of memory holding and additional features of multiple personality disorder.

Gillie was also born with a genetic vulnerability to develop anxiety disorders and major depression. She had a strong family history of both illnesses, and her mother served as an active example of the manifestation of both problems. Her mother was an excessively fearful, passive, and depressed woman. She cowered before her abusive husband and spent much of her time in tears. She saw no way out of her own overwhelming life situation and ultimately died at a young age, leaving Gillie even more alone and fearful than before.

Gillie's genetic vulnerabilities, coupled with her life experiences, led her to experience ongoing anxiety problems and chronic depression throughout the course of her adult life. At the time that she and I began working together, she met diagnostic criteria for two additional psychiatric disorders. She had both generalized anxiety disorder (see Appendix VII) and recurrent major depression (see Appendix I), on top of her dissociative identity disorder. She was truly challenged.

And yet, although Gillie was a shy, timid child who developed multiple psychiatric disorders, she was also born with a passion for life. Perhaps that passion for life was her greatest inborn gift. It enabled her to be an excellent student, a loyal friend, and a doting parent. It enabled her to separate and hide the bulk of her traumatic history in order to function in the universe. It served as the driving force behind her quilting, cooking, and volunteering; and it compelled her to partner with me in her amazing journey to heal.

Her passion for life was the seed of hope and the root of her ultimate redemption. In allowing that passion its full expression, Gillie was blending the *body* and *spirit legs* together. She called upon the greatest healing force in the universe to fuel her salvation: *her passion to live fully*.

Working with the Body Leg

As you recall, what transpired in the initial moments of our first session were crucial to Gillie's whole course of treatment. In those first minutes with Gillie I was working to identify her strengths and weaknesses. I was registering all pertinent diagnostic information available to me, and using it to make powerful and dramatic treatment decisions. Within those first moments, I determined that I was dealing with a massively impaired individual who also had amazing strengths. While I was overwhelmed by the power of her sickness, I chose to be hopeful. From the very beginning of my work with Gillie, I decided to ally myself with her inborn strength. While I realized that her psychiatric illness would require me to provide her with all kinds of support, I also knew I could engage with her through her passion for life.

Were it not for that partnership, I don't know if we would have been able to work together after Dr. G returned. And, as you know from the story, when that partnership was threatened by Gillie's "dishonesty" and overdose, I felt compelled to terminate my work with her.

Luckily, we were able to repair our relationship and mutual trust through a series of sessions where we spoke openly about what each of us expected and were capable of in the therapeutic relationship. I am pleased beyond words that we were able to come to terms with one another and to continue our healing work together.

Throughout the course of my work with Gillie, I was constantly coaxing her passion for life from the pit of panic and despair that enslaved it. For many years, that desire to live fully was but a mere thread of a thing; and at times, Gillie's connection to me seemed to be all that supported its continued existence. Thankfully, she was able to maintain the connection and nurture that profound life force.

Over the course of Gillie's healing journey, I regularly worked with the *body leg* elements of diagnosis, feelings, and inborn vulnerabilities. I used all manner of psychotropic medications to address her depression and anxiety. I educated her as to the nature of her MPD and helped her to understand, reclaim, and ultimately integrate her personal history. I gave her gifts, audiotapes, and take-home notes to support her through her frequent episodes of panic, despair, and experiences of unreality.

I pushed Gillie to be her best self. I refused to allow her to take the passive, self-destructive path. I challenged her weaknesses and supported her strengths. And yet, although I worked like heck to help her heal, it was really *who* Gillie *was* that determined both the course and the ultimate outcome. Who Gillie was, what she came with, and what she was created to express—these were the things that served to determine the route of our amazing journey together. It was Gillie who taught me how to help people become their best selves. She taught me to trust in who I am, and to believe in my ability to help others find the healing force they need within themselves and the universe-at-large.

Identifying Mindset Leg Elements in Gillie's Tale

As discussed earlier, the mind, or *mindset leg*, of the stool encompasses your thoughts about yourself and others. It is dramatically affected by the models you are exposed to or taught, especially during your formative years. It is the *what* in the question, "What do I think?"

Again, let's apply the theory to Gillie's story and see what we find. What did she think about herself and about other people? What lessons did she learn from her childhood? How did those lessons become reflected in her mindset? What growth-enhancing stuff did she learn that needed to be nurtured? What harmful stuff did she learn that needed to be unlearned? What was she ultimately meant to think?

Perhaps the best way to answer those questions is to return to Gillie's list of goals. I have rewritten one of her points below, adding the necessary words for clarification.

> *(I want to) develop trust in adults. (I) see men as unpredictable, taking advantage, hurting you, powerful, volatile, rejecting you because (I am) bad, teasing and laughing (at me because they are) more important. (I see) women as stupid, weak, phonies, liars, abandoning you. (I have) lots of trouble trusting (that I am) not going to be hurt by either (men or women. I want to) learn to relate better so (I do) not have to always feel different, alone.*

• • •

If we examine Gillie's description of self and others as expressed in this goal, we see that she learned to think of herself as bad, unimportant, different, and deserving of abuse. She saw men as dangerous and women as weak and unreliable. She was schooled to distrust others and to loathe herself. Indeed, Gillie had internalized a lot of harmful ideas over the course of her life; and she would have to unlearn many, if not all of these ideas, in order to heal.

What did Gillie learn that needed to be nurtured? How could she possibly have learned anything constructive in the face of all that trauma? What do you think?

Perhaps you recognized that Gillie was able to learn one of the most amazing lessons any of us can ever hope to understand—that she could *survive* in the face of overwhelming suffering. She discovered that she could find her way in the midst of what seemed impossible. Although many of the coping mechanisms that she came to employ in order to do so, such as switching, cutting, and burning herself, needed to be unlearned, that fundamental lesson served her well. That mindset lesson of survival enabled Gillie to agree to my treatment terms even when she doubted in her ability to meet them; it was crucial to her healing.

She also learned the importance of connecting to others for survival and healing. As she says in her first goal, "Reality changes when not connected to anybody." She goes on to write that she thinks she will "break apart, disappear, go crazy if alone." The abuse of her childhood taught her to search for human connection in order to survive and grow. It was out of fear of losing her connection to me that Gillie decided to commit to my treatment terms. She knew that loneliness was deadly, and connection was a lifeline. This aspect of her *mindset leg*, which also blends with the *spirit leg*, was a major determinant of her healing path. It enabled her to choose the path of salvation.

Working with the Mindset Leg

As her psychiatrist, I had to work with the positive and the negative beliefs that characterized Gillie's mindset. Again, I want to take you back to January 3, 1989, when Gillie presented her list of treatment goals to me.

Gillie came to me having learned: "I am bad, unimportant and deserving of abuse. Men are dangerous. Women are unreliable." She came to me with a series of deeply internalized negative cognitive distortions that ruled her life. She had been so deeply schooled in these ideas from such an early age that she had no concept of any alternative. To tell her otherwise, to her mind, was an enormous lie.

So how did we manage to reprogram what was, in computer lingo, such a "hard-wired" system?

If you guessed it was the power of Gillie's repetitive listening to the tapes of her psychotherapy sessions, you hit the jackpot. Remember that Gillie taped almost every psychotherapy session that she had with me. Every session served to challenge her self-concept and view of others. I constantly told her that she was a valuable person. She was neither bad nor unworthy of love. I taught her that her father had been a severely disturbed man, but that most men were caring and respectful. I explained that while her mother was emotionally limited, she was not representative of women in general. I personally demonstrated a different model. I showed her a strong, reliable example of a woman. I could be counted on. In session after session, I verbalized and demonstrated a different model from the one that she had learned.

Although Gillie and I had thousands of hours of direct contact over the years, those hours in and of themselves would not have been sufficient to affect the degree of cognitive restructuring that was necessary for her to heal. In order to effect a real cognitive restructuring—a massive exercise—she had to repeatedly listen to the positive messages from our sessions. Believe it or not, Gillie listened to the tapes of her psychotherapy sessions nearly twenty-four hours a day, seven days a week, for years. She went to bed wearing earphones and fell asleep listening to my voice uttering positive thoughts. She awoke in the morning with earphones on, listening to my voice telling her she was a valuable, wonderful, and deserving person. She bought a Walkman that continually rewound and replayed the tapes and she wore it all the time. She went through batteries for her tape machine like there was no tomorrow. She listened to me as she drove in the car, did her dishes, and read the newspaper. She used my voice to drown out her negative internal voices. Ultimately, she internalized my views and replaced the ones she had become too accustomed to; her use of the tapes transformed her negative mindset.

I should tell you something important about my decision to have Gillie tape her sessions. In urging her to bring a tape recorder to sessions so that she could take my voice home with her, I was engaging in what many of my colleagues would have considered questionable behavior. In my training, I had been schooled to be a neutral party. I had been told not to give patients presents, notes, or tapes. I had been taught to be excessively cautious about sharing anything that could be misinterpreted or used against me in a court of law. I had been encouraged to adopt the belief that to share myself was often destructive to the therapeutic process.

While my training encouraged me to be a compassionate professional, it also inadvertently encouraged me to split the stool legs from the stool, so to speak. By leaving the creative healing force out of the therapeutic process, my training prepared me to be a good doctor and therapist, but it did not teach me how to help people heal.

As I have already explained, I simply cannot leave spiritual matters out of my healing work. I don't know how to do it. And moreover, as a physician, I can only do what feels right to me at any given moment in time. So, in spite of what I learned in my training, I encouraged Gillie to tape the sessions. I did so because every fiber in my being told me that she needed the tapes. The powerful healing force that vibrated between Gillie and me said, "She needs to take you home with her in all ways possible. Give her what she needs so she can heal. Don't worry about what others would think of your actions. Trust your gut. Do what you need to do and it will work out fine. Just do it!"

It is apparent that those tapes had a major hand in transforming Gillie's belief system. But while that point is clear today, I did not think about cognitive restructuring when I encouraged Gillie to tape those sessions—in fact, I didn't think much at all! I simply did what felt absolutely right at the time. Although I was mindful of the power of positive affirmations to effect healing, I was completely unaware of how Gillie would choose to use the tapes or what she would accomplish as a result. In suggesting that she tape the sessions, I was simply trusting my gut; and unbeknownst to me at the time, in electing to trust my gut, I was to have a hand in transforming Gillie's world permanently.

• • •

Now, what about the positive aspects of Gillie's mindset? What did I do to nurture those? How did I nurture her belief that she could survive the impossible? How did I support her in her need for connection?

I challenged and expected Gillie to do the impossible. I challenged and expected myself to do the same. I challenged her to accept treatment terms that were monumental, and I committed myself to being there for her in every way humanly possible to enable her success. I reassured her that through our connection to one another we would find solutions; and I used every trick I could think of to nurture that healing connection. Nothing seemed too stupid or trivial to me—nothing at all! I put myself on the line as I challenged her to do the same. In short, I made sure that Gillie knew we were on this journey together. Our partnership was crucial to her salvation.

Identifying the Spirit Leg Elements in Gillie's Tale

The *spirit leg* concerns the meaningfulness and purpose of existence. It includes notions of a higher calling and one's sense of connection to something bigger and grander than the self. It is also the belief that we are here to help others by sharing our innate gifts and enriching one another's lives. It is the *why* of the question, "Why am I here?" It is the root of life, and the source of the infinite within each one of us. It is the experience of oneness that unites all creatures. It is the *creative healing force* and the miraculous in the mundane.

What do we find if we look for the *spirit leg* in Gillie's life? What was the role of her religious or spiritual outlook in her illness and in her healing? What role did my own spirituality play?

Gillie came to me thinking that God had abandoned her in childhood because she was a bad person. She saw little value in herself. This idea played itself out throughout her life; for example, she was convinced that I did not really want to treat her. She was sure I would ultimately abandon her, just as others had deserted her. Her entire experience of herself was as an unworthy person who lived in a dangerous, chaotic, and unreliable universe.

Yet, cloaked beneath all of those negative thoughts was an active spirituality; Gillie embodied a passion for life and creative self-expression. First, she knew that she could survive the impossible. Second, she was powerfully drawn toward the dream of self-actualization, wholeness, and forging a connection to others and the world. If nothing else, her persistent efforts in the therapeutic process, along with her ability to trust me to help her heal, prove this.

Gillie was driven by yet another spiritual dimension. Rather than allowing herself to be done in and soured by the extraordinary challenges she faced, Gillie had always nurtured her giving and generous soul. Throughout her adult life she had routinely reached out to those in need by sharing her money, food, knowledge, love, and competency. She was quick to pick up on the pain of others, and often took a lead role in caring for those whom she saw to be less fortunate than she. Gillie made quilts for AIDS babies, baby-sat for the children of ill parents, and cooked meals for the sick. She donated as much money as she could afford to worthy causes; she was often the voice for the underdog, and she routinely gave more than she could really afford to part with.

While she was constantly sharing her gifts to enrich the

lives of others, Gillie did not realize that she was as much a child of the universe as those she helped. She did not realize that she had as much right and reason to be here as every other human being. For her to achieve wellness, she would need to expand her self-concept and worldview. She would need to begin to see the divine within herself and in the universe. Only then would she be truly healed. It was my job to help her get there.

Working with the Spirit Leg

In order to show you how I worked with the *spirit leg* in Gillie's healing, I need to take you back to my struggle at the end of August 1988. As you recall, I was anticipating Dr. G's return from vacation and looking forward to being relieved of the burden of keeping Gillie *alive*. After telling me that she had never been open with Dr. G about the extent and severity of her self-destructive behavior, Gillie urged me to continue seeing her for psychiatric care. I was overwhelmed by her request.

Suddenly, I found myself drawing upon the spiritual dimension in my life in order to continue working with Gillie. I kept revisiting my spiritual belief system to help me figure out what to do and how to go on. Ultimately, my spiritual beliefs were responsible for my decision to go on working with Gillie after Dr. G's return; and they were paramount when I resolved to give Gillie the benefit of the doubt when she returned, asking for another chance. Perhaps most important, though, my spiritual beliefs were behind my determination to expect the impossible from her. My beliefs enabled me to reassure her that we had the capacity to meet all of her treatment goals, and they led me to do all sorts of unconventional things to foster the healing process.

Although Gillie came to me thinking that God had abandoned her because she was bad, I always saw the divine in her. Even though Gillie was unable to recognize any value in herself, I was struck by the infinite value of her life, gifts, and potential. When Gillie was convinced that I did not want to meet with or help her, I reassured her otherwise. If Gillie were willing to choose life, I was committed to doing my very best to assist her.

My awe of the sanctity and majesty of all human lives that come before me is unavoidable. It is present in every moment of my healing work. It informs everything that I do. It leads me to draw on all of the resources I can possibly harness, and to disregard all the skeptics. My sense of wonder and oneness in the world leads me to trust my gut and to search for partners in the universal village. It leads me to look for solutions when others would say there are none, and to expect miracles in the most mundane of pursuits. It enables me to coax the phoenix from the ashes and to have a powerful hand in the transformation of lives.

In the final analysis of Gillie's tale, I have to say that my belief system was the cornerstone of my success. Without my faith, I would have become just one more psychiatrist in Gillie's long list of care providers. Without the passion and persistence of my belief system to guide Gillie, I don't know if she would have recovered. In the deepest recesses of my being I choose to believe that *wherever* there is a will, *the creative healing force* will enter in to show us the way. My faith and search for that healing force, ultimately helped Gillie turn her life around.

As we go forward, I hope to help you see the place and power of that force in your world as well. I want to help you transform your life. I will show you how to think about and apply the three-legged stool model to your own experience. Although your story is unique, the principles that guided me in Gillie's treatment process apply to your journey as well. After all, we humans are more alike than we are different. Given our similarities, I can guarantee that if you have the will to change your life, then there's a way for you to do so.

Step One: Body

GETTING A BASELINE
AND ACCEPTING WHO YOU ARE

Let's begin walking through Step One of the healing journey, understanding and addressing the *body leg* of the stool. The *body leg* involves biology, genetics, inborn personality characteristics, feelings, vulnerabilities, and diagnosable medical conditions. This biological dimension concerns what we can call the "givens," those bits of you that reflect your nature and constitution.

Getting a baseline and accepting who you are is the first step in your path. You may be in treatment, but find that you are not making any headway because you haven't been given a diagnosis that is crucial to your recovery. Or, you may have been given an incorrect diagnosis at some point, and find yourself unable to make progress as a result. You can have this experience whether or not your therapist is a physician, or even if you have never been in therapy at all.

Skipping over this diagnostic step altogether, or mislabeling a condition, is extremely common.

You may be wondering, "If my doctor has missed or mislabeled my condition, does that mean I need a new doctor?" I would say possibly, but not necessarily. If you come to think your doctor has erred, I encourage you to revisit your provider and share your newfound understanding. See if you can work through it and move forward together; oftentimes you can, and are better off for the effort. If you find that you are unable to make progress with your provider, I suggest you get a second diagnostic opinion from someone else.

Beyond diagnostic issues, you may be having difficulty accepting and honoring aspects of your biology, constitution, or personality that are unrelated to a disorder. Sometimes a feeling can just be a feeling. In other words, being sad does not necessarily mean you are clinically depressed. Whether or not you have a diagnosable condition, it is extremely important to come to understand your biological givens, vulnerabilities, and sensitivities. Our culture tends to focus more on what's *wrong* with us as individuals than on what *works* to make us special and wonderful. We all have a tendency to find fault with the aspects of our appearance that we have not chosen, vulnerabilities and limitations that seem to hang us up, and our drives and orientations to pursue activities that are considered outside of the mainstream. We are prone to be far more self-critical than is good for our health, and we are usually quite unaware of how severely we sell ourselves short.

In this chapter, I am going to concentrate on diagnoses and identifying feelings. I am including some questions for you to consider as well; hopefully, they will assist you on your own healing journey. These questions are designed to help you identify other significant aspects of your nature, such as your personality traits and innate talents. But please remember, no matter what you discover as you work with the tools in this chapter, *your gifts outweigh all of your shortcomings and vulnerabilities.*

You are *meant* to heal.

• • •

In an effort to get you thinking about self-concept and diagnosis, I want to share what three of my patients told me about themselves when they first came to see me for treatment. I asked them, "Tell me what brings you here and how I can help you." Each of their cases provides us with an example of a missed or incorrect diagnosis.

> Cindy was a teacher who was experiencing such excessive anxiety that she had been unable to go to work for several days. She contacted me after her long-standing therapist suggested that she calm down by either sitting in an easy chair while listening to mood-music, or climbing into a warm bathtub in a candle-lit bathroom. Feeling incapable of sitting still in a chair or a bathtub, Cindy knew that she needed a different sort of help. Her next-door neighbor, a prior patient of mine, suggested that she call me. When Cindy first contacted me, she attributed her symptoms to a job that was too stressful. "I am anxious," she said, "because my job is too hard."

> Samuel, a married businessman who had been successful in a long-term recovery program for an addictive illness, explained his ongoing marital

discord and his checkered career history to me by saying: "I am self-centered and selfish. I want what I want when I want it, and I don't treat my wife well at all. My last therapist told me that I have a narcissistic personality disorder!"

Baxter, an attorney who had recently relocated to Philadelphia for work, told me he had a history of depression and was currently being treated for panic disorder. He explained his ongoing career dissatisfactions by citing his long-standing competitive issues with his father. "My last therapist of several years told me that my anger and competition with my father were causing me to be dissatisfied with my work. My difficulties have nothing to do with my diagnoses or with the career path I chose."

Although we are about to begin discussing biology, proper diagnoses, and self-acceptance in this chapter, I do not want you to be overwhelmed by the prospect of trying to figure out "who you really are" in one afternoon. While it is crucial that you come to know yourself in order to heal, understanding and accepting your biology, your propensities, your genetics, and your inborn talents and limitations is an immense project. While a diagnosis may be applicable to you, you might find it hard to understand and accept that. And again, it is worth noting that some of the biological elements in your character might be related to a medical condition, but they might not. When you engage in self-analysis, it is important that you take your time and stay the course.

If you are like most people who seek my counsel, you are probably wondering, "What is the path to transforming my life? Where do I start? What is the process? How do I know if I am doing the right stuff? How do I stay on track and keep from getting derailed?" You might even be saying, "Never mind how I do it, what I really want to know is *can* I do it? The task seems overwhelming! Can I really get better?"

I hear your concerns and I understand them. They are universal. We all have them. Change is scary. I would like to help you combat your fears. So, before I begin describing Step One of the path to personal transformation, I will offer you some spiritual coping techniques. I will share my model of personal empowerment with you.

When I feel overwhelmed, I call up a series of responses. I remind myself that the longest journey begins with the first step. "Easy does it," I say. "Don't forget that you only need to consider one day at a time." I recite the serenity prayer and allow it to echo in my brain.

*God grant me the serenity to accept the things
I cannot change, the courage to change the things I can
and the wisdom to know the difference.*

I remind myself of the miraculous in the mundane and struggle hard not to get too far ahead of where I am. I think: yesterday is in the past, and tomorrow is yet to come. The only thing you really have is today. Start with the now. Do your best for today and try hard not to obsess about tomorrow. Do what you need to do for today, and tomorrow will be better than yesterday. Don't worry so much. Just get started!

So, what is involved in getting started? What is the first step in transforming a life? Where did I start in my work with Gillie? Where did I start with each of the three patients whose comments you just read? Where do I suggest that you start in your own personal journey?

You probably remember that in my initial session with Gillie, I focused primarily on my questions and observations of the *body leg*. I worked to identify the diagnoses, feelings, strengths, and weaknesses that defined Gillie. I needed to understand, register, and accept where we were starting; I asked myself, *Who is this person in front of me? What did she come with that needs to be nurtured, transformed, or treated? How can I help her to help herself?*

I started my work with Gillie in the manner that all transformational journeys need to begin; I started where she was. I started by identifying and accepting the givens. I did so because no other first step is possible. I started my work with Cindy, Samuel, and Baxter in the same way. None of us can possibly hope to effect any kind of change in ourselves if we cannot first accept who we are. We must start with attempts to gain self-knowledge and self-acceptance.

Let's look at this Step One concept in another way. As you may know, the 12 Step recovery programs are a series of self-help programs that began in the late 1930s with Alcoholics Anonymous. Two alcoholics, who had failed to improve with all other manner of treatment, got together to form the first spiritually based program for healing. They developed the 12 Step approach to recovery. The success of their program in promoting healing was so dramatic that the twelve steps of AA have subsequently been adapted to many other addiction recovery programs as well. These spiritually based programs have miraculously enabled many millions of addicts, who could not imagine living a single day without using their drug of choice, to attain clean, sober, and deeply fulfilling lives.

In spite of the fact that the 12 Step programs have been

so successful over the years, they remain divorced from traditional medicine. The language of diagnosis and medication intervention is strangely absent from 12 Step meeting rooms, and the spiritual message of 12 Step recovery programs rarely enters physicians' offices. This split has always troubled me. We can all learn something if we look for greater integration. Even spiritually based programs have something to teach us about *body leg* issues.

Given the powerful and miraculous transformation that is possible through the active use of the 12 Steps, it behooves us to look at step number one as we begin to answer the questions we are asking here: What is the first step that I need to take in my own personal journey to transform my life?

Interestingly, the first step in the 12 Steps is one of *body leg* acceptance! Even in this spiritually based program, self-acceptance is where the healing transformation begins. The founders of AA, and millions of other recovering addicts, understand that without taking that first step, recovery is impossible. Step number one reads: "We admitted we were powerless over alcohol—that our lives had become unmanageable." While step two of the AA 12 Steps moves on quickly to address the need for a higher power in healing, those founders realized that they needed to accept their alcoholism as a given if they were to begin to recover. Only in accepting the current reality or diagnosis can committed alcoholics have any hope of healing and redemption.

How does this digression relate to you and your path of transformation? I suggest that whether or not you have an addictive illness, you need to take Step One. If you want to change, you first need to take a personal inventory and identify who you are. Be gentle and honest with yourself in this exercise. Be open to the possibility that you have a psychiatric or medical condition that requires medication management or some other form of treatment and support. Do not allow yourself to get stuck in shame and guilt. You have strengths as well as limitations, gifts as well as challenges. Since all psychiatric diagnoses are made on the basis of history, not laboratory tests, you are well equipped to begin to look at whether a diagnosis belongs to you. You know your own history and internal world better than anyone else does. If you are given enough information about the various psychiatric disorders, you can begin to determine whether you have one, none, or possibly a few.

Consider whether you meet diagnostic criteria for any of the following extremely common psychiatric disorders, which will interfere with healing if they go undiagnosed: major depression, dysthymic disorder, bipolar disorder, panic disorder, obsessive-compulsive disorder, post traumatic-stress disorder, social phobia, generalized anxiety disorder, attention deficit disorder, anorexia, bulimia, binge-eating disorder, and substance-related disorder. Diagnostic information concerning these disorders can be found in Appendices I-XI. Additionally, the clinical tales that fill this book will help you evaluate where you fit in. If at any point you begin to think you might have one or several of these disorders, please pursue assessment from a trained professional. Seeking help for diagnosable conditions is a significant part of Step One in your personal journey. The interventions that might be necessary include medications and cognitive tools and techniques.

Find a doctor who is equipped to diagnose and treat your condition. If your circumstances allow, and you are able to find a care-provider who does body, mind, and spirit work, all the better. However, it is not necessary for you to do so.

You can procure appropriate diagnosis and treatment of the aforementioned conditions from someone who may not provide the full course of the body-mind-spirit treatment that I routinely offer to patients in my practice. That said, you can cover Step One with doctors who are equipped to address that dimension of your journey, and look to other resources for the rest. It is very important for you to realize that you do not need to get all your care in one place: over the course of your journey, you might seek the counsel of therapists, physicians, clergy members, social workers, friends, family, and so on.

In continuing to work on Step One in your healing journey, you might want to answer the following questions; they are designed to help you name and accept "givens" about yourself:

Who am I?

What do I know about myself?

What are my passions?

What makes me laugh, cry, scream?

What am I great at?

What am I terrible at?

How do I most like to spend my time?

What do I wish I could do more of? Better? Differently?

What do I want that I don't have?

What am I avoiding? Denying?

What do I fear?

Who do I love and why?

Can I identify my feelings most of the time?
Why or why not?

What feelings am I most comfortable with?

Are they the ones I express?

Am I true to myself or not?

Answering the above questions will help you get more out of the stories and lessons that follow. Feel free to answer them now, or to return to them once you have read the tales that follow.

Cindy and Step One

When Cindy first called me on the telephone to set up an initial appointment, she was suffering from crippling anxiety. Her speech was pressured. She could not stop pacing, and she was completely unable to sleep. Before she could even get in to see me for an appointment, she needed some help in settling herself down. Easy chairs, mood-music, baths, and candles were clearly not doing the trick. I prescribed some anti-anxiety medication for her before arranging to see her the following day.

When Cindy came to see me the next day, she was calm enough to sit still and give me some background. She told me that she was anxious because her "job was too stressful." I listened carefully to her description of the challenges facing her in her position with the school system. I discovered that there were, indeed, some new demands being placed on her there. But when I asked her to tell me about other recent developments in her life outside of work, Cindy described a series of painful losses, including the death of her mother and the breakdown of trust in her relationship with her sister. She talked about being unsure of how to cope with these significant losses of connection in her life. When I asked her to describe her baseline nature, she told me that her family members all considered her to be "too hyper." She went on to say that, although she had never seen herself in the same way, she was now beginning to wonder whether they might be right.

I then asked her to tell me about the specific symptoms of her current anxiety problem. She described discrete periods during which she would experience the sudden onset of intense fearfulness or terror accompanied by a sense of impending doom. During each of the episodes she would be short of breath, feel her heart beating rapidly in her chest, experience a painful smothering sensation, and be consumed with a fear of a complete loss of control. Each episode would come on rapidly, and the symptoms would peak in severity within the space of ten minutes. It would take her a long time to settle down once she had an attack. Her first episode had occurred some weeks ago. The attacks were coming on more and more often as time passed, and she was finding herself increasingly anxious about the possibility of recurrences.

As part of Step One, I said to Cindy, "It is quite possible that your current job is too stressful and that you would be best suited to make some sort of job change, but that is not clear now. What is clear is that you meet diagnostic criteria for panic disorder. You were born with a genetic vulnerability to develop this disorder. Your 'hyper' nature is similar to that of many people who go on to manifest this disorder. Further, the kinds of losses you have recently experienced often herald the onset of panic attacks. In order for us to sort out the job question, we need to treat your panic disorder first. You cannot possibly figure out anything else if your thoughts are coming a mile a minute and you cannot even sit still in a chair. I need to treat you with medications and teach you how to use some cognitive behavioral interventions. Once your anxiety is under control, we can begin to explore the role of your current job in its genesis."

Cindy listened carefully and asked many clarifying questions. She struggled with my take on things. She wanted it to be about the job, not a disorder. She didn't want to accept that there was something "wrong" with her. She kept coming back to the specifics of her job to justify her distress. We revisited her resistance repeatedly. She was loath to admit that it was not the job that filled her with fear of a complete loss of control, caused her to pace the room, and lose her focus. Although I read Cindy the diagnostic criteria for panic disorder, and she recognized her problem in the *DSM IV* criteria, she did not want to accept the panic disorder label.

In that initial session, Cindy was struggling mightily with Step One. She was doing what we all do. She was mustering every argument and defense that she could think of to avoid a "given" about herself, a diagnosis, or a reality that was too disturbing to her. Cindy, like all of us, had been schooled to think that a diagnosis was a bad thing. Somehow, in her mind, having panic disorder made her defective and unworthy. For her to have a diagnosis meant that she was "damaged goods." It was abhorrent to her to consider that notion. She didn't want to be ill. She didn't want to acknowledge the clear implication of a fit between her symptoms and the diagnostic criteria she had heard.

In tackling Cindy's resistance, I needed to call into action all of my medical knowledge and reasoning skills. I shared the available scientific data on the onset, course, and treatment of panic disorder with her. I outlined the great morbidity associated with untreated panic. I explained that

while she had not chosen her biology or particular vulnerability to the disorder, she could choose to either deny the
diagnosis or accept and deal with it. I encouraged Cindy to
do what I suggested you do at the outset of this chapter. I
urged her to take Step One. "Accept where you are to begin
with," I said. I worked to normalize the diagnosis by telling
her that the National Institutes of Health had recently
reported that 2.4 million American adults between the ages
of eighteen and fifty-four, or about 1.7 percent of people in
this age group, in any given year have panic disorder (see
Appendix III). I pushed her to challenge her view of the
diagnosis, and explained that the recovery could only occur
if she would accept and deal with the givens.

While the process was quite difficult, Cindy ultimately
agreed to start at the necessary beginning. She chose to
accept the diagnosis and began taking medication for her
crippling symptoms. In closing that first session, Cindy
admitted, "I guess you are right. I need to accept what this
is. I can't even think straight right now. If I go on like this,
I will lose my job and go nuts. I need to accept treatment for
a disorder I know I have."

Over the course of the ensuing weeks, I taught Cindy
how to use anti-anxiety medication as needed to control her
symptoms. I also showed her how to use a series of cognitive-behavioral techniques to combat the patterns that had
emerged: as soon as a bit of anxiety would show itself, Cindy
would begin to focus on its propensity to overwhelm her.
This would cause her to become more anxious. I taught her
how to stop her thinking from snowballing out of control by
introducing her to a technique called "thought-stopping."
The technique is similar to the one that I used with Gillie
when I encouraged her to use the tapes of our sessions and

to talk back to her negative internal voices. It involves inter-
rupting the worrisome or obsessive thoughts with a specific
type of self-talk and activity.

Whether you suffer from panic attacks or some other
disturbing series of symptoms, you can use the thought-
stopping technique to address just about any cascade of
negative thoughts. For Cindy, the trick was to curb her escalating worry, but it can be equally effective as an antidote to
depressive or self-deprecating thoughts.

The technique involves a series of steps:

1. Identify the negative thought that you are telling
   yourself, i.e., I am worthless, or my anxiety is going
   to escalate out of control.
2. Take a single opportunity to tell yourself something
   that contradicts the negative thought, i.e., I am a
   worthwhile person, or I can control my anxiety with
   the medications I have been given.
3. Then begin to tell yourself to "stop it" whenever you
   find yourself beginning the cascade.
4. Use reminders of any sort to help you remember to
   turn that negative message off. In Cindy's case, I
   suggested stop signs.
5. Rather than allowing yourself to continue focusing
   on the negative thought by "talking back to it"
   specifically, distract yourself in any way you can.
   Use music, a book, a magazine, television, exercise,
   cooking, singing, or anything else that will keep you
   from returning to the thought.
6. Use this technique whenever you realize you are
   engaging in negative self-talk. At first, you will find

yourself falling into a destructive self-talk cycle before you even recognize what is happening; over time, however, you will begin to identify the moments that your negative thinking is getting the better of you.

7. Stay the course. As time goes on you will learn to interrupt yourself earlier and earlier and will need to use the technique less and less.

To make these points clear, listen to how I used the technique to help Cindy. I explained to her that she would have to tell herself to "stop it" whenever she began to obsess. I urged her to place little stop signs all around her house, in her car, and in her purse to remind her to use the technique. I explained that she needed to remind herself that her anxiety could be managed by medication, so she need not panic about it escalating beyond her control. I told her that she needed to stop allowing herself to obsess; she needed to say "Stop it" whenever she began to worry. She then needed to shift her focus to another activity that would preclude her from thinking about her worries. I explained that she might need to use this technique hundreds of times a day at the beginning but, as time went on, she would need to do it less and less.

Cindy began to follow my instructions. She used a favorite song as her distraction and sang it to herself in her head when she could not do it aloud. As she did this, her symptoms began to remit. After a few weeks, she was relieved of her crippling anxiety. We were then able to take on another part of Step One.

As I mentioned earlier, accepting vulnerabilities and diagnoses is only part of Step One; another part involves paying due respect to your ongoing feelings. This part of Step One can be quite challenging. We all have a tendency to avoid identifying our feelings, and a propensity to confuse *feelings* with *thoughts*.

The feelings that I am talking about in the context of Step One, *body leg* work are the ones that concern *emotional states* or *reactions*. They are usually named by the single words that complete the following sentence: I feel _____. Some examples of such words include *happy, sad, excited, anxious, unsettled, depressed, joyous, hopeless,* and *hopeful.* Each of these feeling-words can be a window into the soul. Each word conveys something active and relevant about what a given individual is experiencing at a given point in time.

Feelings are the universal connectors and the greatest equalizers. All people, whether or not they speak the same language or come from the same culture, have the capacity to connect with one another through shared feelings. Words can become unnecessary in the realm of emotional connection; even facial expressions can reflect feelings. Feelings are among the most fundamental "givens" of life. To respect them is to nurture life; to run roughshod over them is to squander life's potential. Before I show you how that happens, however, I want to show you how to separate your *feelings* from your *thoughts*.

Oftentimes we kid ourselves into believing that we are identifying our feelings when we are really expressing our thoughts. It is actually harmful to confuse the two. Registering feelings can guide us toward greater self-knowledge and actualization, but thoughts disguised as feelings tend to do the opposite. Here are three examples of thoughts disguised as feelings.

1. I feel that my boss is unreasonable.

2. I feel as if I am doing my best in my position in the school system.
3. I feel like my ex-husband is taking advantage of me.

While each of these three sentences begins with the "I feel" statement, none of them ends with a feeling-word. In fact, all three sentences include a transition after the "I feel" part of the sentence. Words such as *that, as if,* or *like* change the subject of the sentence from feelings to something other than feelings. What follows the transition is a *thought* about a thing or a person. Whenever we add a transition after the "I feel" part of a sentence, we are tricking ourselves into thinking that we are identifying feelings. We are not; in fact, when we make this mistake, we usually wind up shifting our focus away from ourselves and onto others. In so doing, we become even further detached from our essence.

I often give my patients a list of words, what I call a Feelings Vocabulary, to refer to when they are developing the skills they need to identify their feelings. I encourage them to post the list on their refrigerators or bathroom mirrors, and to refer to it as they work to name their emotional states. While I recognize that the list is far from exhaustive, it is a good start. I often encourage my patients to add feeling-words to it as they grow in their feeling recognition skills. I am providing the list for you at the end of this chapter so you can use it in your own transformational journey. You will probably find that this list will help you to expand upon or change your answers to the questions at the outset of this chapter.

Feelings play a crucial role in diagnosis and Step One work. One of my long-term patients often highlights this lesson by asking me, "What feelings am I supposed to pay attention to? You tell me to respect my feelings. Yet when I tell you that I am a failure, you tell me I am being hard on myself. You tell me to talk back to myself when I feel lousy and put myself down. You encourage me to nurture self-love. I don't get it. What feelings am I supposed to respect?"

My patient's confusion is understandable. I just told you that feelings are windows into the soul, that to respect feelings is to nurture life, and to run roughshod over feelings is to squander life's potential—but are there feelings that need to be understood differently? Are there feelings, or descriptions of emotional states, that are not really reflections of your core? Are there feelings that reflect something else?

The answer is yes; absolutely and most definitely yes. The feelings that would fall into that category are those that serve to define a particular medical or psychiatric diagnosis. While identifying, understanding, and respecting those feelings is crucial to healing, it is not part of the exercise of gaining self-knowledge. It is part of accepting what is, diagnostically. The excessive anxiety felt by someone who has a panic disorder is not a window into the soul, but rather a key to the diagnosis of panic disorder. The excessive self-loathing felt by a clinically depressed patient is not a window into the soul; it is a key to the diagnosis of major depression. The irritability often felt by the individual who has ADD is not a window into the soul. It is a key to the ADD diagnosis.

Making this distinction between the feelings that are part of a medical or psychiatric condition and those that are windows into the soul is a key element in the growth and healing process. In fact, making the distinction is so crucial that I started this chapter, not with a discussion of feelings, but by urging you to consider whether any of the common psychiatric disorder diagnoses might apply to you.

I did so because no growth work is possible if crucial diagnoses are missed and feelings are misunderstood as a result.

So how did I work with feelings in Step One of Cindy's care? Remember what I told you: Cindy's feelings would not lie. Her feelings were there for a reason. If allowed their full expression, her feelings would indicate the path to her salvation. Once uncovered, they would show her what steps she needed to take to further her growth and support her recovery.

Since we humans are more alike than we are different, I could deduce certain things about Cindy. Furthermore, once Cindy's panic disorder was under control, I could understand her anxiety differently. I knew that Cindy became anxious when she ignored or repressed her feelings, because we all get anxious when we push ourselves to do what we don't want to do. I also knew that her anxiety would be quelled when she respected her feelings, because we all feel better when we do what we know we need to do. Helping Cindy to identify and respect her feelings was going to be a crucial element of our Step One work together.

As such, I began to explore Cindy's emotional life with her. Rather than tell you her whole life story, I will give you a few examples of the Step One process involved in her care. The first example concerns Cindy's experience of her workplace. Cindy often began her sessions by recounting detailed stories of how her co-teachers had left her out of the process of making some important team decision. Each time she told me such a story, I urged her to avoid focusing on what her colleagues had done wrong. I pushed her to identify how she was feeling about the occurrence. This exercise made her anxious.

However, once she was able to get past the anxiety she felt each time I pushed her to deal with herself, she would stop blaming her co-teachers for her distress. She would then identify her own feelings of hurt and anger. "Good for you," I would say. "It is very important that you realize you were hurt by their actions. Identifying your feelings is your first step in solving a problem."

I would then ask her whether she had ever tried to talk to her colleagues about her desire to partner with them. Had she told them that she felt pain upon being left out of crucial decision-making? Had she let them know it mattered at all? As time went on, Cindy began to realize that she had never tried to talk to her co-teachers about her desires or feelings.

I continued to urge her to respect the messages her feelings were sending her. Then I would tell her something that has become a crucial theme in my work with many patients. "Ask for what you know you need," I would say. "No one can read your mind. Tell others how you feel and what you hope for, and let's see what happens."

Eventually, Cindy was able to do just that. She began to share herself with others, and was amazed to discover what came back. Her colleagues were happy to work more closely with her! They had not realized that she wanted to have a different sort of working relationship. They were all for it!

The second example of my Step One feelings-work with Cindy occurred several months into our work together. Cindy came for her session and shared that she had been excessively anxious all week. Although she had been using the medication and the thought-stopping techniques, she just could not seem to settle down. She didn't know what else to do.

I asked her to tell me something more about the events of her preceding week. She began to describe the stress she felt in anticipation of an upcoming holiday feast. She was hosting her whole extended family for the meal. "My mother always used to do the holidays," she said, "Now everyone expects me to take over. My sister won't help out and my brother wants to bring extra guests. I hate entertaining. They are all being so obnoxious. I don't even like some of them. No one cares about me. They just want me to take over where Mom left off."

As she spoke, Cindy became increasingly agitated. I could see why she had had a tough week. She was doing something we all do at times. She was relinquishing control of her life and taking on more than she felt able to manage.

"Cindy," I said, "stop talking for a minute, and take a step back. Why are you torturing yourself so much? Do you want to host this holiday or not? You don't have to do it. You do have a choice. No one can make you host your family. You are a grown woman. How do you really *feel* about it?"

Cindy did not register my questions at first. She was on a roll; rather than acknowledge her feelings, she continued to focus on what "other" people were "doing." She kept talking about her relatives critically. While her misguided focus was apparent to me, she was blind to it. She was attached, as we all are, to her way of experiencing things. I stopped her again.

"Cindy, stop for a minute and take a step back, please," I said. This time she paused. Before she could continue saying more of the same, I asked her, "How are you *feeling*, Cindy?"

This time, she heard me. Tears came to her eyes as she said, "I do not want to host this holiday. I feel overwhelmed by the details involved. I feel guilty saying that, though. I know my mother expected me to follow in her footsteps and to keep the family together. She was the glue in the family. She expected me to pick up where she left off. I know that she is watching me from heaven now. She expects me to be the hostess."

There it was. Cindy had just described a self-destructive thought pattern that many of us are prone to enact. "You have taken on quite a burden. Do you really think your mother would want you to be sick?" I asked. "I need to explain to you why I am asking that. Your anxiety disorder is escalating out of control as you try to take on a task that your core being—the place where your true feelings live—wants to avoid. You don't want to entertain, but you are trying to do it anyway. You are forcing yourself to do it because you believe that your mother, who has passed away, wants you to do it. You are ignoring your feelings and making yourself sick in the process. If you keep moving along this course, you may even make yourself too sick to host the family event no matter what. Do you really think this is what your mother would want for you?"

Cindy sat quietly for a long time. I could tell that she was working hard to challenge herself to think broadly. Finally, she seemed to calm down and find a place of peace. She then said, "I know how my mother thought and felt about most things. I know that she would have given up her life if she thought that it would be helpful to me. She never would have wanted me to make myself sick. She would have told me to respect my feelings and let someone else do the entertaining of the family. I guess I need to listen to her, and trust my feelings on this one. Thank you for setting me straight. Can you help me figure out what to tell my family members? I know that they aren't the problem in all of this. I am. I just don't know what to say to them to get out of the obligation I feel."

As is often the case, in identifying her own feelings, Cindy was able to let go of her negative thoughts about others. In doing so, she could calm down and begin to solve the problem. We began to work on setting boundaries between herself and her relatives in a respectful way. This led her to decide to tell her siblings the truth. She would let them know that she was conflicted: she was pushing herself to take on duties that were making her sick; her attachment to certain beliefs about her mother's expectations had been causing her to disrespect her own needs and feelings. The pressure she had put upon herself had been causing her to experience escalating panic. Her doctor had helped her to realize that hosting the holiday meal was having a negative impact on her mental health.

By the end of her appointment, Cindy had even decided to ask one of her siblings to host the event. She was able to leave my office feeling lighthearted and excited. She was proud that she had figured out how to respect her own feelings and take care of herself without treating any of her relatives with disrespect.

There is more to share in Cindy's story, but before we move on, let's pause and have a look at what we can learn here. Cindy's resolution of a common self-destructive pattern has several important lessons in it. First, when we act from a place of guilt or misguided belief, we can do damage to ourselves and make ourselves ill. Second, when we ignore our feelings, we often become critical of others. Third, when we come back to center, or identify our misguided beliefs and core feelings, we can problem-solve and move forward with our growth.

In a final, brief example of how I worked to help Cindy identify and learn from her feelings, I want to share a vignette that concerns her marital dynamic. Cindy's wedding anniversary was two days away, and she came to her psychotherapy session in an extremely agitated state. "What do you think is bothering you so much?" I asked. In trying to understand the reason for her distress, Cindy began to brain-storm aloud. She finally hit upon a crucial set of feelings. She realized that she wanted to take her husband away on a short trip for their anniversary. Yet, she had not allowed herself to identify her feelings or desires because she was afraid to spend the money. The internal desire versus fear of conflict was causing her to be anxious. Once she was able to identify both the desire and the fear, we were able to problem-solve the issue. Cindy and I worked together to plan an affordable getaway for her anniversary. Just like that, her anxiety disappeared and she was able to celebrate!

• • •

How is Cindy's story emblematic of the crucial role the *body leg* plays in healing?

Here is a summary of the key *body leg* points.

1. Although Cindy came to me thinking she was anxious because her job was too demanding, she was actually suffering from an undiagnosed panic disorder. Cindy's absence of a proper diagnosis had been keeping her from healing. Although she had been getting therapeutic support, in her severely debilitated state, she had been unable to make use of the strategies recommended by the prior thera-pist. Step One in her healing journey required making the proper diagnosis.

2. I made sequential use of medications, cognitive-behavior therapy techniques, and feeling identifica-

tion strategies to promote her recovery. Once the proper diagnosis was made and Cindy accepted the treatment plan, specific steps could be implemented to diminish her incapacitating panic symptoms. The diagnosis determined the plan.

3. Once Cindy began to improve, we discussed boundary-setting and problem-solving skills that she would need to incorporate into her life in order to heal. Once Cindy's symptoms were under control, she could begin to learn specific life strategies to mitigate the onset of panic attacks.

What can we learn from Cindy's story?

1. If you find yourself stuck in your growth whether in or out of therapy, you, like Cindy, may have an unrecognized psychiatric disorder that requires diagnosis and treatment. You may even have panic disorder. Do not blame, criticize, or devalue yourself if you are stuck. Be open to the possibility that you need help with something that you did not choose or cannot control. Review diagnostic information on common disorders that may apply. Trust yourself to figure whether descriptions of particular problems might fit you. Then ask for help from medical professionals who can help clarify your suspicions.

2. Once you have ruled in or out diagnoses, you are prepared to take specific steps to address your problem. If medications or specific techniques are required, take and use them until you feel a growing sense of mastery. Do not try to do too much too fast. Medications and specific behavioral strate-

gies can take a while to take hold. As long as you see slow, but steady progress, stay the course. If you do not, challenge the diagnoses or treatment plan.

3. Once your symptoms are under reasonable control, you can begin to look at bigger questions about relationships, interactions, and life choices.

Take-Home Points

1. We all have difficulty managing our anxiety at times. For some of us, a full-blown anxiety disorder exists and can be incapacitating; the rest of us can be periodically overwhelmed by anxiety as well.

2. The steps and tips in Cindy's tale are universally applicable to the management of anxiety. Most particularly, the thought-stopping technique can be used by anyone.

3. Proper self-assessment, cognitive restructuring, feeling identification, and learning to ask for what we need are crucial to our ongoing self-care. We can all develop competence in these skills.

Samuel and Step One

Samuel was referred to me by a friend from his 12 Step recovery program. He requested the referral because he felt "stuck" in his growth plan to transform his life. He had been in regular psychotherapy for some time, but felt as though he was going around in circles. He had no idea of how to move on, and although he had been clean and sober for years, he was still regularly feeling unsettled at home and at work. When he came to see me, he described continued fights with his wife of thirty years, and told me that he had no idea how to understand or stop them. He described an excessive amount of responsibility in a high-level executive position at work, where he had multiple people reporting to him, and no concept of how to be an effective manager.

During his first visit with me, Samuel described a series of contradictory experiences. When speaking of his long-standing marriage, he conveyed a deep affection for his wife. Yet in describing the details of a recent argument that ended in an impasse, Samuel also conveyed some shakiness in his commitment to his marriage. In describing his career history, Samuel told me about a series of incredible accomplishments in his high-powered jobs. But he also told me that he had been unable to maintain many of those positions. He had lost a series of jobs over the years and had experienced several periods of unemployment.

As we sat together that first time, I experienced Samuel to be a caring, competent (but confused), judgmental, and self-critical fellow. In summing up his tale, he told me: "I'm self-centered and selfish. I want what I want when I want it and I don't treat my wife, friends, family, or direct reports well at all. My last therapist told me that I have a narcissistic personality disorder."

As part of Step One, I said to Samuel, "It is quite possible that you have a narcissistic personality disorder, but I have my doubts. Let me read you the diagnostic criteria for that disorder. I would like you to tell me if you agree with your past therapist." Believing in the ability of each person to critically evaluate their own diagnostic fits, I took the *Diagnostic and Statistical Manual of Mental Disorders, Fourth Edition*, from my bookshelf and opened it to the appropriate page. I read the list of characteristics of which five must be present to make the diagnosis. They include grandiosity, entitlement, a need for excessive admiration, a lack of empathy or concern for the feelings of others, envy, arrogance, and a sense of self as better or more special than others.

Samuel listened carefully as I read the criteria. He looked increasingly confused as I went on. When I finished reading, I asked him, "Does that description sound like you? Do you think you have narcissistic personality disorder?" Samuel looked me straight in the eye. With great clarity he said, "That doesn't sound like me at all. I know that I can be arrogant and self-centered at times, but I definitely care about other people's feelings. While I may talk a good line, I often know when I am wrong. I think that most people do a better job than I do. I don't feel better than others. In fact, I often feel like a failure. I don't know why my last therapist told me I had that disorder."

"Well," I said, "I can't possibly speak for your past therapist, but I am glad to discover that he was incorrect in his diagnosis. In his attempt to make sense of your confusing history and current struggles, he came up with the wrong answer. In speaking to me, you have shared a lot of inconsistency in your history, feelings, and behavior. As I have listened to you talk, I have seen that your life is not a consistent reflection of your values and core feelings. Perhaps your last therapist mistook your impulsiveness and propensity to criticize others as a lack of concern for your job and your relationships."

I went on to teach Samuel a crucial lesson about assumptions; it is a lesson I revisit frequently in my clinical work. It is this: we are all prone to attribute the wrong motivation to others when we try to ascribe meaning to their behavior. I went on to hypothesize that perhaps his last therapist had looked at his behavior, made incorrect assumptions about his feelings, and provided an inappropriate diagnosis as a result.

• • •

Since Samuel and I did not have time to explore a more appropriate diagnosis in that first session, we used the remainder of our time to address the argument he had just had with his wife. It had ended in an impasse and he was clearly disturbed about it. In order to help him resolve the argument, I felt the need to establish some givens. As such, I asked, "How do you feel about your marriage, Samuel?"

"I am 90 to 95 percent committed to my marriage," Samuel said. "It is probably only 5 to 10 percent of the time that I think I want out. The rest of the time I want to be married."

That was a shaky foundation. I said to Samuel, "I thought you might say something like that. Your inconsistent behavior and criticism of your wife made me wonder. You need to decide if you can be 100 percent committed to your marriage. I cannot help you to make your marriage better if you are not 100 percent committed to the union." I went on to explain that the marriage commitment ceremony requires an "I do" or an "I don't." When it comes to marriage, 95 percent doesn't work; Samuel had to decide whether he was "in" or "out."

Samuel looked at me long and hard. He began to fidget in his chair. We were in the first step of Step One and he was not comfortable. He was being forced to consider if he was or was not fully committed to his marriage and how he really felt about his wife.

After a few moments, he seemed to calm down. "If you put it that way," he said, "I am in 100 percent. I love my wife and want to have a good marriage. Maybe your way of looking at it can help me fix my marriage. It is clear that my way isn't working at all."

I began to show him how to resolve the recent argument he had had with his wife by revisiting the scene. "During that argument, you said something that you realized hurt your wife's feelings. Yet, you did not apologize. That was wrong." I went on to explain that if he wanted to have a good marriage, he needed to treat his wife in a loving way. Healthy functioning requires our behavior to be consistent with our feelings. I sent him home with instructions to apologize to his wife for his behavior. "You need to tell her how much she means to you, and that you are sorry you have caused her so much pain. This is the first step in repairing your marriage. You need to identify and own your feelings for your wife, accept responsibility for your error, and make amends. I know you can do it. I will see you again next week, at which point we can look to see if a diagnosis other than narcissistic personality disorder might explain some of your difficulties."

When Samuel returned to see me the following week, he reported having done as I instructed. "My wife thinks you are great!" he said. "She couldn't wait for me to come back today so you could help us some more. She asked me to talk with you about some other problems we are having."

Frankly, I wondered why Samuel was not sharing more of his own feelings, but realized that only time would tell. "I would be glad to do that," I said, "These sessions are yours to use as you see fit. If you want to use today's session to work on your marital relationship, we can surely do that. However, I do think it is important to return to the diagnostic question we discussed last time within the next few weeks. I think you may have a diagnosis that could explain some of your difficulties."

I had been wondering whether Samuel would meet diagnostic criteria for attention deficit disorder (see Appendix IX). He had come to me with an addictive disorder diagnosis, and there is an increased incidence of ADD in people who have addictive illness. Furthermore, his impulsive nature, poor job history, marital discord, inconsistency, and self-loathing seemed to go along with an ADD diagnosis. Most important, adults with ADD are often mistakenly told, as Samuel had been, that they have personality disorders. Their distractibility, inattentiveness, and impulsivity are thought to be volitional by therapists who do not know enough about neurochemistry, neurophysiology, and attention issues to make a more appropriate diagnosis.

Although I knew that we needed to revisit the diagnostic question, Samuel and I needed to work on his marital and workplace challenges for a few weeks before being able to do so. He was resistant, just as Cindy had been, to the notion that there was something "wrong" with him. He did not want to have a second diagnosis. Acknowledging and owning his addictive illness was enough for Samuel. He wanted his other problems to be minor and easily fixed. He did not want to have another disorder to contend with; he didn't even want to contemplate the possibility.

Since I knew that Samuel would not be able to recover if a crucial diagnosis was missed, I persisted in my attempts to screen him for ADD. After a few weeks, he agreed to engage in the process. I administered the Brown Attention Deficit Disorder Scale (BADDS) for adults. The BADDS is a self-report scale that measures symptoms of ADD. It was designed and tested by Thomas E. Brown and is one of the screening tools used in the evaluation of persons suspected of having ADD. It taps for symptoms of inattention, cognition, and emotional impairment often seen in individuals with attention deficit disorder. The BADDS looks for problems in organizing and initiating work activities, sustaining attention and concentration, sustaining energy and effort, managing emotional interference, and utilizing working memory and ability to recall information. Using forty statements that are to be read aloud by the person administering the tool, the examinee is instructed to respond to each statement by choosing between: never (0), once a week or less (1), twice a week (2), or almost daily (3). The respondent is told to pick the words that best describe how much the feeling or behavior described in that statement has been a problem in the last six months and the examiner records each response. Each choice has a numerical value assigned to it (above in parenthesis). The tool is scored by adding up the numerical values. A score of < 40 means ADD is possible but not likely, a score of 40–54 means ADD is probable but not certain, and a score of 55–120 means ADD is highly probable.

When I administered the BADDS to Samuel the first time, I had the sense that he was underreporting his symptoms. His assessment of his behavior and feelings did not seem to jibe with the history that he had already shared with me. Nonetheless, he scored a 47. ADD was probable, but not certain.

I wanted further clarity, though. I suggested that he read the book *Driven to Distraction* by Hallowell and Ratey. It is a wonderful book written by two psychiatrists who have the disorder themselves, and it is one of the most readable and helpful books I have come across for individuals who have, or are wondering if they have, ADD. It helps to answer the diagnostic and what-next questions. I recommended it to Samuel because I knew it would help him figure out if the ADD diagnosis fit or not. If it did fit, the book would go a long way toward helping him make sense of his past and current work and relationship difficulties. It would also expose him to the medication management of ADD, and to a series of coping strategies used by many people in dealing with the challenges of their ADD. Finally, it could offer a lot of hope to him going forward since it was filled with tales of successful diagnoses and subsequent growth experiences.

Samuel left my office carrying a piece of paper on which I had written the title of his recommended reading. He vowed to read the book before our next meeting. "I really need to figure out if I have this thing," he said. "Maybe answering that question will help me get better. I sure hope so."

When Samuel returned to see me the following week, he told me that not only had he "read the book," but he was "ready to start on medication" as well. Somewhat surprised at the rapid turn of events, I said, "Not so fast, Samuel. When you left my office last week, you were doubtful that the ADD diagnosis fit. I recommended a book to you to help us make headway in our attempt to find the right fit. You read the book and now you are ready to start medication? Do you think you have ADD? If so, why? What did you learn about yourself from your reading of the book? How did it apply to you? Help me understand your thinking. What struggles do you relate to, and what role do you see medication playing in your life?"

Samuel listened carefully to my response. In a manner typical of ADD sufferers, he hadn't realized that he had skipped over all the details. He thought I knew what he had discovered, even though he had never shared it. He was struck by the silliness of his assumption once I pointed it out. He began to tell me how much he identified with the stories in the book. Even the diagnostic descriptions seemed to fit. He was sure he had the disorder. He went on to say something many other patients have told me, "The book was written for and about me. I have no question that I have ADD."

"What about that screening tool, the BADDS, that we used last time?" I asked. "What do you think about your 47 score? ADD is probable but not certain."

"Oh," said Samuel, "I know I wasn't honest with myself when I gave you those answers last week. I did not want to have ADD. You gave me the right homework, though. After reading the book you recommended, I realize that I won't get anywhere if I am not honest with myself about the diagnosis. I am sure I have ADD. If I were to take the BADDS test again I am sure I would get a higher score."

Because I am committed to using Step One principles, I feel the need to be rigorous in answering all diagnostic questions. If I want to be able to help my patients, I must know whom I am dealing with and what characteristics that person comes with. No diagnosis can be wishy-washy. Every diagnosis must be clear to me. Once it is, I share the information with my patient. We both need to know where we are starting from if we are going to get anywhere together.

In keeping with this Step One approach, I responded to Samuel, "I think we need to redo the BADDS. It is important that we are clear on your diagnosis. If you think that you underreported your symptoms last time, we need to redo the test. The test is invalid if it is not reflective of your actual experience. We need to know for sure where we are starting from if we are to be able to accomplish anything together."

Since I had the sense that Samuel was underreporting his symptoms when we had gone through the BADDS the previous week, I was far from surprised to hear that he felt likewise. Samuel scored an 82 the second time around, which meant that ADD was highly probable. The second score seemed more accurate to me. After redoing the BADDS, Samuel and I could both accept the ADD diagnosis. We were now ready to begin discovering the role of that diagnosis in his history and current struggles.

Having read *Driven to Distraction*, and learning a great deal about the treatment of ADD, Samuel was anxious to get started on medication. But before writing Samuel a prescription, I needed to discuss the role his medication would play in the treatment of his ADD. I had to teach him what he could and could not expect from it; I told him what I tell all ADD sufferers.

"ADD is something you were born with," I explained. "It is a function of the way your brain is structured and the way it works. To date, we have no reason to believe that we will be able to change the fundamental neuroanatomy and neuro-physiology of the brain in a person who has ADD. We cannot make the ADD go away. However, we do have a series of medications that are effective in modulating some of the symptoms of the disorder. The medications are especially useful in helping to control the impulsivity, distractibility, and inattentiveness of ADD. While not everyone with ADD benefits from medication, at least 90 to 95 percent of ADD sufferers will experience a benefit.

"Additionally, while medications have played a dramatic role in enabling many to transform their lives, you need to keep in mind that the medicines are only one tool in the

ADD treatment bag. Medications do not make the disorder disappear, and they do not eliminate the symptoms completely. Furthermore, they only work when you remember to take them—and their action is short lived. At most, a given dose of medication for ADD will treat your symptoms for eight hours. If you miss your next dose, your symptoms will return as they were at baseline. The medications can help you a great deal, especially if you use them in conjunction with other strategies and techniques. They will surely enable you to use those techniques more effectively if you set your mind to taking advantage of the techniques. The medications can help you to help yourself, but they cannot do it for you. As long as you understand all of that, we can begin developing a medication plan for you."

Samuel and I went on to pick a medication and a dose to start with. The medication management approach I used in Samuel's case is the most commonly recommended approach to the pharmacologic treatment of ADD, and is therefore universally applicable. We picked a stimulant drug, as the stimulants are the most effective and best-studied ADD medications and because Samuel had no health problems that contraindicated the use of such a drug. We started at the lowest reasonable dose so as to minimize side effects, and the possibility of overshooting the level necessary without realizing it. We identified the target symptoms, or the ADD symptoms that are known to respond to medication, that he would be monitoring throughout the week to see if he was benefiting from the drug. We reviewed the side effects and created a dosing plan. We discussed the fact that he would need to stay on each dose for a week to determine its effectiveness. Even though the medication would begin to work right away, it would take some days for us to recognize its full benefit. We would increase the dose incrementally each week, until we saw no further benefit from a particular dosage increase or until side effects (which are dose-dependent) became a problem.

Since medication is *always* only one piece of the puzzle, I urged Samuel to study the tools and strategies described in *Driven to Distraction*. I wanted him to begin thinking about how he could implement some of them in his life. Making an appropriate diagnosis of ADD and beginning a medication management plan was only one step of what would be a very long journey to transforming his self-concept, workplace experience, and marital life.

In urging Samuel to take on this big challenge in a reasonable way, I called upon a series of 12 Step affirmations, which you, too, can use. "Easy does it," I said. "Take one day at a time. Do what you can with medication and strategies this week. You will be able to get to where you want to be if you are diligent, conscientious, and patient in your efforts. Do your best for now. I am sure you can succeed. Pay attention to your symptoms, thoughts, feelings, and reactions throughout the week. Bring me your observations, upsets, confusions, and questions next time. We can make sense of them if we take one step at a time and go easy."

Over time, Samuel and I developed a reasonable regimen for the medication management of his ADD. He was then able to implement some of the time management strategies outlined in *Driven to Distraction* to help him gain greater control of his time. We moved on to address other *body leg* issues in his life. We began to examine his relationship snafus in an attempt to discover respective roles of his ADD and his core feelings in each interpersonal challenge. Each time we engaged in this exercise, it pointed us toward a path for the problem's resolution. I will share one example of this Step One work. It concerns a challenge that Samuel was facing in his workplace. I choose this example because it is particularly representative of the unique challenges that ADD-affected adults face in the workplace.

One day Samuel arrived at my office exasperated with work matters. "I think I have to let Michael go," Samuel sighed. "He holds one of the most crucial management positions in my organization, but I can't get him to give me a budget plan for his department. I have to be prepared to present the budgets for all the departments to the management board in two weeks, and I can't seem to get this guy to give me his. I am really angry with him. He just won't cooperate."

When Samuel paused to catch his breath, I jumped in to ask him questions that seemed fundamental to me.

"Tell me, Samuel," I said, "Does Michael know what you expect from him? Have you outlined your expectations clearly? Have you shown him how to prepare a budget for his department? Have you communicated your time-line to him?"

Samuel looked at me as if I had three heads. He responded in a way that is typical of many adults with ADD. Although he was skipping over key functions that are necessary to a successful workplace relationship, he was unaware of it. "What do you mean?" he asked me. "I am his boss. I just told him what I wanted him to do and I expect him to deliver. That is the way I have always done it. I don't see why I need to do it differently now."

"Well, Samuel," I began to explain, "perhaps the way you have always done it has led to some of your workplace disappointments. Your way of being a manager doesn't fit with my notion of successful management. In the model I subscribe to, the manager is responsible for helping the people who work for him succeed. Each manager has to figure out how to best use and develop his staff. The manager needs to determine how to deploy his resources appropriately.

"In my model, you would guide Michael through the budget planning exercise to help him learn how to do it. If you found that he was ill-suited to the activity once you provided clear guidance, then you would need to decide if his talents would be best deployed elsewhere. You have told me that he does a great job running his department. It seems to me that you would be ill-advised to let him go over budget-preparation, especially if you have never taught him how to do it. Would he be easy to replace?"

Samuel was deep in thought. He considered my words for a few moments. "I see your point," he said finally, "Michael would not be easy to replace. His position is crucial. I have never taught him how to do budget planning, and yet I expect him to be able to do it. I am feeling anxious about what *I* need to present to *my* boss. I am really afraid that I won't deliver! So, I am blaming and criticizing Michael instead of empowering him to give me what I need. Why do I do that?" he asked.

"Wow, Samuel," I responded. "I am really proud of you. You got the lesson immediately and took it further! You used what I suggested and saw your approach to managing Michael in a new light. Realizing your error, you were then able to use your insight to do some self-examination. As a result of your self-reflection, you were able to identify your own fears. You are doing great work here. You are well on the way to becoming an amazing manager! I am thrilled with your desire to grow, and with your interest in under-standing why you do things ineffectively at times."

I began to answer his question by explaining that, at times, his ADD could get in the way of being an effective manager. Many managers who have ADD skip over seeing and communicating key expectations and steps to their direct reports. As a result of their failure to recognize their own oversights, they become frustrated with employees whose work falls short of their secret desires. Because they don't see their own flaws, they go on to attribute their distress to their subordinates. Thus, they get stuck in a "blame, criticize, and failure" cycle that leads to someone losing his or her job. As I am sure you are beginning to see, it doesn't have to be this way.

I said to Samuel, "You told me that you were worried about falling short of your boss's expectations in this budget-review process. Do you feel equipped to get him what he wants, or do we need to get you a consultant to help you produce?" I was working to determine whether gaining insight into the nature of the problem would be sufficient to enable Samuel to address it, or whether more help was necessary. I was raising a crucial question that we would all do well to consider on a regular basis. We need to ask ourselves: "Am I able to do what needs to be done, or do I need help to accomplish it?"

"I think I can do it without external help," Samuel said.

"Good," I said and went on to ask, "Can you teach Michael how to give you what you want from him, too?"

Samuel paused before responding. "I think I can do that."

I responded with encouragement, saying, "Okay, then, stop worrying and blaming. Use your newfound under-standing to turn this frustration and fear into a success for both you and Michael. No one has to lose in this situation. Turn it all around. You can do it."

Samuel left my office with a newfound understanding of

the respective roles of his ADD and his feelings in regard to the challenges he faced in his workplace. By working through that one specific example of his difficulties, he began to understand his long-term pattern of inefficiency and managerial failure. Armed with an explanatory diagnosis, appropriate medication to enable success, and some clear guidance on how to implement a different model of management, Samuel was able to empower himself. He was able to begin transforming his feeling of fear into one of pride. He was coming to realize that he could experience success by helping Michael to succeed. He was learning how to turn the sour lemons he had brought to my office that day into sweet lemonade.

Samuel was beginning to understand that, in using and implementing these lessons and principles, he could become a fantastic manager. By using and respecting Step One principles, he could transform his experiences in the workplace. As time went on, Samuel and I worked through many examples of this workplace challenge. Ultimately, he was able to prevail. By accepting who he was to begin with—including all diagnoses, limitations, fears, weaknesses and strengths—he was ultimately able to turn an area of repeated failure into an area of abundant success. Today, Samuel has an even greater degree of responsibility in that same workplace. He has been rewarded repeatedly for his management skills and is now an *awesome manager!*

● ● ●

Before moving on, I want to summarize the Step One points of Samuel's tale.

1. Samuel came to me believing that he had a narcissistic personality disorder when he actually had

undiagnosed attention deficit disorder. In this case, an improper diagnosis, rather than the absence of a diagnosis, was keeping him stuck and causing him great difficulty. It is important to note that Samuel also had an addictive illness. Thus, he had two diagnoses that often appear together. Many people who suffer from ADD have addictive problems and many addicts have undiagnosed ADD.

2. In order to facilitate Samuel's recovery, I needed to use medications, teach him strategies for coping with his ADD, and help him develop an understanding of the impact of his behavior on others. Once a proper diagnosis was made, a specific treatment plan to address the attention issues could be implemented. The particular treatment approach to ADD modeled here is applicable to all who suffer from the disorder.

3. Once Samuel began to improve, I could teach him the conflict resolution and employee management skills that he would need to implement in order to succeed. Only after the ADD was understood and reasonably well managed with medication and strategy implementation, could Samuel begin to work effectively on the common, problematic behavioral manifestations of his ADD.

How is Samuel's tale relevant to you, and what should you do about it?

*   If you find yourself stuck in your growth process, you, too, may have ADD and/or an addictive illness. If something in Samuel's tale speaks to you, please review diagnostic information on attentional prob-

lems and addiction and pursue further assessment if it seems appropriate. You can then follow the step-by-step approach to treatment described above, and in the lesson points that follow Cindy's story as well.

Take-Home Points

1. On occasion, we all have difficulty managing our time, materials, and impulses. For some of us the problem is the result of a full-blown disorder, an abnormality in brain chemistry that can be overwhelming without professional intervention. For the rest of us, our organizational challenges and impulsivity can present periodic problems.
2. While the medications used to treat ADD are diagnosis-specific, the strategies and tips that help people who suffer from ADD are universally applicable. We can all benefit from implementing the time, responsibilities, and self-management techniques that are described in the ADD management books found in bookstores.
3. While we can all become more competent in our life-management skills and learn a valuable lesson from Samuel's journey, those of us who have undiagnosed addictive illnesses or ADD are in need of some significant Step One interventions to achieve success in our journeys to health.

Baxter and Step One

When I think back to my first meeting with Baxter, I still shudder. The poor man had recently relocated to

Philadelphia from another East Coast city, moving from one law firm to another, hoping the job change would help him calm down. His psychiatrist of many years had given him two referrals of doctors in Philadelphia. I was the second psychiatrist to see Baxter for an initial consultation.

When he came to see me, he shared a long history of depression, anxiety, confusion, isolation, and self-doubt. Although he was married, he was unsure if he wanted to be. He was a lawyer, but he "hated" being one. In fact, he did not know if he wanted to work at all. And yet, as anxious and distressed as he was with his current situation, he told me that he had no idea what he would rather be doing with his life.

He went on to describe the many years he had spent in intensive psychoanalytic psychotherapy. He had seen one therapist four times a week for years, and had most recently been seeing the referring psychiatrist twice a week for many more years. He had been told that he had a panic disorder (which you will recall was Cindy's diagnosis), but that his panic was due to unresolved relationship issues with his father.

Additionally, Baxter described how he suffered from recurrent, intrusive, obsessive thoughts that he knew were absurd, but that he could not seem to stop. These thoughts often concerned sleep issues or details of a project at work. Sometimes, upon examining his workload on a given day, Baxter would realize that he would be delayed in getting out of his office. He would anticipate getting home very late and, as a result, would realize that he would have to sacrifice two hours of his usual sleep time. While knowing that he could function fine on less sleep and would be able to catch up on sleep in a day or two, he would find himself unable to stop worrying about the two hours he might lose that night. In fact, he would work himself into a frenzy and have trouble functioning at work.

At other times, Baxter would leave work for the day and, once home, he would begin to worry that he had done a sub-optimal job on a minor detail in a work document. In spite of knowing that the tiny point had no major significance, he would be unable to stop worrying about it. Again, he would become overwrought.

These obsessive thoughts about sleep or the caliber of his work would pop into his head at the most inopportune times and run around in an escalating fashion until they reached a pitch that could not be quelled. He would grow increasingly overwhelmed and exasperated, feeling foolish, angry, depressed, and ultimately too distraught to function at all.

As I listened to Baxter's description of his history and symptoms, I began to doubt that the diagnosis he had been given was correct. In considering his experiences, I thought that he might have an obsessive-compulsive disorder (see Appendix IV), with some superimposed episodes of depression. These two diagnoses often coexist. Even though he complained of extreme anxiety, I did not hear evidence of panic attacks in his story at all.

As I am prone to do during Step One, *body leg* work, I took my *DSM IV* off the bookshelf and read him the diagnostic criteria for panic disorder. "Does this sound like you, Baxter?" I asked. "Do you think you have this disorder?"

Baxter was surprised that I asked him to reconsider the diagnosis he had already been given—so much so that he asked me to read the criteria again. He became very reflective as he sat in a big armchair in my office and registered my words. "You know," he said, "I don't really think that fits. I do get excessively anxious at times, but my anxiety escalates without all those other panic symptoms. Further, the anxiety does not come on abruptly, and it does not peak within a few minutes. Maybe I don't have a panic disorder after all. If not, what do you think could be causing me to get so anxious?"

"Well, Baxter," I said, "that is what I am wondering. Although you have been in psychotherapy for years, you do not feel that you have gotten any better. You are not happy in your life. You are anxious most of the time, and you are troubled by worrisome thoughts that escalate out of control. I wonder if you have obsessive-compulsive disorder." I went on to explain that OCD tends not to respond to psychoanalytic psychotherapy. It is a function of genetic vulnerability and neurochemistry that is best treated with medications and behavior therapy. The disorder is extremely common. In fact, approximately 2 percent of people in the U.S. have it. It can cause crippling anxiety and is associated with episodes of depression in about 70 percent of sufferers.

After explaining all this to Baxter, I said, "I would like to read you the diagnostic criteria for OCD so you can tell me if they seem to fit you better than the ones for panic disorder did."

With that, I opened the *DSM IV* to the appropriate page and began to read. Rather than rewrite the criteria I read to Baxter, I will reprint a description from an obsessive-compulsive disorder pamphlet provided by the Department of Health and Human Services, *DHHS Publication No. (ADU) 91-1597, 1991,* to make the diagnosis clear to you. The key features of OCD include:

> ***Obsessions:*** These are unwanted ideas or impulses that repeatedly well up in the mind of the person with OCD. Again and again, the individual experiences a disturbing thought, such as, "My hands may

be contaminated—I must wash them"; "I may have left the gas on"; or "I am going to injure my child." These thoughts are felt to be intrusive and unpleasant. They produce anxiety.

Compulsions: To deal with their anxiety, most people with OCD resort to repetitive behaviors called compulsions. The most common of these are washing and checking, as in the first two previous examples. Other compulsive behaviors include counting (often while performing another compulsive action such as hand washing), and endlessly rearranging objects in an effort to keep them in perfect alignment or symmetry with each other. These behaviors generally are intended to ward off harm to the person with OCD or others. They usually are quite stereotyped, with little variation from one time to the next, and are often referred to as rituals. Performing these rituals may give the person with OCD some relief from anxiety, but it is only temporary.

Insight: People with OCD generally have considerable insight into their own problems. Most of the time, they know that their obsessive thoughts are senseless or exaggerated, and that their compulsive behaviors are not really necessary. However, this knowledge is not sufficient to enable them to break free from their illness.

When I finished reading the criteria to Baxter, he said, "You are right on. I think that's it. Although I don't have many compulsions, I definitely have repeated obsessions. I usually worry that I won't get enough sleep and start obsessing about every minute of sleep that I will lose, or that I made some serious error in a document for work and somehow the world will fall apart as a result. I go over and over the document in my head. Even though I know that I am being ridiculous, I cannot stop myself from thinking the thoughts and getting anxious. I have had this problem since I was in college. My therapy has definitely not changed the frequency, character, or nature of my problem. Do you think I can get better? I am just as unhappy in this job as I was in the last one. I thought I was making my life better by accepting this job and moving here. Now, I don't think the job has anything to do with my distress, and it surely doesn't have anything to do with the recent stresses that have emerged in my relationship with my father. What do you think? Can you help me?"

"Well, Baxter," I said, "I am sure I can help you if you choose to work with me. First, I would need to get you on the appropriate medication. The medications traditionally used to treat OCD are different from those prescribed for panic disorder. Second, I would need to teach you how to employ behavioral strategies to combat some of your symptoms. Third, I would need to help you explore your lifestyle choices to help you establish a series of work and home-life involvements that fit your needs and nature. It seems to me that you have been tortured by obsessive anxiety and depression for years, and that you have made impulsive life-altering decisions in the hope that taking action would quell your anxiety. I understand that you chose to take a new job and move to Philadelphia for that reason. I am truly sorry that your last therapist was not able to help you see how unlikely that move would be in enabling you to calm down. You and I may ultimately discover that the environment of any large city law firm is a poor fit for your nature. Time will tell. Although that would not be a surprising development, it is too soon for us to try sorting it out. What I want you to focus on right now is deciding which of the two psychiatrists you have been to see is a better fit for you. If you need to meet with the other psychiatrist again before deciding, that is fine with me. I will see you once more in a week's time. At that point, we will need to resolve the question of who will take on your care."

As I spoke these words I was saying to myself, "I feel so sad and sorry for this man. His OCD diagnosis makes it extremely difficult for him to make a decision about where to get his psychiatric care. He is prone to argue with himself incessantly and indefinitely about which choice is more correct. He has no psychiatrist to call his own as he struggles with the extreme anxiety and depression his move caused. His past psychiatrist unwittingly set him up to suffer. Rather than making it simple by providing Baxter a single referral with instructions to call for more if the first didn't work, his psychiatrist created a dilemma which Baxter is having a devil of a time sorting out."

As my time with Baxter was running out, I gave him some pamphlets and articles about OCD to review and discuss with others. Perhaps that would help him make a decision.

As Baxter closed his first meeting with me, he said, "You have given me a diagnosis in the space of one visit that seems to fit me better than the one I have been carrying around for years. Yet I am not sure whom I should ask to be my psychiatrist. I need to meet with the other person again to discuss all of this. I think I will call my old psychiatrist too. I am so confused. Thank you for all this reading material on the diagnosis and treatment of OCD. Maybe it will help me sort this out. I do understand that I need to make a decision about my continued care by our next meeting. I look forward to seeing you again."

• • •

Before we go on to finish the *body leg* lesson of Baxter's tale, I want to remind you of the crucial role feelings play in diagnosis and Step One work. Feelings that define the diagnosis are not core to expressions of self and desire. I raise this point now because of the striking role that feelings play in the experience of a person who has OCD. Baxter left my office with a clear sense that he had finally been given an appropriate diagnosis. He did not doubt the new diagnosis. Yet, he still felt confused and unable to decide what to do next. His OCD, and the obsessive doubt and anxiety that it entailed, were keeping him from identifying his core feelings. Because he could not keep himself from running around in circles in his own head, he could not figure out how he felt about his continued care. His obsessive behavior and anxiety was blocking his access to his true feelings. His disorder-feelings were masking his core-feelings.

Knowing how much Baxter was suffering in his new job, and knowing how hard it was for him to choose a care-path, I sent him more reading material by mail. I wrote him a supportive and encouraging note, and reiterated my sense of his potential. I was trying to prevent what we call in medical language, his decompensation—his mental and emotional deterioration in the face of his massive anxiety and confusion. I was reaching out, as best I could, to help him.

By the time Baxter returned to see me for our second

visit, he had been to the other psychiatrist three times. He was starting to get clinically depressed. He knew my diagnosis was "right on," but could not commit to working with me. It felt too "scary."

Fearing Baxter's further deterioration, I told him that he would need to come to a conclusion over the weekend. I would only see him for one more consultation visit. I was not willing to participate in prolonging his agony by continuing to meet with him while he remained committed nowhere. I would not support a process that would make him sicker.

Over the weekend, Baxter decided to work with me. In doing so, he allowed his intellect to prevail over his obsessional worry. He knew that what I had told him made sense. He was smart enough to understand that a proper diagnosis was a necessary first step in his healing journey; he therefore believed that it was far more likely that I would be able to help. While he was unable to take much pleasure in having made a choice, he knew that it was the right one. He decided to go with his logic: a proper diagnosis had to be the first step of his treatment.

While it is beyond the scope of this chapter to share Baxter's entire story with you, I will tell you that he has been my patient for five years now. His OCD is under excellent control with the medicines I have prescribed. He has gained a great understanding of his obsessional pitfalls. He regularly uses the strategies that I have taught him in order to cope with his hamster-and-wheel way of thinking. He left the law-firm setting several years ago, and is now in a work environment far better suited to his nature. His marriage is quite good, and he has a satisfying relationship with his father. He is increasingly able to access and talk about his core feelings.

As I write this paragraph, Baxter and I are meeting only

twice a month. We are almost finished with our work. Our sessions now focus on matters of meaningfulness, fulfillment, and spirituality. While his OCD will never disappear, Baxter's life has been transformed: purpose has replaced panic as its driving force. While Baxter has learned that he will need to respect and address his obsessional nature forever, he has also come to understand his diagnosis for what it is. He has learned to delve beneath his obsessional worry to find answers. He has learned to respect what his core-self has to say. He is truly a changed man, *and he knows it!*

• • •

Before moving on to the next chapter, I want to summarize the Step One points of Baxter's tale.

1. Baxter came to me believing that his anxiety and depression were results of a panic disorder and unresolved issues with his father, when he actually had a depressive illness and an undiagnosed obsessive-compulsive disorder. Baxter's misdiagnosis led him to make a dramatic lifestyle change that paradoxically increased his pain and suffering, rather than providing him with much sought-after relief. Step One in his healing journey involved acknowledging and addressing two common disorders that frequently coexist.

2. I needed to use medications, teach cognitive behavior strategies, and educate Baxter about the implications of his OCD diagnosis in order to promote his recovery. Again, the proper diagnosis dictated a specific approach to symptom relief.

3. Once he began to improve, I was able to help Baxter explore and address his issues of workplace fit. Only with his symptoms under a reasonable degree of control could Baxter begin to consider larger issues of geography and career path.

How is Baxter's tale relevant to you, and what should you do about it?

* If you relate to aspects of Baxter's journey, you, too, may have undiagnosed depression or OCD. Please review the diagnostic information that seems relevant to you and pursue further assessment if it seems appropriate. Do not allow yourself to go around in escalating obsessional circles that promote your decompensation. Trust your intellect, rather than your worries, and get the necessary help.

Take-Home Points

1. We all tend to search for geographic cures, believing that if we move to another city or town our troubles will disappear. While a geographic change can often nurture and support our growth journey, the only way to change or cure a diagnostic issue is to address it.

2. It is often hard to alter the familiar patterns and notions that we have come to think of as helpful. Baxter struggled with how to let go of his previous therapist's advice. When you begin to sense that the problems raised by what is routine outweigh the

benefits you clearly experience from it, you would
do well to question the status quo.

3. Be sure to go easy on yourself in your growth
journey. Until you address paralyzing symptoms
and diagnostic issues, do not push yourself to
answer major lifestyle questions.

We have come to the end of the *body leg* chapter. Before
moving on, you might want to make note of what you have
learned about the *"Who* am I?" question. What is the place
of *body leg* issues in your recovery path? If you have yet to
consider the questions posed at the outset of this chapter, I
suggest you answer them now. They can help you identify
the role that biological and diagnostic issues play in your
growth journey.

Feelings Vocabulary

Abandoned	Baffled	Desolate
Absurd	Barraged	Despairing
Abused	Battered	Desperate
Accepted	Better	Despised
Acknowledged	Belittled	Despondent
Activated	Betrayed	Destroyed
Adversarial	Bewildered	Disconnected
Affectionate	Bitter	Discouraged
Affirmed	Blah	Discredited
Afraid	Blessed	Disgraced
Agitated	Blocked	Disinterested
Aggravated	Blue	Disliked
Aggressive	Bothered	Dismal
Alarmed	Bored	Displeased
Alert	Brave	Dissatisfied
Alienated	Brittle	Distant
Alone	Broken	Distressed
Amazed	Bruised	Distrustful
Amorous	Burdened	Disturbed
Amused	Bypassed	Dour
Angry		Doubtful
Anguished	Calm	Downcast
Annoyed	Capable	Downtrodden
Antisocial	Cheapened	Dreadful
Anxious	Clueless	
Apologetic	Cheerful	Ecstatic
Appreciated	Debased	Embarrassed
Appreciative	Defeated	Empowered
Apprehensive	Defective	Empty
Ashamed	Deflated	Encumbered
Awed	Dejected	Energized
Awful	Delighted	Enraged
Awkward	Demoralized	Entangled
	Depressed	Enthusiastic

Envious	Healthy	Left out
Estranged	Helpless	Lifeless
Euphoric	Hindered	Limited
Exalted	Hopeless	Limitless
Excited	Hopeful	Lonely
Excluded	Horrible	Lonesome
Exhausted	Humble	Lost
Exhilarated	Humiliated	Loved
Exposed	Hurt	Loving
		Lousy
Fantastic	Ignored	Low
Fearful	Ill	
Fine	Impaired	Maligned
Foolish	Impatient	Marvelous
Forgiven	Impotent	Miffed
Forgiving	Imprisoned	Miserable
Fortunate	Inadequate	Mistreated
Frantic	Incapable	Misunderstood
Free	Incompetent	Morose
Frightened	Ineffective	Needed
Frustrated	Inept	Neglected
Fulfilled	Inferior	Nervous
Furious	Insecure	Noticed
	Insignificant	Numb
Gifted	Inspired	
Glad	Intimidated	Offended
Gleeful	Irritable	Open
Glorious	Irritated	Oppressed
Good	Isolated	Optimistic
Grand		Ostracized
Grateful	Jealous	Outraged
Gratified	Jilted	Overlooked
Grumpy	Jittery	Overwhelmed
Guilty	Joyous	
	Judged	Panicky
Happy	Jumpy	Passionate
Hateful	Justified	Perplexed

Playful
Pleased
Powerless
Powerful
Pressured
Proud
Puzzled

Rebuked
Regretful
Rejected
Rejuvenated
Relaxed
Relieved
Resentful
Respected
Restless
Ridiculed
Ridiculous
Rotten

Sacred
Sad
Safe
Satisfied
Scared
Sensual
Serene
Sexy
Shaky
Shocked
Sickened
Silly
Skeptical
Slighted
Sorrowful
Sorry
Spiteful

Stable
Stifled
Stuck
Startled
Supported
Surprised
Suspicious
Swamped

Tense
Terrible
Terrified
Thankful
Threatened
Thrilled
Toppled
Tormented
Triumphant
Trounced
Trusting

Unappreciated
Uncertain
Uncomfortable
Uncooperative
Undervalued
Unencumbered
Understood
Uneasy
Unhappy
Unimportant
Unloved
Unstable
Unsure
Unwilling
Upset
Uptight

Valued
Valuable
Vengeful
Vindicated
Victimized
Victorious
Vulnerable

Wanted
Welcomed
Welcoming
Well
Whole
Wonderful
Wounded
Willing

Step Two: Mind

FIGURING OUT YOUR MINDSET, ATTITUDES, AND IDENTIFYING FAMILY-OF-ORIGIN ISSUES

In this chapter we are moving on to Step Two, and therefore into the mindset realm; that said, Step One never really ends. Remember, there are three discrete legs of the stool, but each leg is required to support the whole structure. In other words, just because you have tackled identifying diagnoses and core feelings in your healing journey does not mean you can leave Step One behind. You will need to revisit it forever. Over time, and as you progress in your journey, your diagnoses and core feelings will grow, change, and evolve. Whenever you ignore or neglect them, you will suffer consequences. We all do.

In this chapter, I intend to walk you through the second step of your healing journey: understanding and addressing the *mindset leg* of the stool. The *mindset leg* cncompasses your thoughts about yourself and others. The models you were exposed to or taught during your formative years dramatically affect your mindset. For most of us, our primary learning laboratory is our family of origin. We learn how to think about ourselves and others from what our parents teach us by word and example. Although our teachers, class-mates, and religious leaders may exert powerful develop-mental influences on us as well, we experience the messages contained in our "home-base," or our family home, as the most powerful. Obviously, if you were raised in an environment other than a traditional home with parents, then you were exposed to messages and models of a different nature. While it is beyond the scope of this chapter to give examples of alter-native home-base environments, the principles are the same. The home-base environment has the greatest power to affect the mindset of a developing child, whatever form it takes.

It is also beyond the scope of this chapter, and in this book in general, to define causality. The complex interplay of nature, nurture, and developmental forces in the genesis and perpetuation of psychiatric pathology is far from clear. The relative roles of genetics, biological vulnerability, inborn personality characteristics, and developmental challenges are an area of active research as I write this book. I would not presume to know exactly what causes what or why.

Think back to my discussion of Gillie's *body leg* issues and recall that I described her unique nature, and how she responded to her father's sexual abuses. Further, remember that this combination led to her development of MPD. Who she was biologically, affected who she became in the face of repeated episodes of sexual abuse by her dad.

Does that mean that her father caused her to develop MPD? I would say no. He surely exerted the ongoing environmental pressure that led her to develop the disorder, but he did not establish her particular vulnerability. He cannot take credit for who she was to begin with, nor can he lay claim to her creative problem-solving skill in the face of his abuse.

So how do I see Gillie's father in all of this? Do I think he is a bad person? Do I dislike him or wish him ill? Do I think he did the best he could have done as a parent? Could he, or should he, have done better?

It is crucial that you understand my answer to those questions before you go on to read the rest of this chapter, as I want you to understand how deeply I believe that doing a "bad job" does not make any person "bad." On occasion, we all do a bad job. Even with the best of intentions, we are humans, and humans are known to mess up. As we operate from our blind spots and misguided positions, we wreak havoc. We all do "bad things" at times, but none of us are "bad people."

At one point during our work together, Gillie asked me what I thought of her father. We had been talking about the recurrent episodes of sexual abuse that she had endured at her father's hand when she asked me, "Do you think my father is evil?"

Somewhat taken aback and mindful of the danger that she would misinterpret my response to mean that I approved of her father's behavior, I thought carefully before saying anything. Finally I said, "I do not know how to think about people that way, Gillie. I do think your father did many terrible and horrendous things to you. He had an obligation to provide for you and protect you. You were his dependent child and, as a result, completely at his mercy. Yet, he abused and violated you repeatedly. Rather than care for you, he traumatized you. He engaged in criminal behavior each time he violated you sexually. He did awful, awful things.

"But was he evil? I can't think about people that way. Your father was an extremely sick man. There must have been something terribly wrong with him. He convinced himself that his treatment of you was justified. Perhaps he was totally insane! I am not sure. There is no question that he did a terrible job of parenting you. But I do not think he was evil.

"Although we are all capable of engaging in behavior that is evil, I believe that there exists a piece of the divine in us all. We are each created with a piece of the infinite. Some of us become so sick that our potential is never realized. Some of us become sick enough to engage in behavior that flies in the face of all that is divine in the universe. I don't know why that happens. I don't know what caused your father to become so abusive and disturbed. However, I do know that we can turn around his influence on you and repair the damage. I know that we can turn his evil behavior into something that is good for you. We can resurrect your life from the wreckage, and nurture your amazing self. Although we need to hold your father accountable for the negative influence that he had in your development, we do not need to damn his person in the process. You see, Gillie, we are all imperfect beings. We all mess up without realizing our mistakes. God willing, neither you nor I will ever get as sick as your father clearly was. We are fortunate to be healthier and freer to become our best selves. We need to have compassion for those who are more challenged than we are, even if we abhor what they do."

• • •

It is important to recognize that all parents and primary caretakers are somewhat imperfect; they convey some messages that are constructive, as well as other messages that are harmful. We will discuss the nature of parenting and the inadvertent foibles that it can entail throughout this chapter; suffice it to say, most of us are raised by parents who have the best intentions in mind—even if it doesn't always feel that way.

You may recall that while I was in my first few years of medical school, I was terribly depressed. I kept looking for the humanism that I naively expected to characterize medicine and, unfortunately, I was disappointed time and time again.

During that time, I sought counseling. It was way before I had formulated any of the ideas in this book, including the steps to take in order to begin a transformational journey. So, I began therapy with a massage and gestalt therapist. During my first meeting with her, she asked me to describe my earliest memory.

Although I had never consciously been aware of this memory before, I immediately saw myself as a young child, perhaps about three years old, standing at the front door of my childhood home. I was standing inside the house, holding the door open. A large standard poodle, which was many times my size and had been our family pet for about a month, came bounding toward the door and me. The dog knocked me over as she ran out the door, down the driveway, and up the hill near my home. No feelings were attached to this memory.

When I described the scene to my new therapist, she told me that I must have felt pushed or run over a lot in my child-hood. I was quite taken aback by her interpretation of the memory and skeptical of her view of things. At the time, I was completely unaware that being run over was an organizing emotional experience of my childhood. I was nowhere near ready to learn that. Since her interpretation was premature,

I could not use it. As a result, I simply squirreled away her comment, with no idea what to make of it at the time.

Although I did not continue to work with that therapist for very long, I have always remembered her comment. As I sit here writing this chapter today, both the childhood memory and the therapist's comment are calling to me.

Since that first session with the gestalt therapist, I have been engaged in many years of my own growth work. I have visited my share of therapists and counselors. I have done a lot of looking at myself in the mirror. I have also looked long and hard at my own parents. I have struggled to identify the constructive, growth-oriented, and healing lessons that they transmitted to me, as well as the negative, destructive lessons that they taught. I have worked to nurture the constructive ones and rewrite the damaging ones. Sitting where I sit today, I can tell you that the gestalt therapist was right in her interpretation of my memory. The vignette is one symbolic representation of my experience growing up.

As a young child, I loved that dog. I desperately wanted her to love me back. But she towered over me and knocked me down to run back to her previous home up the street. She did not want to stay with me (or our family) and ulti-mately she got her way. We had to give her back to our neighbors. When that big, lovable dog knocked me down to get out the door so she could run home, she knocked down and ran over my feelings as well. While the dog was only respecting *her* feelings in the act—she missed her prior home and prior owners—she hurt me a great deal.

I have come to understand that this memory speaks to an aspect of my relationship with my mother. For while my mother had nothing but the best of intentions at all times, she had a tendency to run roughshod over me and disparage my feelings. She was too depressed to recognize what she was doing most of the time. Therefore, rather than own her mistakes and limitations, she routinely insisted that I was "too sensitive" and needed to be less so. In telling me to toughen up, she believed that she was truly being helpful.

Today, I know that there is no such thing as being "too sensitive." Remember what we reviewed in the last chapter: feelings are *givens*. We do not choose them. We can only choose what we do with them. Sadly, my mother never learned that lesson; she died before ever learning it. She never came to understand the difference between feelings and thoughts. She never realized how destructive her comments and judgments were. She remained a victim of her disordered mindset and never came to see it for what it was.

• • •

Internalized messages affect the course of our lives in many ways. You already know that the lessons we learn about ourselves in childhood serve to determine our adult self-concepts in dramatic ways—whole books have been written about the process and power of that learning experience. While I cannot possibly convey the breadth of their wisdom in a few paragraphs, I want to offer a few of the major highlights, so you can make sense of the exercise questions and the story that follows.

As children, we learn and store away information with the degree of cognitive development we have at the time of the lesson. So, for example, if we are young and still very concrete or literal in our thinking, we may simply store away a lessons like: "I am a bad boy" or "I am a naughty girl." Since our capacity to understand what might make a person

good or bad has not yet been developed, we store the information as a simple fact. Without being consciously aware of
these stored self-concepts, we are influenced by them
throughout our adult lives. Since these old self-concepts can
cause dysfunction and intense pain, we may find ourselves
questioning our ideas and choices enough to identify some of
our negative core beliefs over time. Having identified them,
we can use our adult cognates to talk back to our childlike
ones. By recognizing and subsequently challenging our
internalized beliefs, we can change and replace them with
more constructive and positive ideas.

But how is it that those negative lessons actually affect
us? What do we do with them? What does it really mean to
be influenced by our past?

Strange as the idea may seem, we all re-experience our
pasts in the present. We tend to hear our self-concepts and
world-views reflected back in the words of other people,
even when those people are not saying what we think we
hear. Similarly, we tend to re-create familiar family
dynamics in our adult relationships, even if those dynamics
were and still are painful to us. What is familiar somehow
feels right! Hence the popular notion that "many women
marry their fathers" and "men marry their mothers."

In spite of our adult desires to experience joy, fulfillment,
and pleasure in our relationships and pursuits, we often
unknowingly re-create the pain, sadness, and loss of our
childhoods. Our biggest life challenge can be trying to figure
out how to live the life we are meant to live, as opposed to
the one someone else might have taught us to re-create.

I am anxious to help you live the life you were meant to
live. To assist you, I have created a list of questions for
reflection that you can use to identify some of the mindset

issues that govern your life at this moment. Try to keep the above lessons and my vignette in mind as you answer the following questions as best you can.

As you go through this exercise, think back to those formative years. What lessons did you learn in your child-hood that were, and continue to be, constructive? What lessons did you learn that were harmful? What do you think about yourself and others? Suspend judgments. Allow scenes and words from your past come into your mind. Make notes of what you recall. Each bit of your personal history is invested with a power of some sort. Just write down the words, thoughts, and images as they come to you. If you find that strong feelings accompany a memory, respect the feelings, and make note of them. Document everything. Even if you cannot make any sense of what comes to you as you do the exercise, honor it. I guarantee that if you continue to engage in this transfor-mational journey, the lessons and power of your memories will eventually become clear.

What do I think about myself and others?

What is my earliest memory?

How would I describe my mother, father, siblings, and significant other adults from my formative years?

What did I learn that I value?

What did I learn that has caused me pain?

What are my happiest childhood memories?

What are my most painful childhood memories?

What recurrent dreams and/or nightmares did or do I have?

Is it hard for me to say "no" when I am asked to do something I do not want to do? If so, what do I tell myself? Whose voice is that?

Do I do things because an internal voice tells me I should do them? Whose voice am I hearing?

What constitutes success in my mind? Where do my ideas about success come from?

What constitutes failure in my mind? Where do my ideas about failure come from?

Do I feel guilty about any of the choices I made? Who told me my choices were wrong?

What relationship patterns am I replaying in my life that I learned in childhood?

Which of those patterns serve me well, and which are harmful?

Which parent am I more like? Different from? How?

Am I happy with my answer to the above question? Why or why not?

Is there anything about the way I think that I want to change? What? Why?

Engaging in the exercise of describing what you think and why will help you get more out of the tales and lessons that follow.

The Tale of Two Ladies

They were so alike. They were so different. Two healthy baby girls were born within four years of one another. Liza was welcomed into her birth family, while Shari was welcomed into an adoptive home. Both babies were anxiously awaited and joyously received by the parents blessed with the opportunity to raise them. Both fathers were doctors. Shari's mother had her own career, while Liza's mother worked in her husband's office. Both families were Jewish, but neither was engaged in active religious practice. Both families were upper middle class and lived near a major East Coast city.

Liza was born a shy, anxious child. Shari was born an outgoing and fearless child. Liza maintained a small cadre of friends growing up, but otherwise kept largely to herself. Shari was friendly with everyone growing up and was constantly involved in a series of extracurricular activities. Liza was slow to sign on to things, but was steady and consistent once she did. Shari was quick to sign on to things, but impulsive and inconsistent with them thereafter. Both girls established dating relationships with depressed, unavailable men. While Liza's boyfriends tended to be scary and abusive, Shari's were merely inattentive and disengaged. Both girls were good students and anxious to please. Both went to extremely respectable colleges where they experienced a series of challenges including episodes of depression that went untreated. Each of them became a patient of mine while enrolled in graduate school, and I should mention, they did not know one another in the slightest.

Liza came to me when she was in dental school. She was given my name by her closest childhood friend, who happened to be a patient of mine at the time. When I first met Liza, she was in the depths of a severe major depression. Having found herself ill-equipped to succeed in her clinical studies, she had stopped attending her dental-school classes. Prior to her total decompensation, she had tried to modify her educational program. Her efforts had been fruitless. She described how she had begun to lie on the couch in her apartment and cry for hours at a time. When she found herself unable to go on any longer, she had called her parents to come and get her. "I can't do it anymore," she told them. So, they had come to get her and bring her home. Within a few days of her home-coming, I met her for the first time.

Shari came to see me when she was in graduate school for education. She had been referred to me by a psychiatrist-colleague who worked in student health at the university. When I first met Shari, she was also in the depths of a severe major depression. Like Liza, Shari had stopped attending classes; but in Shari's case, she hadn't been going for months. Shari had finally realized that she might be clinically depressed after watching a television show describing the illness. She had eight of the ten symptoms. This realization led her to visit student health, where she was referred to me. Shari, unlike Liza, had not told her parents much of anything about the length and depth of her depression. In fact, fearful of disappointing them, she had been pretending that she was doing quite well with her classwork. When she finally found herself unable to pretend or go on any longer, she had sought help at school. Since that first contact, she had told her parents of her diagnosis but had not told them much of anything else. Within a few days of her diagnosis, I met her for the first time.

• • •

When I first met Liza, she told me that she had chosen to go to dental school because she didn't know what else to do. "I took the GREs and the DATs in college. I applied to dental school really late, but I got into a school anyway. I decided to go because I had no idea what else to do," she said.

She described having had a difficult time in dental school from the get-go. Most particularly, the dental laboratory classes were overwhelming. She could not create and work with the three-dimensional models of teeth. She could not translate the ideas she learned in class into the models of actual practice; as such, she continued to come up against this limitation time and time again. She became progressively more depressed until her condition ultimately escalated to a point of incapacitation. That was about the time that she called her folks to come and take her home.

• • •

When I first met Shari, she told me that she had embarked on a graduate-school program in education because she wanted to work with children and be a classroom teacher. To her great horror, she had a miserable experience in her student-teaching stint. She had been completely unable to manage the complexity of classroom life. Juggling disciplinary issues, lesson plans, and a relationship with her supervising teacher had gone so badly that she had been turned off to teaching completely. Rather than allowing herself to take careful stock of her situation and decide what she should do next, she had simply transferred into another education department at her school. She began pursuing a graduate degree in a different field of education, but it still held little promise for her. To make matters worse, her mentor left the university. She no longer had any idea why she was even *going* to school.

• • •

Liza and Shari were so similar. Both had histories of major depression and were in the midst of their worst depressive episodes yet when they came to see me for the first time. Both had embarked on graduate-school pathways that were recipes for disaster. Neither lady was well suited to the demands of her "chosen" career. In fact, in both cases, neuro-physiologic makeup would explain why lady and path did not fit together.

Liza was spatially challenged. Perhaps this was a function of the ADD that I discovered her to have. Perhaps it was the result of a separate learning issue unto itself. Whatever its origin, Liza's brain did not cooperate with the demands of dental practice. She could not translate the lessons of the classroom into three dimensions. She could not separate mirror images from one another, or tell which side of the tooth she was meant to be working on. This turned out to be a *biological given,* which we uncovered as we addressed Liza's *body leg* issues. She came with this challenge and it could not be altered.

Meanwhile, Shari was easily distracted and overwhelmed by multiple, simultaneously competing demands. I discovered, over the course of our time together, that she, too, had ADD. Her inability to juggle multiple tasks and requests could have been the result of her ADD or some other neuro-physiologic element of her constitution. Whatever its origin, Shari's brain did not cooperate with juggling the many demands of classroom teaching. She told me that this inability to multi-task had been a part of her forever. She had come into being this way and realized that it was a *biological given* about herself. It could not be altered.

Both Liza and Shari met diagnostic criteria for recurrent major depression and attention deficit disorder. Both became excessively depressed in attempting to pursue ill-suited graduate school programs. Both came to me feeling terrible about themselves, their histories, and their futures. Both have been with me for a long time now.

Liza has been my patient for six years and Shari for eight. Liza, who intended to become a dentist, is now an accountant. Shari, who thought she would be a teacher, is now a neonatal intensive care nurse. Both have worked very hard to find the right career paths and pursue them. I wish I had enough time and space to describe their incredible journeys in this chapter, but it would simply be too much! Instead, let's concentrate on the task at hand—determining the role their family dynamics played in their respective mindsets.

You are probably thinking, Liza and Shari are so similar that they could have come from the same family. They are almost two peas from the same pod. If you are thinking those thoughts, you are somewhat right. In terms of diagnosis and tale, Liza and Shari are very much alike. They share many inborn traits, and they do have similar family histories.

However, if you met these two women, you would realize they are very different as well. Remember, Liza is a shy, anxious, and withdrawn kind of person. Shari is a gregarious, interactive, and verbal kind of person. Their manner of dress, body habits, and ways of being are quite different. Liza and Shari differ in *who* they were to begin with, as well as *how* they dealt with their undiagnosed ADD over the course of their developmental years. Most important, they differ in what they were taught to think growing up, and what they came to believe about themselves and the universe as a result of those lessons. Bear with me as I tell you something about each woman's family history to show you how powerful that difference in upbringing turned out to be.

• • •

Liza's mother was always too involved in her daughter's life. As far back as Liza can remember, her mother insisted on becoming a best friend to Liza's friends. Rather than play the parental role, her mother was a peer, and later a judge. She would routinely criticize Liza for being different from her friends. She would regularly say things such as, "Why can't you be more like Nancy? She is so friendly and outgoing." As if those words were not painful enough to Liza's ears, her mother would often go on to say, "If only you would get a life, I would be happy. You are responsible for making me miserable." And miserable Liza's mother was!

Liza's father, on the other hand, was never much at all involved in his daughter's emotional life. He participated in her life through recreational activities and paying her expenses, but he refused to engage in caring for or participating in her emotional life. He made it clear that he was quite aware of how hurtful his wife could be, but he also made it abundantly clear to Liza that he did not want to "hear about or deal with it."

The way her family dynamic played itself out in Liza's care with me was as follows: within months of Liza's decompensation, her parents began to insist that she stop treatment. Her mother would tell her that she needed to move on with her life, and her father would threaten to refuse to pay for her sessions. When I offered to speak with her parents, her mother jumped at the opportunity and her father refused to speak to me. Once he even went so far as to have his wife call me to express his concern about Liza's therapy. He then had her put the phone on speaker so he could hear my report. Although he was listening to my voice, he declined to speak or participate in the conversation. His wife spoke for him.

Liza was quite aware that she needed my continued help. She would fight her parents, giving them detailed history and information about her current challenges, just so they would continue to pay for her sessions. Their support remained reluctant at best, but Liza persisted in spite of them.

Over the years, Liza has managed to climb out of a big hole. Although she has not finished with her growth work yet, she is about 85 percent of the way there. She still has areas of self-care and interpersonal relationship that require therapeutic attention and help, but I have seen amazing things from her and—most important—she sees her progress, too!

Unfortunately, to this day, her mother continues to berate and criticize her. She is unable to see much of any progress in her daughter. When a peer of Liza's gets married, her mother goes into a tailspin tirade. She starts by saying to Liza, "Why can't you be like Janice?" and then she goes into her traditional accusations: "You have no life. You have no friends. You don't care about how you look. You don't care about me. You don't care about anything. You are ruining my life by the way you are. Why can't you just get married?"

If Liza does not somehow excuse herself from the room, the tirade can go on for hours. Liza's father will walk away without even attempting to stop his wife or offer a counterpoint. He will later tell Liza, "Your mother is crazy and abusive," but he never tries to help Liza deal with her mother. He is also unwilling to help his wife address her own psychopathology.

Early on in my work with Liza, I suggested to her mother that she get some help for herself. She was clinically depressed and somewhat delusional at the time. She finally went for two psychiatric visits with a colleague of mine. She then cancelled all her subsequent appointments. Her husband refused, and continues to refuse, to encourage or push his wife to get treatment. Although he has always recognized her dramatic need for treatment, he does not want to "deal with or talk about it."

So how did this family dynamic play itself out in the development of Liza's mindset? What lessons did she learn about herself and the universe?

Liza learned to expect abuse in intimate relationships. She learned to bury herself, and share little of herself with others. She deduced that anything she communicated about herself would be used against her. She would be attacked and annihilated. Her whole personhood might be erased. No one would help her. She learned to re-create abusive relationships in her adult life. Overwhelmed by the prospect of obliteration, she learned to hide herself so much that she eventually lost the entire notion of who she was!

When Liza first came to see me, she told me that she had no interests. She could not identify anything she wanted to do with herself or her time. She had been unable to find herself for many years. She believed and insisted that there was nothing inside of her at all. She believed that she was meant to suffer. She told me that I could not possibly be correct when I said that she had gifts, passions, and talents that she was meant to pursue. To her mind, she simply did not deserve to be nurtured or treated with respect.

Over time, Liza and I have worked long and hard to find the wonderful person that is buried under all that fear and self-doubt. We have had to negotiate great resistance to enable her to get to a place of openness. We have fought hard to interrupt her pattern of dating abusive men. In the process, we had to establish a fair amount of distance from her parents. To this day, their abusive influence continues to set her back.

After five and a half years of work with me, Liza was finally able to tell me that she believed she was totally rotten inside. This revelation and disclosure was possible because she had grown from the process of self-discovery and actualization. She had succeeded in finding a joyous and fulfilling career. She had dramatically altered her pattern of dating abusive men. During our sessions, she had come to realize that she was sitting with someone who saw her amazing potential—an experience that changed her. She began to believe in her potential as well. In the wake of this growth, she was finally able to acknowledge and share her deepest internalized belief and fear: "There is nothing at all good about me. I am afraid I am really rotten at my core." She was able to tell me that she had learned to loath herself by her parents' example.

That was eight months ago. As I write this today, I can tell you how much more Liza has grown. Liza now knows that her parents were, and are, the disturbed ones in that family dynamic. She knows that she is a worthy, wonderful, and gifted individual. While she has yet to rewrite every line of that negative, internalized diatribe, she is well on her way to doing so. She is increasingly able to nurture herself

and treat herself with respect. Although she is still afraid to
stop therapy, the end is clearly in sight.

• • •

Unlike Liza's mother, Shari's mother had a life of her own.
She had her own friends, an active career, and a much
clearer sense of herself. However, like Liza's mother, Shari's
mother was unduly critical at times. As someone who was
extremely concerned about social mores, customs, and
appearances, Shari's mother was prone to be overly critical
of her daughter's inattention to social graces, self-care, and
proper dress. She would say, "I don't understand why you
can't just dress nicely. Why do you have to go out looking
like that? Why can't you remember to call your grandmother
on her birthday? Did you remember to send your sister a
card? Why don't you stop eating so much? Can't you just try
to lose weight?"

Although Shari's mother could be critical and unrelenting at times, she never diminished Shari's personhood
in the process. If anything, she chose to push her daughter
to pursue her many strengths and talents. Her biggest
mistake in this area may have been that she pushed Shari
too hard at times; but even if she did, it was because she
recognized her daughter's talents.

Shari's father was emotionally engaged and supportive
of his daughter. If Liza's father was an icicle in the
emotional realm of parenting, then Shari's father was a
teddy bear. He was loving, affectionate, encouraging, and
supportive. He told Shari, "You are a brilliant girl, and you
can do anything you set your mind to." If anything, he might
have been a little too pushy; he always wanted Shari to

shoot for the stars. Shari came to feel that great things had to come from her; anything less would be a failure.

The way that Shari's family dynamic played itself out in her work with me was dramatically different from how Liza's did. As soon as Shari became my patient, I told her that we needed to tell her parents about her deception; they needed to know that it had been months since she had attended classes. They needed to be informed of her needs, limitations, diagnoses, and challenges.

Shari was very worried about telling them the truth. She feared their disappointment and anger. She knew they would be terribly upset, and she did not want to cause them any pain. I offered to tell them by myself or to tell them with her present in a family session; she elected the latter.

When her parents came to meet with me for the first time, her father asked me where I had gone to college and medical school. I had the sense that he wanted to be sure his daughter was in good hands. Once he learned that I had graduated from Cornell University's College of Arts and Sciences and the University of Pennsylvania's Medical School, he seemed to relax. He truly wanted to help his child, and he was able to see me as his ally. From that moment forward, he chose to rely on me and defer to my judgment. He was anxious for his daughter to have as much care as she needed at all times. In contrast to Liza's dad, Shari's father preferred that Shari have extra psychiatric visits as opposed to too few. He surely did not want her to decompensate ever again.

As in Liza's case, I needed to confront Shari's mother. I needed to suggest to her that she get some help of her own to address her critical approach to her daughter. Although she was angry with me for telling her to grow herself, she chose to do it anyway. Unlike Liza's mom, Shari's mother started and maintained a therapeutic relationship of her own. She worked on self-care and acceptance. Through the process, she learned how to become a better mother to Shari.

I also needed to confront Shari's father. I had to help him adjust his high expectations and impatience with his daughter. Since he experienced me as an ally, he was able to trust me. I validated his belief that his daughter was truly gifted, but explained that she could not do *anything* by simply setting her mind to it. She could achieve amazing things in her life, but only if she started from a place of self-acceptance. Shari needed to recognize and pursue her strengths, while working with her own unique learning style at the same time. He needed to encourage her to take on challenges, but he could not judge her to have failed if she found some choices to be ill-suited to her abilities. He worked hard to adjust himself according to my instructions, and he learned how to be a better father to Shari.

So how did this family dynamic play itself out in Shari's mindset? What did she learn about herself and the universe while growing up in this context?

Well, for starters, Shari had learned to pursue romantic relationships with men who expected very little from her and offered her even less in return. Growing up, Shari deduced that she was meant to reach for the stars. She also learned that she was expected to succeed. Although she knew that there would always be a safety net for her if she floundered, she feared sharing anything but success. She avoided asking for help. She feared the disappointment of her parents and others. She dreaded the self-flagellation that she knew would follow their critical comments. She learned to pretend that things were better than they were in order to avoid feeling bad about herself. Although she feared falling short and dreaded sharing her difficulties, she never learned to feel rotten at the core because no one ever told her she was. At worst, she felt like a lazy, willful failure. At best, she felt okay about herself.

Once Shari began to understand the impact of her ADD on her history and continued struggles, she was able to adjust her self-concept. She learned to give herself permission to do a less-than-perfect job in most pursuits. She began to share her difficulties with friends. She started to learn what she needed to do to be wildly successful. She has worked hard in many areas and she is almost completely there! She has a satisfying career, good female friends, and she is finally involved in a healthy romantic relationship. Shari is currently engaged to a man who challenges her and gives her the love and support she needs. All in all, the *body leg* lessons she has come to grips with have transformed her life.

In contrast to Liza's parents, once Shari's parents learned how to make sense of her ADD diagnosis and adjust their expectations and measures of success, they were able to revel in her growing accomplishments. They were able to take pleasure in her continued progress. They are currently amazed to see how far she has come.

Shari now has a wonderful relationship with her parents. She lives much closer to them geographically than she did when we began our work together, and she cherishes the time she shares with her family.

Shari has become actively involved in religious practice as well. She finds her religion nurtures her growth and healing. She recently said, "You know, I have to tell you something really strange. When I read *Soul Prints: Your*

Path to Fulfillment by Rabbi Marc Gafni, I already knew everything he was teaching. It is a spiritual guidebook to living your own story—and I learned all the same stuff from you, although you never talked about God or the Bible. I have come so far. I am finally living the story I was meant to live. I have a good relationship with my parents. I understand my limitations, and I recognize my gifts. I no longer feel the need to hide or pretend. I can accept myself for who I am. I can share myself and be accepted. My whole family has grown up. Thank you for showing us the way."

We have come to the end of the "Tale of Two Ladies." Here is a summary of the key Step One and Two points.

1. Proper diagnosis of depression and ADD was a crucial first step in the treatment of both ladies. (Step One.)
2. Even though I found both ladies to have a lot in common, I discovered that the messages they received from their families of origin were quite different. (Step Two.)
3. My long-term recovery work involved addressing each lady's particular mindset. Each lady faced a different set of challenges, and therefore, each lady's path was quite different.
4. While one lady was able to grow closer to her folks, the other lady needed to establish space from her family in order to recover.

Lessons:

How is the "Tale of Two Ladies" relevant to you, and what should you do about it?

1. If you find yourself derailed on your career path, you, too, may be pursuing a vocation that is a poor fit for your nature or makeup. Be open to the possibility that what you thought would be a right fit for you, may not adequately respect your personal gifts and challenges. Pursue input, guidance, and assessment from mentors, career counselors, therapists, friends, and even co-workers to help you find your way.

2. You may find yourself derailed on your life journey as a result of an unrecognized disorder that requires intervention. Revisit *body leg* issues now if this notion resonates with you.

3. If you still feel unfulfilled or stuck in your journey after adequately revisiting and addressing the issues of diagnosis and evaluating your innate gifts and limitations, it is probably time for you to begin to identify internalized messages and ongoing relationships that undermine your efforts. If you feel down, or if you sense you are stuck, and neither of the two points above helps to assuage your pain, then it is likely you are in a mindset rut. Begin looking at your personal history and self-concept.

4. While you may be able to work on mindset lessons without a therapist, you may feel the need for external help. Books, tapes, seminars, journaling, and exercises like the one I have included at the end of this chapter can serve as helpful tools as you work to identify and challenge your mindset snafus. You may need to create some distance from family members in order to heal. Alternatively, you may need to build in more time with nurturing relatives

or friends. If these tools and strategies feel inadequate, you may need a guide or mentor to help you move along. Search for what you need.

Take-Home Points

1. We all internalize constructive and harmful lessons from our childhoods. For some of us, the harmful lessons become incapacitating without intervention. For the rest of us, the lessons hang us up periodically and require episodic identification and confrontation.

2. We all deserve to be free of the mindset chains of bondage. We are entitled and meant to find our own voices in the chorus of the world. We need to give ourselves the chance and opportunity to express our best selves.

3. Here are some tips to use in finding your own voice:
   * Give yourself permission to engage in self-reflection. Regularly ask yourself questions like those provided in the opening exercise of this chapter.
   * Banish guilt. Do not allow yourself to hold on to beliefs about what you *should* or *ought* to do if the doing is not of your own choice. (Revisit Cindy's belief about how she "should" host a holiday meal in order to study this concept.)
   * Silence judgment. Avoid all statements of good and bad, right and wrong. Critiques of this sort tend to be damning and self-destructive. (Consider the reprogramming efforts crucial to Gillie's recovery to help you stay on track with this.)
   * Pursue self-love, acceptance, and self-nurturing activities. Healing is about growing the parts of

you that *work*, as much as it is about silencing the parts of you that *do not work*. Hugs, hot baths, massages, celebrations, and leisure time with loving, safe people can do wonders for you in this realm.

* Avoid abusive and hurtful relationships. Find respectful ways to create a healing circle around you and keep traumatic interactions away. You cannot afford to feed anything that might eat you up.

* Nurture your spirit by adding Step Three to your path. This step will mitigate much of your self-loathing and hopelessness, while growing your sense of self-love.

Here is an affirmation exercise that you can use to nurture the constructive mindset lessons you have learned, and to reprogram the negative ones that bind you. The exercise embodies much of what I do in my ongoing clinical work with patients:

Revisit your reflections and reactions to the questions posed at the beginning of this chapter. Make a list of all the negative core beliefs or destructive mindsets that you have identified. List them in a column on one side of a page. When you finish, start another column by writing a positive statement beside each negative statement—think of the positive notions as the antidotes to the unhealthy ones. Some of the affirmations might even be the constructive lessons you already have learned from your upbringing that need reinforcing. You should wind up with a page that looks something like this:

Mindset	*Affirmation*
1. I am a failure	1. My best is good enough
2. I am a bad person	2. Bad behavior does not make a person bad
3. I can never succeed	3. Where there's a will, there's a way
4. No one cares about me	4. I am a lovable person
5. Nothing ever goes my way	5. I can find pleasure in little successes

If you cannot come up with the antidotes and affirmations, do not despair. Sleep on it and try again tomorrow. If you are still stuck, ask for help.

Once you have your list of affirmations, write each statement on an index card. Post them in safe places and read them regularly. Do this even if you have trouble believing what you are telling yourself. You will be amazed at how successful you can be at reprogramming negative mindsets if you continually challenge them. It may sound silly to you now, but this technique can work wonders so give it a good chance. Try daily affirmations for three months and see what happens. I am sure you can accomplish a lot.

We all need reminders to challenge our negative beliefs periodically. We all need to talk back to our critical selves and nurture the parts of ourselves that will help us grow. In the next chapter, which concerns the *spirit leg* in healing, I will discuss ways you can begin to engage in the ultimate affirmation: embracing the wonder of yourself and the mystery of the universe.

Step Three: Spirit

INVOLVING MEANING AND PURPOSE IN YOUR HEALING JOURNEY

The *spirit leg* of our stool involves the purpose of existence, notions of a higher calling, and one's sense of something bigger and grander than the self. It entails our beliefs about the gifts we have been given and how we need to share them with the world; it includes the need to recognize our unquestionable value and potential. The *spirit leg* concerns the realm of mysticism, wonder, and religion, and finally, what I call the *creative healing force*—the intuitive side of ourselves that vibrates with the healing energy in the universe.

I have come to believe, beyond any shadow of a doubt, that spirituality is the cornerstone of mental and physical health—but I want to be absolutely clear about what I mean when I say *spirituality*. To my mind, spirituality is a sense of meaning and purpose, and an ability to see what is possible in the world. It is an awareness of and a respect for one's inner wisdom. It is a receptiveness and an open-ness to the love, potential, and healing power in the universe. That said, spirituality does not necessarily have to involve organized religion. Many people are extremely religious, but they may not be spiritual; others are extra-ordinarily spiritual, but have no affiliation to a church, temple, or a congregation.

It should not surprise you then, that unless my patients tell me they are believers in a given faith, I do not speak about God or specific religious teachings with them at all. Further, when it comes to Step Three work, it is usually my patients who lead *me* into a discussion of spiritual ideas. Sometimes spiritual questions are posed from the outset, and if they are, I will work with my patients to answer them; however, it is far more common that my patients formulate these questions after having tackled the *body* and *mindset legs* of their journeys first.

Earlier in this book, I mentioned that the vast majority of my patients leave my care with a greater spiritual aware-ness than when they entered it. If you pause to consider this, you will see that it is actually a logical evolution. After meeting the challenges of biological and mindset issues, patients tend to look at their lives with a fresh pair of eyes. With this new perspective, they have the capacity to pose deep questions concerning their purpose and their need to give back to the world. They have worked very hard to iden-tify and alter the factors that kept them from being happy with themselves or their environments previously; and being further along the way, they are—more often than not—inspired to seek the meaning and purpose of their exis-tence. They have moved beyond the experience of pain and everyday challenge and are looking for greater fulfillment.

It is one of the most significant aspects of human nature that we embody some sense of purpose and seek to express this meaning in our lives. We would do well to recall that the timeless search for meaning is no different from the current day search for healing. Just as matters of well-being are ultimately spiritual matters, spiritual matters are very much philosophical matters. The Greek word *philosophy* literally means "love of wisdom," and in our journeys to come to know ourselves, we are seeking inner wisdom, as well as what it means to be a part of this wonderful and mysterious world. While the journey to self-actualization encompasses a lifetime of steps, it is a progressive exercise where we continually learn to trust what we already know but have not fully realized. As we become less encumbered by our biology and mindset issues, we can become more humble, grateful, giving, and connected; we are able to discover our unique gifts and share them with others. *Spirituality* in this context is about honoring the journey toward self-awareness, self-acceptance, and nurturing our connection to the world-at-large.

• • •

Whether you are a devout religious follower or not, the search for universal meaning offers a person a sense of hope, a sense of community, and a sense of worth. If nothing else, a spiritual connection to the world-at-large can lift you out of yourself, shed new light upon the struggles you face, and offer you a momentary reprieve from those challenges. In a world as chaotic and complex as ours, it is certainly easy to lose our way; a sense of faith and purpose can be our guiding thread through this labyrinth. Just as you have considered how your biology and upbringing have played a role in your life, in order to truly move yourself from a place of longing and despair to a place of hope and joy, you need to consider what role you play in the universe and how open you are to allowing the healing power of its wonderment into your life. Do you find solace in the mysteries of the universe? Do you find joy in nature? Are you humbled by the thought that we are the inhabitants of one planet in an infinite sea of space? Do you feel God's presence when you look at your children or spouse? Do music and art move you?

We simply cannot underestimate the power of spirituality and faith when it comes to our physical, mental, and emotional well-being. I have personally seen the miraculous emerge from a tiny sliver of hope, and devastation take over when all hope was snuffed out. I have seen the power of connection and love to transform lives, and the power of isolation and alienation to destroy them. I have seen children excel when told they are smart, and fail when told they are not. I have seen patients with hope survive illnesses that were thought to be fatal, and patients in despair die of curable disease. And finally, I have experienced the healing power of love, hope, and acceptance in my own life. I have been lucky enough to learn how to offer these gifts to my patients. I have found that my faith in the value, purpose, and potential of each of my patients helps them to heal; and I have discovered that by teaching them to see themselves in kind, they blossom.

• • •

Before going on to discuss the *spirit leg* in full, I want to share a personal tale that demonstrates how openness to the *creative healing force* can transform a painful experience into one of joy. The story began a long time ago, in my home in Philadelphia, and in a kingdom far, far away.

As far back as I can remember, I dreamed of marriage and children. Growing up, I visualized my adult-self sharing a life with a loving husband and four children whom I would call my own. I saw myself raising two girls and two boys. Don't ask me why that was. I cannot possibly tell you. I do not really have the faintest idea. Why we dream what we dream is a spiritual question that cannot be fully answered; it is like trying to reduce the infinite to the realm of cognition. It is one of the questions we will ask, but may never answer during our time on this planet.

What I can tell you, however, is that my life did not quite unfold according to my childhood vision. Although I did find and marry a loving man early enough to build the life I dreamed of, the demands of medical school and my psychiatric residency training did not support it. I chose to put off conceiving my first child until I had been married for more than six years. As a result, I had only two sons by the time I was in my mid-thirties, but no daughters; and for reasons that are irrelevant to this chapter, I was not in a position to attempt further pregnancies.

My pain was like a bottomless pit. Years passed and each time the notion of daughters crossed my mind, my spirit would weep. The passage of time did not seem to heal my wound. The pain would just not go away.

Then one day I was sitting with my patient, Rachel, who longed for children but could not conceive. I found myself responding to the pain of her predicament by saying, "There are other ways to become a parent, Rachel. Have you ever considered adopting a child? You do not need to live with this pain forever." It was as if the Messiah had just stepped into the room. Rachel looked at me in awe. A smile as bright as the sun itself appeared on her countenance. "You are brilliant," she said. "How did you know to say that?"

Stunned at her remarkable response, I answered, "I don't really know, Rachel. It just came to me and I said it. I am touched by how much my words affected you. Trust your reaction to them and do what your inner wisdom is telling you to do about your life. This is all for a reason."

Rachel did go on to adopt an adorable child from Russia. She transformed her life through that one moment in my office; she heeded my words and altered her life forever.

What is even more amazing to me about those words is the role they came to play in my own life. For on the day of that session with Rachel, those words had a powerful resonance for me as well. They continued to echo in my brain as I drove home from work. Suddenly, as if the Messiah had stepped into my car, I found myself saying aloud, "I can do that! I can adopt a child. In fact, I can do that more than once. I can have *four* children! I can have *two* daughters. I can give wonderful lives to *two children* who might otherwise not have that opportunity. I will live my dream after all!"

As I entered the door of my home, my spirit was singing. My husband looked up at me from his place at the table and said, "You have that look in your eyes. I know that look! What's going on?"

I gazed back at him, unable to put this wonderful idea into words. He began to guess.

"Are we taking a vacation?"

I shook my head.

"Are we moving?"

Again I shook my head. "Bigger than that," I said. "I want to adopt a child." My husband's face betrayed his awe and fear. "In fact," I continued, "I want to do it *twice*. I want to adopt *two* little girls who need families. I want to have those two daughters I always dreamed of having. My spirit is singing, and I *must* dance."

After hours of conversation, my husband took a deep breath and looked at me, "I know how you are when the fire starts burning. There's no stopping you. You have seen the future and you'll rush to grasp it. . . . So, what do you need me to do?"

The well of pain that I had harbored for so long, suddenly turned to overflowing joy. I would have two daughters after all. I would! I would! I would!

Although the journey has been fraught with roadblocks and dead ends, today I am the mother of four children. I have two sons and two daughters. My sons, Benjamin and Gabriel, are my biological children. And my daughters, Shira and Glory, came to me on the wings of angels. My daughter Shira Leora, whose name means "song of light," was born in China and became my child when she was ten month old. Our amazing relationship began six and a half years ago. My daughter Glory Beth was born in Cambodia and became my child when she was three and a half years of age. That amazing relationship began one and a half years ago.

When Shira first learned that she would be getting a sister, she began to dance around the room. "I'm so excited! I'm so excited! I can't wait! I'm going to have a sister! I am going to have a sister! I really am!" My husband and I took Shira and her grandfather to Cambodia with us. While there, Shira gained a sister who looked like her, and I realized a dream I thought had died.

• • •

Because my life and my work have shown me how fundamental faith is to the recovery process, I am committed to
helping you find your way to seeing the wonder in you and
the potential in humankind. You may already have a deep
sense of faith, trust, or spirituality, but have no idea how to
use it to support yourself in your journey to heal. By
contrast, you may be skeptical of religion and spirituality,
and feel challenged by the mere notion that faith heals or
that belief matters when it comes to your mental well-being.
I have worked with individuals from both ends of the spectrum, and respect you wherever you are.

That said, it has been my experience that many
sufferers believe in God or have a profound sense of spirituality—and yet they do not know how to apply that sense
of faith, purpose, and wonder to assist them in their
healing. For example, how can you be a failure if some
element of the divine rests within you? The two beliefs
simply do not fit together; they cannot co-exist. If you have
a sense of faith, then your Step Three work will focus on
challenging your self-concept with what you know to be
spiritually true about humankind.

Those of you who have steered clear of the notion of faith
in your lives tend to face a different set of challenges. Your
Step Three work will involve nurturing a sense of hope in
what is possible. You will also need to increase your involvement in activities that offer the opportunity for human
connection and sharing so you can experience the healing
power of love and meaningfulness in life.

In order to help you figure out where you are on your
spiritual path and what you might need to nurture it, I have
included an exercise. As you go through this exercise, reflect
on the meaning and purpose of existence. What is your

notion of a higher power or God? What gifts do you have that you are meant to share? What matters to you? Why do you think you are here? If you happened to have had a religious upbringing, what did you learn from it? What was constructive and what was not?

As you go through the exercise below, document whatever comes to mind. Doing this exercise, or engaging in any attempt to describe your spiritual outlook on life, will help you figure out where you need to start your Step Three work. And of course, please remember: there are no right or wrong answers here. You can feel moved and uplifted when you are singing in a choir, climbing a mountain, donating your time to a charity organization, or sitting in a quiet chapel. Your spiritual connection to the universe can take many wonderful forms.

What do I value most in life?

What are my most precious memories? What are my most precious belongings?

Whom do I respect the most? Why?

Where, when and with whom do I feel most calm or at peace?

What words heal me?

What words harm me?

Do I have a spiritual home? If so, where? If not, why not?

Do I see myself as a child of the universe? If so, do I treat myself like one? If not, why not?

Do I treat myself with as much love as I treat my

children? Pets? Partners? Friends? Relatives?
Neighbors? If not, why not?

Do I offer to help others?

Do I allow myself to ask for help when I need it?

Do I treat my body like the physical temple that houses
my soul? If not, why not?

Do I give and receive love with a full heart?

Do I act from a place of self-love and love of others?

Do I allow judgment and criticism to rule my life?

Do I approach pain with humility and a desire to learn
from it?

Do I give thanks for the many blessings in my life?
Do I even know what they are?

Do I take time to watch the sunrise or sunset? To smell
a flower? Or to say a prayer?

Do I strive for peace and harmony or would I rather
be right?

Do I say I'm sorry often enough? Too much?

Do I believe in magic? Miracles? Wonder?

Do I allow myself to experience pure joy?

Do I give myself permission to be silly? Playful?
Creative?

Do I allow myself to laugh and cry enough?

Do I hear my spirit when it sings? Do I allow myself to
dance to its music?

At the end of my days, what do I hope to be remembered for? Am I living a life that supports that vision? If not, why is that?

Do I surround myself with people who nurture my spirit? If not, why don't I?

Do I spend the bulk of my time pursuing what matters most to me? If not, what gets in the way?

Am I generous with my time, money, self, gifts? If not, why not? Am I afraid they will be exhausted?

Now that you have completed this exercise, read Chris's Tale to see what you may be able to learn from his journey of personal growth.

Chris's Tale

Chris was referred to me by his treating psychiatrist of many years. She hoped he would be a candidate for the long-term psychotherapy group I was running for recovering addicts. This psychotherapy group was designed to augment their individual work, as well as their 12 Step recovery work, by teaching recovering addicts how to conduct their lives in the context of interpersonal relationships. In giving me some relevant background information, she said, "Chris is in his early fifties and has been with me for seven years. I don't think he will ever graduate from my care. He has been in treatment since he was twenty years old and is still deeply troubled. He is isolated, disconnected, poly-addicted, and stuck. He has no intimate relationships in his life. He has never really had any. He lives alone and has no real friends. I have hit a wall with him. I don't know what else to do. I hope you can help him. I see no endpoint to his therapeutic need!"

Needless to say, I was concerned about Chris before I even met him. I arranged to see him for an intake assessment. From his psychiatrist's description, I was expecting to find a recalcitrant, somewhat uncooperative fellow who was troubled, but unwilling to do much about it. I was shocked by what I found instead.

When Chris came to see me, he shared a history consistent with the one his referring psychiatrist had already provided. However, he also provided me with a different perspective on his situation. "I have been in therapy for many years, but I am not happy," he explained. "I am depressed about how little progress I have made. I want to get better. I know that I need to do something different. Do you think you can help me?"

Somewhat surprised and relieved to find Chris open to change, I offered hope and encouragement. I told him of the requirements for acceptance into the therapy group. He needed to be clean and sober for thirty days prior to starting the group. He needed to be attending 12 Step recovery meetings on a regular basis. He had to maintain a relationship with a therapist. He was required to commit to coming to every group session for at least a year. Although planned absences of an occasional nature were allowed, the expectation of all members was a commitment to attend, and thus organize their lives around the weekly sessions of ninety minutes.

Chris listened carefully to the requirements. He immediately agreed to meet all of the terms. He signed the commitment letter, in which he pledged to abide by the group rules, and we arranged that he would start coming to group sessions several weeks hence.

Once Chris began attending the group, he showed

himself to be a model patient in many ways. He maintained all the commitments he had made in agreeing to the group rules. He never faltered. He *immediately* stopped acting out in his addiction. He attended regular 12 Step meetings. He showed up for every single group and routinely followed up on homework assignments issued in session.

However, Chris also severely lacked interpersonal skills and the capacity for empathy. He criticized and attacked other members, carrying on in a holier-than-thou manner on a regular basis. He often operated from a place of right and wrong, and was quick to point out to others how wrong they were. He could be intense and unrelenting in his critiques, and it was easy to see—from my vantage point— why Chris was as lonely as he was.

Although group members all made a year commitment before starting group, the vast majority of the participants stayed for five to eight years. Chris was no exception. This particular group was meant to be extremely long-term; its aim was first, to teach addicts how to live without acting out in their addictions, and second, to teach them life-building and enhancing skills through the experience of learning and practicing with one another over time. While long-term group work for recovering addicts has a place among treat-ment options, it is surely not the only way for you to promote and sustain recovery: active and consistent partic-ipation in 12 Step recovery programs, along with brief therapy, for example, can work as well.

In Chris's early years of group, I needed to confront him regularly about his critical and judgmental nature. I would jump in and stop his tirades, showing him, along with his peers, how feedback needed to be offered. While the lessons I taught are ones we all need to review from time to time, they are crucial to the success of any therapeutic group. Every statement Chris and his peers made had to be in the "I" form, as opposed to the "you" form. Rather than telling someone what he or she *should* do, Chris and his peers needed to comment empathetically, and therefore, from a place of personal sharing. This is fundamental to effective communication; it is far easier to hear how others relate to our struggles than it is to receive their unsolicited assessments of what we are doing wrong.

I gave Chris examples of how to connect to others from a place of empathy as opposed to one of judgment. A useful model for this is the sentence: "When you _____, I feel _____." The first blank is meant to include the behavior of the person to whom you are speaking. The second blank contains a feeling word that describes your emotional state. Often I would even need to tell Chris, "You have to be quiet and listen now. You cannot continue to respond to others' sharing. You must sit quietly and take in what other members need to express. Sometimes we can learn more by being quiet than by talking. You need to do that now."

Although Chris did not like what I was saying, he would always do as he was told. He would sit quietly and try hard to grasp my point. Sometimes, he would forget to be quiet and I would need to remind him to hold his tongue. Rather than rebel, he would respect my instructions and try harder.

• • •

Let's take a step back from the group session for a moment so I can explain how I saw and experienced Chris. I want to do this in order to demonstrate how a spiritual vision and approach served to transform Chris's life.

When Chris came to see me, I was struck by what was amazing about him. Here was an unhappy man in his early fifties; his life was not working out the way he wanted it to, and instead of giving up, he continually tried to fix it. Although he had sought help for many years, he was still willing to do whatever a new provider suggested. He came to me full of passion, willingness, and promise. However, his intensity and sometimes critical manner of dealing with others conflicted with my sense of him. And while I truly felt that Chris's passion came from his desire to connect, it was clear that he didn't know how to articulate or channel it to achieve that end.

When I looked at Chris, I saw beyond a lonely, middle-aged man, to a joyous, connected, fulfilled man in the future. I saw the potential for his boundless energy to be converted into deep expressions of love and caring. I saw a man searching for meaning, purpose, and oneness, who had lost his way and was alone, screaming in the dark.

Unlike his referring psychiatrist, I had no question in my mind that Chris would graduate from therapy. I trusted in his commitment to grow himself and in my ability to help him get where he was meant to go. I knew that I would be able to channel the healing force to lead his spirit from its cave of loneliness and despair. I had *faith* in his potential. I *knew* that he could heal, so I *expected* him to do so.

● ● ●

Several years into Chris's group therapy work, he stopped meeting with his referring psychiatrist. He did not feel as though he was growing as a result of meeting with her. He saw himself growing in group and through the increasing number of friendships that he was establishing with group members and other recovering addicts. Before reaching his decision to leave his ten-year therapy relationship, Chris spent a long time considering the possibility. He shared his concerns and questions with his fellow group members. He worked hard to figure out what was best for himself. He went back and forth a lot. Ultimately, with the blessing of his long-standing psychiatrist, he bid her *adieu*. For a while, he was flying solo.

As Chris continued to grow himself, he began to experience intense challenges in the relationships that he was developing outside of the group therapy room. He did not know how to be intimate with others and still maintain personal boundaries. He looked for all or nothing in his relationships, but could not really tolerate either state.

One day he called me by phone and said, "I am having a nervous breakdown." His relationship with a friend was going poorly and he could not concentrate on anything else. He could not even stop crying.

I arranged to see him for an emergency psychiatric visit the following morning. I offered necessary hope. "I am sure we can figure this out," I said. "Can you come in to see me tomorrow?" Relieved to be taken seriously, Chris thanked me for my willingness to fit him in and agreed to come in at the appointed time.

When he arrived, Chris and I began to work in earnest on his long-standing relationship difficulties. He asked me if I would be willing to continue to see him for individual visits. He needed help in implementing what he was learning in the group. Would I help him take the lessons home?

I agreed to take on Chris's care but first explained that, since his problems had been some fifty years in the making, the process of transformation would be long and arduous. Chris was undaunted by my words. Suffering with incapacitating distress, he was willing to agree to almost anything. He knew that his life could not go on and on the way it was. He needed to get better.

Chris and I embarked on a remarkable journey. Over the course of the ensuing years, we worked hard to address his relationship challenges. He had many lingering family issues that affected his capacity to be intimate. We needed to tackle them in our therapeutic work. I taught him to be honest, open, intimate, but to maintain boundaries. I showed him how to be revealing without losing himself, and how to keep those boundaries without being hurtful or offensive. He and I visited the same issues many, many times. The lessons took a long time to take hold because his old ways of seeing things and behaving were deeply entrenched. Still, Chris hung in there. He kept coming back for more guidance. He kept trying to do a better job.

His hard work began to pay off in a progressive way. He began developing an ever-expanding circle of friends and mentors. Soon his life became full of shared meals and phone calls. Connection ultimately replaced isolation as the governing force in his life. Although Chris did not experience this growing connection as part of his spiritual evolution, I did. I saw the love emerging between him and others as transformational. Perhaps the next piece of Chris's tale will help you see why.

Some years into our work together, Joyce, a long-standing member of the therapy group, was ready to graduate and move on. Although Chris felt a very strong connection to her, and I knew that he would miss her terribly once she was gone, he was not planning to tell her how he felt. To be that honest and self-revealing frightened him.

During Joyce's last group session, I told Chris, "You need to tell Joyce how you feel about her leaving." I wanted him to learn how to show his love in an appropriate way. Chris gave me one of those deer-in-the-headlights looks, but I did not relent. "It is important for you to learn to express your feelings of caring appropriately," I said. "You need to tell Joyce how you feel about her leaving."

Rather than do as I instructed, Chris hemmed and hawed. Finally, he began to tell *me* about how he felt about Joyce. I stopped him. "You need to talk to Joyce, not to me. Tell *her* how you feel."

After what seemed like an eternity, Chris turned to Joyce. Tears filled his eyes as he began to tell her how much she meant to him. As he went on to say that he would miss her, he began to cry. His body shook as he sobbed, and the love that he had kept hidden within himself for all those years began to emerge.

He was now channeling his incredible passion into loving expression. His spirit was beginning to emerge from the cave! This development meant we were closer to the end than the beginning. Rather than suffer in silence, he was beginning to dance.

Some years later, one of Chris's parents developed a life-threatening illness. As a result of Chris's incredible growth work, he was able to cry and love aloud. Rather than avoiding the pain of the impending loss and its aftermath, Chris was able to embrace it and comfort his family members.

When his parent ultimately passed away, Chris found himself turning to religious ritual and practice for support. While this was something he had never done before, it became a heartfelt source of nurturing and sustenance for him. In embracing religious practice, Chris began to glimpse the divine in the universe. He began to study the teachings of his faith and found mentors in his religious community. He formed many friendships among his fellow worshipers and began to adjust both his life and business practices to be more in line with the principles of his religion.

One day when he came to see me, he shared his sadness that he did not have a family of his own. He had been spending time in the company of families with young children and had begun to realize how much that sort of life appealed to him. "I only wish things were otherwise for me," he said. "I am too old and set in my ways to have that life now, and I did not see it as a possibility when I was younger. I am in my early sixties already. I just wish I had known I could have done it all differently."

If you pay careful attention to what comes next in Chris's tale, you will see how the identification of feelings, a Step One lesson, is fundamental to a person's spiritual growth. You will realize why I told you that feelings are a window into the soul. You will see how inseparable biology and spirit really are in recovery.

"Chris," I said, "do you really mean that? Do you want to marry and have a family of your own? I want you to think long and hard about this. If you really want that for yourself, I will help you get there."

Chris looked at me and said, in an incredulous sort of way, "I can't start dating now, at my age. I have never been able to have a successful romantic relationship. I can't even imagine doing that."

"You did not answer my question," I said. "Do you really mean what you said? Do you wish for marriage and a family? It is crucial that you think about the question enough to be honest with yourself. Do you really want what you spoke of moments ago?"

Chris thought and thought. Finally he said, "I do, but I do not see it as a possibility."

But where there is a will, there is *always* a way.

"It is possible," I said, "If you really want it, it is possible. You *can* have the life you want to live."

You see, I believe in the *possibility* of what seems *impossible*. I know that miracles happen all the time. I try always to look for and trust in them, and I urge you to do the same. Just like Chris, and all the others whose tales fill this book, you, too, can have the life you want to lead.

In that session, Chris and I embarked upon the second part of our journey together. It has been a five-year-long effort thus far, and one of the most fantastic and rewarding experiences I have ever had.

Chris and I went to work, long and hard, on what would be involved in realizing his dream. What did his envisioned family life look like? What sort of partner would be a good fit for him? How would he find a suitable match? How would he know if and when he had found her? On and on we went with theory and practice, trial and error, hope and fear.

That is, until one day, when Chris came to see me with a light beaming from his eyes. I knew it as soon as I saw him; he had met his intended! While he had not yet realized that the woman he had just met was going to be his wife, I could tell from looking at him that his search was coming to an end. It did not take him very long to discover what he had already shown me.

Several months passed and Chris became engaged to that lovely woman, who had two children from a prior marriage. Chris then wondrously found himself in the heretofore unimagined position of having some trouble finding a wedding hall large enough to accommodate all of the people whom he had grown to care for during the years of our work together!

On a magical day some months ago, Chris was married. As he stood before members of his therapy group, family members, friends, many religious leaders, and members of his spiritual community, Chris cried tears of joy. His life had been transformed from a place of desolation to a place of joy and meaning. His spirit had emerged from the cave to find its blessed home.

Here is a summary of the *spirit leg* points in Chris's tale.

1. Chris was stuck in therapy when I met him because:
   * He had an active addiction. (Step One.)
   * Chris suffered from unresolved family issues and entrenched behavioral dysfunctions as a result of those issues. (Step Two.)
   * He had a lack of faith in what he could achieve, as did his referring doctor, who feared Chris would never graduate therapy. (Step Three.)
2. Because I saw the possibility of a wondrous future for Chris, and he was willing to continue to work in therapy in spite of repeated failures, I was able to help him walk through the steps necessary for growth.
3. As Chris experienced progressive growth and connection, he was able to open his heart in an increasing manner to the spiritual messages he heard during his sessions with me. I conveyed the message that hope heals, love matters, and where there is a will, there is a way.

4. Eventually Chris internalized those spiritual messages and found comfort and support in a faith-based practice that continued to enhance his growth.

5. For Chris, an active religious practice offered a new vision of what was possible in life. His faith opened new doors to friendships and gave new meaning and direction to his life. As such, Chris was able to move on, marry, and create the family he longed for.

Lessons:

How is Chris's tale relevant to you, and what should you do about it?

1. If you find yourself stuck in your growth journey, it may be because you have inadequately attended to Step One or Two; or it may be because you lack faith in what is possible.

2. If a lack of faith is the root of your problem, please surround yourself with spiritual messages. Spend time with those who believe in you and pursue any activities that will nurture your spirit. While we all could stand to engage in more spirit-care, those of us who are stuck as a result of its absence need to pursue it more often.

3. Take a careful inventory of the confidantes, therapists, and other helpers in your life. Ask yourself if they can support you in your efforts to heal. If the answer is no, do not be afraid to ask for something different or move on. Surround yourself with people who believe in you, even when you doubt your own potential. You deserve to recover.

Take-Home Points

1. We are all enhanced by pursuing what nurtures our spirit.
2. If we are able to find an active religious practice that nurtures us, we are well served to pursue it.
3. Many studies have actually shown that prayer is good medicine!

Questions for you to reflect on:

* Do I sell myself short or neglect to see my own potential?
* Do I search for guides, teachers, or mentors in my journey toward self-actualization?
* Do I allow myself to trust in people who believe in me?

• • •

Rather than tell you another tale to bring the *spirit leg* lessons home, I have decided to share some brief exchanges that demonstrate common struggles and spirit-based lessons. The conversations that follow were all one-time interactions that occurred in my office.

Mary

Mary came to see me at the suggestion of her internist after an extensive workup for her chronic abdominal pain found no abnormality. During our first visit, she said: "My doctor says the pain is all in my head and that there is nothing wrong with me. I am very upset. My belly really hurts. I know I am not imagining that, and I am not crazy."

Concerned about Mary's take on the matter, and armed with many tools to address somatic symptoms, I said: "Mary, I think your doctor meant to convey that there was nothing seriously wrong with your *belly*. I have no doubt that you are in pain and that something is causing you to experience discomfort. Our job is to figure out how to decrease your experience of pain, not to judge your sensitivity to it. I am sure we can do just that."

Mary responded: "This may sound strange, but I feel better hearing that. Knowing that my feelings are legitimate and that you can help me diminish the pain makes a big difference."

Lesson: Mary came to me in emotional and physical pain. In *accepting* her experience without judgment, and by offering her *hope*, I was able to help her.

Moral: Search for acceptance and hope in your journey to heal.

Eric

Eric, a man I was treating for depression and addictive illness, brought this dilemma to a session: "I know I am supposed to believe in a Higher Power to heal me, but I don't think I know how to do that. My experience of religion as a child was punitive and critical. I feel really turned off to this notion of a Higher Being and powerlessness. What do you think I should do?"

"Is there anything you already do, or can begin to do, that might increase your sense of meaningfulness?" I asked Eric.

Eric looked at me, looked away, and looked back again. After a moment he said, "You know, when I donate the unsold food from my restaurant to the homeless shelter, I experience meaning. Perhaps I will start to volunteer there once a month. I can see how doing that good deed might help me see a greater purpose in life. You know, those homeless folks even say 'God bless you' to me when I deliver the food. Now that I think about it, maybe their blessing has something to do with why it feels so good to go there. I am definitely going to do it more often."

Lesson: Eric came to me in a specific spiritual crisis. In considering my question/suggestion, which addressed one element of the *spirit leg*, Eric was able to figure out a next step. That particular step even offered him the opportunity to begin to restructure his notion of God from a punitive being, to a benevolent one!

Moral: Invite spiritual questions into your journey and take small steps in the direction of greater meaning.

Lynne

Lynne, a woman I was treating for an eating disorder, began a session with the following statement: "I have been using all the techniques you have taught me, but I have not been able to get myself to stop bingeing for two weeks. Whenever I have time alone, I binge. I haven't had this much trouble for years. I don't know what is wrong with me."

Struck with Lynne's inability to be at peace when alone, I wondered if she was trying to avoid a recurring thought or feeling that plagued her unless she found a way to distract herself. "Lynne," I said, "do you think you are using the binge behavior to avoid something scary, hurtful, or otherwise upsetting?"

Lynne thought for a moment before realizing and saying,

"I need to pursue my photography. I never told you, but I used to be an avid photographer. I quit taking pictures after several exhibitions of my work failed to yield any work for pay. I have been trying to avoid visiting that old hurt, but I am happiest when I am taking photos. I guess I need to acknowledge the pain and not eat over it, so I can return to doing what matters to me. I don't need to get paid for my work, but I definitely need to pursue it. If I don't take pictures, I am not sure what will become of me!"

I commended Lynne for identifying what mattered to her and for realizing the fundamental importance of pursuing her passion. When she returned the next week with the new photos she had just shot, she reported, "No binge episodes this week! I used my alone time to reconnect with my camera instead of the cookie jar."

Lesson: When Lynne came to see me, she was overwhelmed by a symptom she could not make sense of or control. I helped her to understand her symptom differently when I asked a question that honored her deeper wisdom. In my search for meaning, I enabled Lynne to identify her passion and return to something she was meant to do.

Moral: Look for meaning, purpose, and the feelings that may be driving your symptoms. Expressing symptoms is one of the ways your body is able to communicate your feelings to you.

• • •

I encourage you to refer to these brief vignettes and lessons as you continue to concentrate on your own growth. I *believe* you can heal. I *believe* in your amazing potential. Having shared many different *spirit leg* lessons with you, I want to offer you a spiritual development exercise that you can use to grow yourself at your own pace.

List three action-steps that you are willing to take within the next two months that will serve to nurture or grow your spiritual self. The steps could be anything from beginning a workout or weight-loss program to attending a religious service. They ought to be related to the answers you gave when doing the long exercise at the beginning of this chapter. Review your answers to those questions in developing your three action-steps.

Once you have written the steps, commit to taking them. I guarantee you will see incredible results if you choose to take this on. Of course, the more you take and grow your list of steps, the more fulfilled your life will become.

Remember, easy does it.
One step at a time, but never give up.
Nurture faith in your potential.
You can do this!

Step Four:
Putting It All Together

HOW TO STAY THE COURSE
AND MAINTAIN HOPE THROUGH
THE PROCESS

The steps I have shared with you thus far have demonstrated how you can integrate body, mind, and spirit in order to achieve dramatic results on your journey to greater health—but there is still much to say about the actual process of growth and change.

First and foremost, I want to reiterate that the process of growth and healing is not a straight line. None of us moves from dysfunction to fulfillment without a lot of setbacks, pauses, and mistakes. The path to health is a bumpy road.

Personally, I tend to think of the healing journey as akin to climbing a mountain. As we start at the mountain's base and begin climbing, we discover steep areas, plateaus, treacherous slopes, and peaks that come in and out of view. We may think we have seen the summit only to realize, upon reaching that spot, that the mountain goes on and on. We may choose to camp and rest for an extended period of time along a particular plateau. We might even choose to abandon our climb and resume it at some other point in the future. Sometimes our own limitations will give us pause, while at other times, the forces of mother nature will send us scurrying home. We may ultimately climb as far as the mountain's summit, or find ourselves content to have arrived at an elevation somewhat shy of that lofty peak in the clouds.

As an avid hiker who thrills in reaching the summit on all occasions, I can tell you how difficult it can be to take pleasure in the trek when it must be abandoned shy of the goal. And yet, while the goal of reaching the peak is significant, taking joy in the sport, as well as appreciating the wonders encountered along the trail is just as important. I have wonderful visions of hikes I have taken over the years lodged in my mind's eye; I hear the sound of the wind rippling through the aspen leaves in Colorado, I see the Stellar's Jay in the peaks of the Teton Mountains, I watch the play of light throughout the day in the Grand Canyon, and I observe an ominous storm blowing onto the peaks of the North Cascades. These beautiful visions exist like a gallery of glorious experiences which I will always be able to delight in.

But that brewing storm over the North Cascades is a particularly good example of a hike that was both disappointing and yet wonderful in another way. The looming threat of bad weather forced my husband and me to abandon our six-day backpacking loop; had we continued on, we would have been stranded above tree line at the mercy of strong winds and snow for countless days. I still have a sadness about "the hike that wasn't," but I will never forget the drama of that storm as it blew in across the sky. You can bet we high-tailed it out of the park pretty quickly once that powerful image appeared! I still think about that hike and the storm we almost encountered. When I do, I relive the excitement, anxiety, and the humbling effects of Mother Nature's ability to send us running for cover. "The hike that wasn't" is still a loss, but it has also become a blessed memory of another kind.

• • •

I use this climbing metaphor to represent our growth process because loving the natural wonders of the world is really no different from loving the world within each one of us. As we continue to mark time on this planet, we are either growing ourselves or slowly shrinking. We can either challenge ourselves to live more fully, or allow ourselves to shirk life so we slowly wither away.

Just as the mountains beckon us to make the climb, our uniquely gifted selves persist and long to be nurtured and expressed. We can either choose to climb the mountain, or we can shut our eyes to it. We can take on the challenges our growth requires, or we can deny their call. We can grow ourselves for a while and then give up—effectively never reaching the mountaintop we aspire to gaze from—or we can continually push ourselves to keep going. We can attribute our difficulties to the external world when in fact they are within us, or realize that we can accomplish more than we ever expected. At times we may think we have finished the arduous climb, when the truth is we have only just begun. We can take five steps forward and two steps back every time we venture forth. We can take pleasure in our accomplishments however small, or strive for perfection and devalue everything short of it. We can delight in climbing the mountain, or curse its presence in our back- yard. We can see lessons in our mistakes and strive to do more, or we can treat our mistakes as bad omens or failures, and allow them to trip us up time and time again.

In the healing work I do with my patients, I have seen people avoid becoming their best selves out of fear; it is the greatest derailing force there is. What's more, people rarely identify their fears when they avoid or abandon their growth work. I have come to appreciate how the most predominate fears—of failure, alienation, abandonment, pain, annihila- tion, or death—work to keep people from embarking upon their healing journey, or cause them to abandon their "hike" midway through its completion. Ultimately, fear can keep individuals from experiencing fulfillment.

Of course, there are other folks who are anxious to heal, but remain stuck in place because they have no idea about what to do differently. Perhaps they have key diag- noses that have been missed and need attention. Perhaps they have mindset lessons that have conspired to keep them stuck. Perhaps they lack the faith that they have the potential to heal. Perhaps they fail to see the wondrous possibilities of the universe.

If I can offer you nothing else, I want to offer you hope. You need not get stuck in fear or confusion. I have the utmost confi- dence in your potential to heal. In all my years of practice, I have never met a single person who truly wanted to heal but couldn't. Where there is a will, there is *always* a way.

That being said, what is the way? What is the answer to

all your troubles? What is the quick fix, easy solution, take-home message?

Fortunately, or unfortunately as the case may be, there is no easy answer to these questions. All of those self-help gurus who tell us to do this or that and then everything will be fine are appealing to our desire for quick solutions to complex problems. We want our upsets of today to be fixed by yesterday. We are surrounded by marketing messages for products that guarantee to bring us joy, health, fulfillment, or satisfaction immediately. We live in a quick-fix, "drive-through" culture that plays to our childlike desires for everything to be made right in the world with a hug or mother's milk. If only it were so simple!

In reality, the path to fulfillment is simple. It is just not easy. Just as the notion of starting a mountain climb at the base and establishing a goal to reach the summit is simple, its actualization can be fraught with challenge. A pleasant, straightforward idea can become complex to the nth degree. Whether you are climbing mountains or tending to your self-growth, the concept is simple, but the actualization is not easy. The trek is wondrous, but extremely challenging.

Whenever I take on new patients, I try to convey something of what my role will be in their healing journeys. My place is to walk with them side-by-side for some period of time. Of course, we can't do everything together. We are not, thank heavens, fused at the hip. Though some of us may choose to learn from and partner with one another for extended periods of time, we are not meant to travel each other's growth paths. Each human is unique, and so each journey to self-actualization is as well.

Whenever a patient is ready to graduate my care, or decides to take a break from our work together, I respect the value of the parting. I know that I have done what I was meant to do along the path of that healing journey. It is time for our paths to part and for other partners to step into the space freed up by our separation. Letting go is a big part of healing. Just as we all need helpers, mentors, guides, and supports, we all need space and distance to find our own true and special selves.

To love is ultimately to give of ourselves so as to be able to let loose. It is to honor and respect the wonder in one another, and to do our part to share our vision of that wonder with other travelers. We are all more alike than different, and yet there is a magical gift and uniqueness in each one of us.

So how do I suggest you work with this body-mind-spirit leg model in your own healing journey? How should you start? Where should you go and when should you stop?

Start your healing journey with the *body leg* work of Step One. Identify feelings and diagnoses first and always. Get whatever help you need to do this now and in the days to come. This is the touchstone you need to start growing and healing. Unfortunately, this vital step is too frequently left out of the popular self-help literature; please do not leave it out of your personal ongoing self-help project. Whenever you need help in this area, get it. Don't allow yourself to get stuck in permanent idle. There are too many skilled and wonderful people out there to help; you need not go on suffering without assistance.

Continually grow and challenge yourself in this area. Use psychiatrists, internists, and primary care doctors to help with matters of diagnosis and medication management. You can use other guides and caretakers who know how to work effectively with your particular diagnoses to help you deal with the issues you discovered when you examined your capacity for feelings identification. These guides and care-takers should also be able to assist you with incorporating behavioral interventions to address your problems.

Remember that you are the best steward of your journey. Do not be afraid of asking "professionals" to outline their goals for you. In fact, be sure to ask them about the experiences they have had in dealing with problems similar to your own. Ask them to share their diagnostic impressions, and to summarize your treatment plan. Be sure the plan feels right for you before you agree to take it on. While the process of change can be scary, the approach your doctors or counselors take should not be. You need to be comfortable with your partners in this journey; otherwise, you may find yourself unable to engage in the process. Trust your gut: if it feels right with a given healthcare provider, it is probably right. If it feels wrong with a given provider, it is probably wrong. There is a match for everyone.

If care that felt right as you started down the path begins to feel wrong somewhere along the road, don't be afraid to change your mind or move on to another provider. But be sure to share your impressions with your provider before giving up on a treatment that initially seemed like the right fit. Sometimes a misunderstanding or misperception can be the culprit in such a shift, and a productive discourse can reset the track of the relationship. If discourse does not serve to heal the discomfort, it may well be time for you to move on. Don't second-guess yourself too much. Just try to remember that we are not meant to stay together forever. If it feels like it is time to move on, it probably is.

• • •

What about the *mindset leg* of the stool in your healing journey? Do you need a therapist of some kind to help you there? It is a crucial question, but you must answer it for yourself. If you reflect back on your responses to the stories and exercises in the mindset chapter, you may know the answer to that question already. Sometimes, exercises such as the ones provided in Step Two are enough to enable an individual to start challenging negative internalized beliefs and behavior patterns; and sometimes they are not.

In order to challenge the negative mindsets taken on in childhood, we need to allow our adult-selves to talk back to our child cognates. For example, a child may have come to believe that she cannot do anything right after having been told so repeatedly by her mother. Yet as an adult, this child may have achieved great success in her chosen career. But because her internalized childhood belief is locked away in her unconscious, her adult experience of success may never challenge it. She may walk around feeling bad about herself without quite knowing why. However, once she is able to call up that childhood belief and identify it for what it is, she may be able to talk back to it, saying, "I *can* be successful. I just won an award and got a promotion for my professional accomplishments. My mother was *wrong*. She taught me to think of myself as a failure. But I am really a *huge* success. I don't need to walk around feeling like a failure anymore. I am not what she told me I was. I am okay!"

If that adult-child is really evolved, she may even begin to take that lesson into other experiences of self-perception. She could continue to talk back to the internalized negative cognate until she comes to feel really good about herself. Each time she begins to doubt in herself, she may challenge the negative self-concept that hinders her. In continuing to articulate her adult knowledge, she will nurture her growing sense of self.

Although we can all do some of that mindset work without help, it is not unusual to find that we need periodic assistance in identifying and challenging some of the negative mindsets that we have internalized. Additionally, we often need help to identify the role those negative mindsets play in our adult propensity to unknowingly recreate the destructive patterns of our childhoods. If you find yourself in need of assistance here, please procure it. Use the same approach to finding a suitable provider as outlined above in the *body leg* section. Remember there are right fits and there are wrong fits; additionally, nothing has to be forever.

Perhaps it will help you to know that I needed a great deal of help identifying and challenging the negative self-concepts and worldviews that I had unwittingly internalized in my childhood. Growing up, I had been exposed to a series of contradictory messages. While my religious background and relationships with my father and maternal grandmother taught me to value myself and the universe, my relationship with my mother sometimes challenged my notions of worth. When I grew up, I knew that I had internalized the conflict, but I still needed a lot of help identifying and changing its manifestations in my adult life. Some of the help I received was better than other help. None of it was all bad, but none of it was a panacea either. In the end, I have to say that the best help I received came from my own personal spiritual journey as a healer and as a human looking to be healed.

• • •

As I have tried to show you throughout this book, addressing the *body* and *mindset legs* inevitably bring us to the *spirit leg* in healing. What can you do in order to nurture your spiritual connection to yourself, others, and the universe? What steps should you take when it comes to the *spirit leg*?

In his book, *Eyes Remade for Wonder*, Rabbi Lawrence Kushner writes about a lesson he learned from a professor in rabbinic school. The professor taught Rabbi Kushner that most rabbis have only a few sermons that they work to refine, polish, and deliver over the course of their lives. Kushner goes on to express the hope that his readers will glean a few good lessons from his book—something I hope you will be able to do with this book as well—but I mention the story for another reason. When Rabbi Kushner speaks of the key sermons each rabbi is meant to deliver, what I hear him talking about is the spirit voice—the wondrous gifts our lives embody, the piece that makes each individual unique and necessary to the universe. We each have and hold our own piece of the infinite. We each have our own individual story to tell. For some of us, the story will burst forth in sermon form. For others, the gift will be revealed in another way—we will write a novel, donate our time to charity, become teachers, or devote ourselves to our families. We each have our own way of contributing to the universe. We each have our own "sermon" that we need to refine and cultivate over the course of our lives. Our challenge is to figure out what that "sermon" is and pursue it.

I recently came across a journal that I had kept during my medical school days. Having thought I had lost it in one of my many moves, I was thrilled to find it again. The journal contains several entries concerning aspects of my own spiritual journey.

For me, the journey has always been about pain, healing, and growing myself by helping others. The events of my life, including all the trials, tribulations, moments of pain, moments of joy, and every one my achievements as well as mistakes, have led me to where I am today. Like all of us, I was at times hard-pressed to see the significance of a given event or moment in my life while I was in the thick of it. But when the history of my own journey is spread before me like a tapestry of events, emotions, and lessons I have learned, I see the course of my spiritual journey writ large. I am not surprised by what I see, because I have come to realize that this was the path my life was *supposed* to take.

Whether it was a poem I wrote while standing at the stern of a cruise boat on the San Francisco Bay, or the day-to-day moments captured in the ink-stained pages of my medical school notebook, each entry shows the progress of my journey whether I knew it at the time or not. Lines such as *Struck by an overwhelming faith in God /Aware of the precarious balance between wonders and horrors/ Seeing dancing mermaids beside drowning children in that wake/ Unable to comprehend the misery/ Still struck with an over-whelming faith* wash over me still. Entries speaking to my search for meaning in the face of despair remind me that this was a path I was *meant* to travel.

In February of 1982, I wrote:

Today was another episode in the continuing saga of Medicine. On rounds with our attending this morning, the fifteen of us went to see a patient who had been in a somnolent state for close to a week. The etiology of her condition remains a mystery. As we all stood about her bed, I was struck by the focus of my educators. Beside this woman's bed stood her husband. Both his love for his wife, and his deep concern over her condition, hit me like a ton of bricks as we stood there. He watched, in fright, as these mountains in white coats poked at his wife and spoke gibberish over her prone body. Only one of the white mountains was considerate enough to throw him a bone by way of explanation. As my team left the room, I remained with this man only long enough to put my arm round him and let him know I understood his fear and trepidation. As I walked out of the room, my eyes welled up with tears and I fought desperately to maintain my composure. How horrible can be this glorious profession. How absolutely horrible.

From moments of seemingly overwhelming dismay in my chosen profession to the healing power of life in general, my journal chronicles the stepping-stones I followed. In the same month as the above passage, I wrote the following:

My favorite season is spring; the bursting forth of new life, the vibrancy of bright greens against brown barks, the freshness, the promise, the joy of spring...! These have always swelled my heart to near bursting. I grew up in the woods and was never more at peace than when walking among the blooming trees and flowers.

I have always been preoccupied with growth and equate life with it. My preoccupation with growth, with beginnings, has been behind my continual uprooting and relocating. I thrive on the challenge of a new environment.

My interest in medicine stems from my interest in growth. My ultimate aim is to grow by helping others to do the same, to come to know myself better by helping others to get in touch with themselves.

I am a visionary and have always pictured a life, a world, other than the one I function in today. One of my most cherished mottoes embodies the concept: *She who cannot dream, cannot effect change. For dreams are the stuff the future is made of.*

I have always been acutely aware of eyes and fear nothing more than losing my sight. Perhaps this is why I have such trouble looking into people's eyes with the ophthalmoscope.

Finally, I feel somehow like a tree. As a tree gives evidence, by the character of its rings, of everything it has experienced, I feel that I am very much a composite of my experiences. Each stage of growth, of readjustment, of life has merged with all others in some unique and special way to create the *me* I am today. I regret nothing I have done, for had I done otherwise, I would be someone else. I rejoice in my growth and would not, for one moment, switch places with another.

It is a curious thing that reflecting upon moments from our past will often send us even further back in time. I have seen this happen time and time again with my patients, and I understand it well. When I look at these journal entries from my young adulthood, childhood memories flood my mind. Like the entries above, these memories demonstrate the enduring pull that psychic pain and healing have had upon me over the course of my lifetime.

I recall a time in elementary school. It was recess time on a glorious, sunny day. We were outside playing in the schoolyard when I stumbled across a classmate whom I barely knew. She stood crying behind a spreading oak tree on the school grounds.

"What's wrong, Brenda?" I asked. "Why are you crying?"

Brenda looked at me as she sniffled and sobbed, "I am too fat and nobody likes me," she said. "I have no friends."

Now Brenda was a tall girl who towered over me, but she was in no way *fat!* I was puzzled by her words and said, "I don't think you are fat, Brenda, and I will be your friend."

"Really?" she said. "Do you really mean that?"

"Of course," I said. "I would not say it if I didn't mean it."

Brenda seemed relieved. A smile replaced her tears just as the bell rang indicating recess had come to an end. We exchanged quick good-byes and went inside to our classrooms.

While I don't really know if Brenda's assessment was accurate when she told me that she had no friends, I do know that she had friends thereafter. I know that because I became her friend. Since I was a popular little girl in elementary school, the other children followed my lead. Brenda's life was definitely filled with friends after I came across her crying on the playground that fateful day.

There is another childhood memory that comes to me as I reflect upon my path. It involves an experience I had during junior high school while participating in a volunteer project. Once a week, a number of us would pay a visit to the local home for preschoolers who were wards of the state. The children were in the home for reasons of parental loss, abuse, or negligence. My classmates and I went to the home to read to the children, color with them, or just simply be present for emotional support.

Each week when we would arrive, countless tiny children would converge upon us. As I write this passage, I see myself barely able to sit down as a crowd of little bodies hangs from every piece of my body. In my mind's eye, I am filled with love and panic. I love every one of those beautiful, affection-starved children while I am simultaneously overwhelmed by my limited capacity to meet even a fraction of their boundless needs. This memory touches me now, as the experience touched me then.

And finally, there is a third memory that echoes in my mind. It concerns a conversation I had with a dear high school friend. I am not quite sure when it occurred; it was either during high school or college, but I remember the actual exchange vividly.

"What do you want to do when you grow up?" she asked me. "What do you see yourself doing with your life?"

I had never really thought much about it before, but I found myself saying, "I am not exactly sure what it will look like, but I do expect that I will have some sort of a place that people will come to in order to heal. I will teach them how to take better care of themselves."

Interestingly, my friend no longer remembers the conversation we had some twenty-five years ago, but I have never forgotten it! In fact, it is probably one of the most important conversations I have ever had, because it was the first time I articulated the vision my life now reflects.

• • •

My draw to psychic pain, my search for another way to see and do things, my ache to find oneness in healing, my love of connection—and searing pain in its absence—my need to change the world and be changed by it, my drive to find meaning in the face of despair, and my passion to grow and help others to do the same have been there all along. These are the forces that continue to drive me today. They are, to borrow the words of Rabbi Lawrence Kushner, the sermon that I was put on this planet to refine, polish, and deliver.

The road to wellness and fulfillment can be bumpy and elusive at times, but there is always a purpose and a path. Each one of us has a spiritual journey we are meant to travel. Each one of us has a spiritual self that longs to be expressed. Each one of us has the potential and possibility of finding our own unique and wondrous spiritual home. Just as I have my sermon to live, so, too, do you; you have a story that is just waiting to be told.

You may be wondering what you should do to stay the course when the road gets bumpy or how to nurture hope in the face of despair. You may have read my "sermon" and thought, *Well! That's your life, but I am different. My life is not for a purpose. There is nothing unique about me or what I am meant to do.* Perhaps you are wondering where to go from here.

I always encourage people to start from where they are. Whatever feels most pressing, powerful, or onerous right now is where you are meant to begin. No matter how massive your recovery project feels to you, I guarantee you will feel better as soon as you begin to honor your challenges and take small steps in the direction of help, growth, and health. Even though the path may seem unclear, I know that you will find your way if you search for it.

I can't tell you what steps to take to find your own unique place in the universe, but I can show you the road and promise you that your place does exist. Remember the courageous blind woman that I introduced you to in the beginning of this book and follow her lead. Find "Seeing Eye dogs" you can trust. Surround yourself with books, mentors, guides, and friends that nurture your spiritual self. Take a series of steps, one after the other, that evolve from all of the exercises you have done in this book.

Where there's a will, there's a way. One step at a time will get you there. Just begin, and keep walking. Give yourself the future you deserve. Learn to hear the melodious voice of your own spirit when it sings. Learn to dance your glorious dance when the spirit sounds. Discover the story within yourself and share it with the world. Give yourself every chance you can. Remain committed to your dreams, and to your infinite potential. Choose to grow yourself just a little bit more today than you did yesterday. Reach out like the blind woman and call to the universe for guidance.

You will be answered.

In the Words of My Patients

WHAT IT FEELS LIKE TO SUFFER AND HEAL

Before getting into the body of this chapter, I need to tell you something rather amazing. At the time that I wrote the conclusion of the previous chapter, I had no idea that I was going to ask my patients to talk to you. But suddenly I found myself thinking, *I believe I am supposed to ask my patients to write a part of this book with me. How fitting, yet how odd. Whoever would have thought that I would ask them to write a component of this healing guide?*

Over the course of the ensuing days, I found many opportunities to help my patients by asking them to help me help you. As I sat with six of my longest-term patients, all of whom were close to graduation, I found myself asking them if they would find it helpful to write something about their course of therapy in order to help others.

A truly miraculous thing occurred! Each patient responded to my question with such will, gusto, and appreciation at being asked that I found myself overwhelmed by their passion. Several patients even told me that writing something for me to share was the least they could do to give back! They were all excited about the opportunity presented to them. They would each learn something more about themselves by reflecting on their healing journeys. They would each play a significant part in helping others in pain.

I gave very little instruction to my patients. I explained the premise of this book and shared some pieces of its content with them. Beyond that, I said very little.

Each of them took the assignment very seriously and arrived at their next session with the material that you will be reading here. I made some suggestions when grammar or points were unclear. I made no recommendations to change or embellish the content.

The only "reflection" that I played a part in organizing is the first one. As you read through Sally Jean's reflections, you will understand why I chose to become involved in her material as I did. All of the other reflections came to me as they are printed here.

While some of my patients chose to include diagnostic information in their pieces, others did not. Even where diagnostic information is included, it is often only a part of the full diagnostic picture.

Finally, I want to tell you why these reflections are of such long-term care. I stopped taking on any new, even potentially long-term patients over two years ago. I knew I was going to start writing and teaching more. Since I did not know where that journey would take me, I did not want to start with new folks whom I might not be available to help arrive at a point of graduation.

Since I have no shorter-term cases at the moment, I only asked folks who have worked with me for years to talk to you. I don't want you to think that all therapy experiences have to go on for years. They surely do not. That being said, the healing journey itself does go on for years. It goes on forever. As long as we live, we have opportunity and obligation to grow our amazing selves. While the following reflections concern experiences of long-term growth in the context of a therapeutic relationship, much healing and growth can occur in other forums. There is a time and a place for everything.

I am privileged to be able to share what some of my patients have agreed to tell you about their experiences of the therapeutic process. Their words bring a different voice of wisdom to the dialogue. They experience the therapeutic relationship in ways I do not.

Listening to others who have visited the pain you may now face can be an empowering tool. You can learn some of your greatest life lessons from fellow seekers. Searching your own soul for lessons, as you listen to the tales of others, can provide perspective and hope. Look for yourself in their words. You are present in them.

We all are.

Sally Jean's Reflections

Sally Jean came to me in January of 1997. She was referred by her gynecologist with the following letter:

Dear Eve,

Sally Jean is a patient of mine who underwent a modified radical hysterectomy in March of 1993 for an invasive squamous cell carcinoma of the cervix. Since then, she has done very well and has been disease free.

At her last visit, she stated that she has been experiencing bouts of depression that have been increasingly more severe. She does admit to some suicidal ideation, however, when questioned about the manner in which she would carry this out, it is apparent that she has not thought about this in any great detail. I do not think that she is looking to use this as an escape from her depressive episodes, but I think it shows that she is getting tired of dealing with the symptoms. Her most recent examination fails to reveal the presence of any evidence of disease and I am referring her to your capable care in hopes that you will be able to help this very nice lady.

If I can be of any further assistance, please do not hesitate to contact me.

Sincerely,

Timothy B. McGinness, D.O.

Sally Jean became my patient in January of 1997. I still see her today. Although she was able to share her clinical depression with me from the get go, she needed to hide her alcohol addiction for years to come. It took many years of therapy before she could trust anyone enough to let them into her private world.

Sally Jean has allowed me to share a series of excerpts from her journals. They concern her referral to me, her alcoholism, her family-of-origin issues, and her growing sense of what the healing journey is really about.

On her referral:

I was just thinking about how shitty I used to feel—I mean *really, really* low. My guts told me EVERYTHING was wrong with my life.

Where I was living. How I was living—my jobs, my hobbies, my decisions—all way out of line.

But I did what I did until one day—when I figured no one was listening anyway. I responded to a physician's question during a routine exam. When asked, "How are you feeling?" my response was, "Okay, I guess; physically." To which he responded, "Do you know you said that last time?" All I could feel/think, is why would he notice? I sure didn't realize it, but I believe now it was the very last speck of me, part of me that keeps me going—it wasn't even a conscious effort—but thank God for the conscious response—I'd just about given up on them. Following was a conversation about psychiatry and the potential I might have for feeling better simply by talking to someone. The tears sprang forth and it was the first time I felt like anyone truly cared about how I felt—or at least got me involved with how I was feeling. Thank you, Tim McGuiness

On trusting herself and others, on her alcoholism, and on spirituality:

> Numbers are not my forte, but I think it took me a solid six years of therapy to realize I didn't trust anyone, myself notwithstanding. The result of developing a "lack of trust" in the world is that I have an issue with honesty and truth.
>
> What I never incorporated into my journey for understanding was the truth about me, because the only thing I could hold on to was me. On some level, I had to be okay, right? What I managed to omit from my health picture was a virile career in alcoholism. Well, I always drank—so how could my problems have anything to do with alcohol? I've always had relationships and jobs—so the alcohol couldn't be interfering.
>
> Not as long as I maintained relationships that weren't intimate. Oh. Intimacy. What the hell's that? Lord knows I never had a relationship with myself, let alone anybody else that wasn't at the very least enabling me in my behavior. And guess what? I'm angry about it—but that's good because in the past I'd just be drunk about it and it would go away...and I LOVE things that "GO AWAY...."
>
> But in time, and thanks to AA, I have learned that we all have shortcomings and the only way to narrow the gap is to own that about ourselves, and realize that some people will and some won't, choose to own their own behavior—but it is our understanding of this that allows us to accept each other and tolerate the "in-betweens."

The work to be done around the word "acceptance" is huge. It has been pivotal in my understanding of myself and others.

This, I believe, is where the spirituality work enters.

I have a distinct understanding that we are sums of the parts. The more parts you accept and acknowledge, the richer the whole will be.

On the place of family-of-origin issues in her healing journey:

What I know now, that I didn't know then, is that I'd spent my entire life doing what I thought I was supposed to be doing—taking my clues from a woman who was doing what she was supposed to be doing and teaching me what I was supposed to do without knowledge of what that was, because her mother did what she was supposed to do. None of which ever felt "right" for anyone, but nobody knew the wiser because we simply did what we were supposed to do and that was as close to doing the right thing as we came.

The problem is: there is no genuine "ness" when you don't integrate your *feelings* into what you do and how you do it. Your feelings guide the truth which guides the action, which guide the essence of you, the Spirit.

If you don't give shape to your feelings, you can't give shape to anything about you. And when feelings have been as dormant as mine have, well, there's a "mess-o-chaos" in store for you.

Who knew? I just felt what I was supposed to feel—

things went smoothly that way, until what I was really feeling kept bugging the shit out of me, and it's taken a very long time to dig down to me. But Eve has been my "miner," "mentor," and "Mom" unearthing the vast layers of dirt and rubble, showing me how to sift through and identify what's valuable and what's not, in starting my collection of things that are truly me.

And thank God for the commitment I've been fortunate enough to experience, because where I come from, there's no commitment to self. Just commitment to what you're supposed to do.

I passed the test with flying colors, but felt no reward. It's kind of like scuba diving—yeah, I did it, but guess what? I don't really like it—so what. I didn't do that for me. But it's taken a long time for me to understand that is how I feel...

On the pain of her alcoholism:

I think finding out I had alcoholism was more devastating than the news I had cancer. What's up with that?

You can take my uterus, but don't take my bottle. God, is that a sick thing to write.

But it is how I felt.

(I'll never be able to recover unless I can say that, which I have.)

My desire to die is directly correlated with my use of alcohol. Fact. I hear it in the rooms too.

Alcoholism is like being HIV+. If you don't take care of it by preventative measures, it will kill you.

Around the pain of her experiences growing up:

> It bothers me that my mother told us she had three miscarriages and adopted us to replace those children.

> Dad always said: "Children should be seen and not heard."

• • •

I was struck by something I just read and want to note my curiosity about my Mother's obsession with keeping her encyclopedias. Of all the books in her library, she insists on keeping the encyclopedia handy. I can't tell you how many times we've moved them. I feel blessed she didn't make me pack up the edition she bought for the shore house.

It's about life, I'm sure. It's about the tangible, the finite, the facts. It's about what happens, and why what happens, happens. It's a comfort to her.

God, this is sad. No questions unanswered, no ma'am—the only resource you'll ever need—keeps you independent—no need to ask questions—it's all right there.

In the book I'm reading, the character reflects on the women in her life and her memory of them. Ironically, although from a close group of women, four aunts (siblings), a mother and sister, she identifies most with her black nanny as the only continuity in her life. She could determine what day it was by what chore was being done; and the devastation she feels when that changes.

It is my belief that my parents have never read for pleasure.

If fiction wasn't based on non-fiction, they had no interest in it. It's as if things not rooted in actual experience have no value. It was impossible to feel in any way productive while I was growing up.

• • •

I have never felt "in the day" in my life. I have never felt "in my life" in the day.

• • •

Emily asked me the most wonderful thing: "Mom...do you still love me when I'm not cooperating?" "Of course I do. I love you no matter what."

• • •

Deciphering life. That's what I feel like I've been doing for a very, very long time. The words, the gestures...the body language—the contradictions, the idiosyncrasies. You say one thing, but it means another. I'm so confused and all I want to do is the right thing. I want you to love me, accept me, but I'm not fitting in, it's not in the cards—I don't know what you need from me and what I am—dear God, help me—I'm not going to make it—no one's coaching me but they threw me the ball—Christ! I didn't even know I was in the game.

Some years ago, Sally gave me a gorgeous decorative plate. It was a montage of a grown woman, a classroom blackboard, a bowl of fruit, flowers, and beauty. Across the bottom were sprawled the words: "I am still learning." The plate hangs on the wall in the entry hall of my home.

Although I have always loved it, I never understood its full significance until Sally Jean shared the following journal entry with me:

I pride myself on deciphering my feelings now. They come to me in thought and then I need to strip them down, like sounding out the vowels in a word for the very first time. I'm learning to read, but the inside part this time. The part that isn't in the books, but the part I bring to the book to make it come alive for me. It's invigorating now. Once it scared me to death...but I had to learn to understand that fear. I had to learn that everybody has that fear, and it is so debilitating...Talk about being "my own worst enemy."

There's help. There are people that have had very different experiences. But you have to want a different way, you have to be willing. Willing to deal with the truth about all things. Willing to have Faith that only good can come out of being genuine.

I am still learning.

• • •

I am still learning...
I am still learning...
I am still learning...
As I contemplate Sally Jean's journal entries, I find myself identifying with her words. I, too, am still learning. I am learning how vital a bottle of wine can be to an emotionally starved child, how damaging the feeling of being unwanted or unseen can be to a child's innate sense of trust, and how healing patience, persistence, and love

can be to anyone in pain.

Although Sally Jean felt unable to organize her journal reflections for publication when I asked her if she would be willing to share some of her experience with you, she wanted to be of service. She did an amazing thing. She brought her journals to a therapy session. Having finally grown to trust someone, she handed them to me, saying, "I trust you. You keep them till next time. If there is anything in them of value, you can use it. Pick out whatever you want." I could not have been more moved by anything else Sally Jean could have said. She had finally moved from a place of complete distrust of the universe, to a place of growing openness and love.

I would like to share a final entry from Sally Jean's journal and the blessing it evoked in me in response. The closing entry:

The only map you need is the one you create in the process of discovery. These are the tools to navigate life with:

Body is the Ship

Ocean is Life

Oars are the Will

Wind is the Spirit

Sails are the Heart

And my blessing in response:

May the wind always fill your sails for joy.

May the sun drench your body with its warmth.

May the sea part to enable you to walk through on dry land,

Or carry you gently and buoyantly home.

May you have the strength to row against the current when necessary,

And the wisdom to relish the journey no matter where it takes you.

With love, gratitude, and blessing, I say "thank you" to Sally Jean and Tim McGinness.

Delilah's Reflections

Delilah chose to describe her experience of therapy by using a well metaphor. Her rendition is printed here as I received it. No changes have been made.

A journey up from the bottom of a well.

I am at the bottom of a well. No warmth, no light, no escape in sight, only anxiety, fear and hopelessness.

I met Dr. Eve Wood while I was suffering with severe post-partum depression ("PPD"). I could not care for myself or for my newborn daughter. I could only sleep two to three hours in any twenty-four hour cycle and had trouble eating. I had developed a stutter and was experiencing debilitating anxiety attacks. Not even my favorite books, magazines, television or radio provided any escape from my misery. Although not actively suicidal, I felt my connection to life slipping away rapidly. After a horrible outpatient visit to an emergency psychiatric facility, I was steered to Dr. Wood by my daughter's pediatrician.

A rope appears above my head,
but I cannot reach it.

Dr. Wood threw down a rope. She immediately increased the dose of medication I had been prescribed at the psychiatric emergency room and we began to talk. She explained to me and to my husband that I would get better eventually, but that my condition was serious and required serious attention. These first few months in therapy are difficult to remember. I was very unhappy and impatient to feel better. I saw the rope back to my old self dangling above me, but it was beyond my reach.

I begin to climb up the rope, inch by painful
inch, often slipping back down.

After about six months, I was almost myself. I was caring for my daughter and returned to work part-time. We spent a lot of time discussing my previously unrecognized history of depression, which I had inadvertently documented in journals dating back to my childhood. I began to understand that my parents were incapable of providing the emotional support that I needed as a child, adolescent and young adult. Going forward, I would need to mourn that loss, learn how to seek emotional support from other sources and become emotionally healthy myself, so that I could nurture my child. Although I understood this project on some level, change was difficult and slow. Interacting with my parents was a struggle that often left me exhausted and depressed.

Questioning the rope: Is Dr. Wood's rope the right way out or is there a better way?

After about a year, issues of intimacy in my primary relationships became a focus of therapy. This was very difficult for me, and especially so as it related to my marriage, because I had placed pretty much every emotional egg in my marriage basket. Although my husband is a very caring, loving, and loyal spouse and father, Dr. Wood helped me see serious problems with our marital dynamic. I placed my husband on a pedestal and looked to him to care for me and make me happy. To make matters worse, my husband felt threatened by the issues I was raising, and was concerned that Dr. Wood was intruding inappropriately into our family.

I felt very torn. On the one hand, I had improved greatly with Dr. Wood's help, and I sensed that if I stuck with it, it could change my life dramatically for the better. On the other hand, it was expensive, inconvenient, and was making major waves in my marriage. I felt like I was being "re-programmed" and wondered if I would somehow lose my identity. I was thinking about letting go of the rope, but my fear of falling back down to the bottom of the horrible well kept me hanging on.

I continued with Dr. Wood. With time, effort, and what I now recognize as tremendous personal courage, my marriage began to change for the better, despite my fear of conflict. I came to realize that I loved my husband deeply, shortcomings and all. With this understanding, and an acceptance of my own limitations, my husband and I were able to blossom as parents and create a marriage that was stronger and healthier than ever.

Now I know I need to keep climbing the
rope to get to the top, but wonder how
long it is going to take.

Over the next couple of years, I continued to meet with Dr. Wood and discuss my marriage, parenting, work, and the stresses that arose in my life. I was basically stable, but had some real rough patches. She helped me learn from my mistakes and figure out that I had to make better, healthier choices, choices that would support my well-being and growth. I came to feel very dependent on Dr. Wood, who I appreciated more and more over time. Sometimes I felt I was at the lip of the well, almost there, but other times I felt myself slipping back down. Was I going to be in therapy forever? Why couldn't I figure things out myself by now? Why was

I repeating the same mistakes?

My marriage continued to improve and my husband's resentment abated, but I felt frustrated at times, wishing he would find his own rope, and focus on his journey upward as much as I was focusing on mine.

I do not worry anymore when I'll reach the top and instead focus on putting one hand on top of the next.

Here I am, closing in on my fourth year of therapy, knowing it is going to end sooner rather than later. I am much more confident and happy in all aspects of my life than I have ever been. I finally appreciate the importance of self-care. Nevertheless, I am anxious about losing my weekly sessions with Dr. Wood. She has become the mother I never had—compassionate, insightful, helpful and focused on my being. How can I give this up?

I have begun my own spiritual journey, with baby steps. I joined a synagogue and attend services with my daughter, often welling up with tears when we sing together. My husband and I decided, after much deliberation, against risking another bout of PPD and instead are well into the process of adopting a little girl from China. This is a choice that would never have occurred to us if I had not experienced PPD, but it is a decision that seems so right and so life affirming. My daughter has developed into an amazing preschooler, whose strong will and charisma amazes and challenges me constantly. I volunteer for "Depression after Delivery," and speak with women in the throes of PPD. I think I help them. I share the insight I've gained in therapy with my friends who ask for advice. I am certain that my parenting skills have been helping them a lot.

I look up out of the well and to the vista.
I see beauty and challenges all around me,
and so many options.

I do not know if I will climb mountains, stay in the valley, fish in the rivers, or sail on the ocean. Sometimes I worry about falling in a well again, but I feel that I have so much more wisdom and the tools I will need to scale a rock face, plant a crop, hunt, fish or build a boat to sail across the ocean. Or even to climb out of a well, if I fall that far again.

Will I be on medication for depression for the rest of my life? Probably. Will I always be vulnerable to depression? Yes. But I will be so much more than that. I will be a caring and loving parent, wife, and friend. I will contribute to the world around me in ways I cannot even yet imagine.

I have specific goals going forward: to recognize and then keep appropriate boundaries, especially with my daughters, husband and parents; to support the nurturing relationships I am blessed with, while letting go of some less healthy ones; to invest the necessary time and energy into spiritual, emotional and physical health; to accept my limitations and the limitations in those around me and embrace what each individual has to offer; and to get help when I need it.

Most importantly, I will strive to be a compassionate person, even to myself.

Nancy's Reflections

Nancy wrote the following rendition of her treatment experience as part of her therapy graduation exercise. She felt that it would be helpful to document her growth. She wanted to put her remaining challenges in perspective.

My ten years of therapy with you have taken me on an incredible journey. Today, I leave the safety that I have found in you, for the safety that I feel within. My heart and soul are filled with gratitude to God for making this experience a reality.

Eve, when I first came to you, I came with a broken spirit and a disparaged soul—but I had hope. Many of my dreams have been realized beyond my expectation. I came to you scattered and unintegrated. I had little if any sense at all of myself. And I was filled with self-hatred because I was almost totally unable to accept myself, especially since I barely knew myself.

I will be more specific. The first area I would like to discuss is the uncontrollable rage that consumed me when we first met. I was filled with hate and anger. Most of this anger, which manifested itself in temper tantrums, throwing objects, cursing, and screaming, self-abuse, etc., was directed at others. The main target was my ex-husband. I now believe it was really rage at myself. Today, I am able to "live and let live." I wish my ex-husband well, although I do not go out of my way to have much to do with him. But when our paths do cross, I treat it as a pleasantry. I no longer feel "the victim" when things do not go my way. I can handle not having things my way as a natural part of life—and it's okay.

So many wonderful and exciting things happened to me in therapy. All were related to the core process of helping me to become whole, rather than fragmented, and to enable me to face life on life's terms as an independent, coping being. When I first came to you, Eve, accompanying my intense anger was a lack of any sense of self. I knew no boundaries. I knew not where I began or where someone else ended. My relationships were completely and totally enmeshed.

For instance, there was the pivotal relationship that existed between my mother and me. All of my life I had clamored to win my mother's love, attention, and approval no matter what it would take. The cost was high—I lost touch with my core and my own feelings. I failed to realize my potential as a person. Upon entering therapy, I did not know my own mind. I was fearful of life. I was unable to make decisions. I was extremely engaged in people-pleasing because of my terribly low self-esteem. I lacked all sense of self and was filled with self-hatred. I saw the world entirely through eyes produced by black and white thinking. I was dependent upon my mother. I thought the thoughts I believed she wanted me to think. I made decisions based upon what I thought would please her. I idolized her. I was angry at her, at the same time, for not really being the mother that she represented herself to be.

If she was angry at me and withdrawn from me, I would suffer what felt like a deep, empty hole within myself. I felt helplessly abandoned. The way I dealt with this empty hole was to enmesh myself with others so that there could be no separateness. Therefore, all of my relationships at the time were dysfunctional and unhealthy.

I actually shook at the thought of my mother dying someday. I felt lost. I envisioned myself floating somewhere in space with no grounding. In all of my relationships I would choose controlling people who would tell me what to do. I would become addicted to those relationships. I was attempting to fill the emptiness within me. I would allow people to be abusive of me, as well, just to stay in the relationship. I repeated the pattern with my mother over and over again.

When my mother died, after about eight years of therapy, I was able to handle the loss in a healthy manner. I accepted that it was time. I handled my grief appropriately and maturely. I was in touch with myself and my feelings. I did not panic or feel empty or abandoned. All of my relationship skills had globally improved by this time. This growth was evident in my friendships and my parenting.

Regarding my parenting skills, when I first came to you I did not have any real relationship with my daughter, my only child. Nor did I have any clue as to how to build a relationship. My example of parenting had been control and enmeshment. Through your constructive mothering of me, I began to see a different, much healthier picture of what good parenting was. I learned that good parenting is the ability to help our children realize who they really are and not who we want them to be. Therapy has helped me to let go of my desire to control Alice. Because of my strong sense of self, I have been able to be open and honest with my daughter. We share true intimacy today, as I have learned to allow her to know me.

These skills have affected all of my relationships. I am able to be present for the people in my life. I can be myself because I know who I am. I have healthy relationships with others because I now have a healthy relationship with myself. I no longer need obsessions and addictions to fill me. My connectedness to myself and others fills me.

It was during my therapeutic experience that I realized that I have ADD. All of my life I had been plagued with an inability to focus and concentrate. I had always had a dream of attaining my master's degree, but believed it to be an impossibility. I neither believed in myself nor was able to stay with something long enough to see it through.

Through your belief in me that I could accomplish these things, and with the treatment of ADD, I began to have faith in myself. I was able to attain my graduate degree. I went from being in a job that I hated, to one that I love. At last, I began to experience the feeling of personal empowerment. I learned that I can make a commitment to myself without letting myself down.

My mind began to get clearer. With crisper thinking, I began to feel centered and uncluttered. I began to have insight into where I was, where I was going, and who I am. I began to establish my identity in my own mind. I was able to see things that needed to be worked on. I could fulfill personal commitments to work on them and change. I began to experience a satisfied feeling of self-like, and then self-love, acceptance and true happiness.

I have also been able to let go of materialism to a great extent, realizing that the relationships with people I love, including myself, are the most important things in life.

Today, I exist as a mature, happy, independent person. There is much work behind me and also much work still to be done.

One of the biggest areas that I must work on is my spirituality. I do not yet fully understand this, but I know that my eating disorder is directly connected to my lack of spirituality. The commitment to surrender and to steadily work a 12 Step program in order to give up food has to be redeveloped. I have done this before, but I have failed to grow spiritually. Therefore I do not stay committed to turning to God instead of to food.

Tied into my eating disorder is self-acceptance. As I work on confronting the issues of spirituality, I hope to become more accepting of the fact that I have this disorder and that it is part of me. I want to become more integrated in this area, and less rejecting of it. Connected to spirituality is the concept of honesty. I still have trouble at times with people-pleasing because I am afraid that others will not like me. I need to be myself and accept all of me. I need to be rigorously honest about my life. Work still needs to be done here. Either/or thinking still appears, and I have to be reminded that things are not black or white. There is a lot of gray, and there are not always answers. There are no guarantees. Even when there are answers, they might not be the ones I want and I need to surrender. All of these things are connected to my eating disorder and weight problem. I know that I must face these issues as I go on. I need to put more structure into my life and keep it there so that I may succeed.

Even though I will no longer continue my weekly therapy appointments, I will take the knowledge I have attained with me. What you have taught me is now a part of me and I will take it with me wherever I go. I have God, my support groups, my friends, and family. Most importantly, I have myself to rely on. I am not alone.

Today, I know who I am. I am not afraid. I feel full inside. I have healthy priorities. I feel centered, capable of facing life, and at peace. Walking up the steps to my apartment, I feel:

* Empowered

* Satisfied

* Queen of my own domain

* Able to make it on my own!

It's my place. I pay for it. I never had that before. I have a lot to show for my life. I love my life. I feel free.

Dominick's Reflections

My journey through adulthood has taken some interesting turns. In 1973, I married my high school sweetheart. We started our family in 1976, with the birth of a son. In 1979, our second son was born and one year later I started my own business. The year 1981 brought the birth of our daughter and everything seemed wonderful. Life was good.

In the spring of 1989, my world came crashing down around me. I entered a treatment facility for addictive illness. In spite of a number of years in therapy and 12 Step meetings, I couldn't get control of my life. My marriage was in trouble and I felt terrible about letting down my wife and kids. Life was not good.

This was a turning point for me. It was time to get honest and face myself, and what I despised about the man in the mirror. My therapeutic experience needed to change directions. It was time to get honest, be accountable, and learn to trust others. I had to begin to love myself and cultivate a belief in a power greater than myself who loves and cares for me.

Today, as I speak of the journey I am still on, I feel good about myself and grateful for the opportunities presented to me. I am thankful for the love and support from my family, friends, and the special people that made up my therapy group. We, as a group, growing together for close to ten years, shared a common bond of wanting to be at peace with ourselves. We aimed to develop a spiritual connection with a Greater Being, so that we could recognize what God wanted for us and be able to accomplish it.

I learned through that process that I need to accept that my past and my family of origin played a huge role in who I am today, and where my strengths and weaknesses come from. Being born the fourth of six children into a rather dysfunctional family played a big part in creating the issues that, after all these years of therapy, still challenge my very core. My issues are many, but easier to recognize today than they were a few years ago. I fear conflict and confrontation at any level. I struggle with self-esteem and self-acceptance. Throw in eating, sexual behavior, and workplace issues, all of which can provide avenues of excess for me, and you can understand why my journey is not a smooth sail down a lazy river.

It's been a long, bumpy ride with new challenges around every bend. Just when I get one part of my life on the right path, another seems to unravel. I guess this is just the process of self-discovery. It's not something I can do on my own. With the help of my therapist, wife, family, and a couple of very supportive friends, I have been peeling the layers of the onion, or my issues, away.

There are days when I feel I can't go on any further or that I don't want to work this hard anymore, but I'm learning ways and developing tools to help me through these times.

Just as important as my family-of-origin issues,

we've identified that clinical depression and attention deficit disorder also play a large role in how I got to where I am. Successfully treating those problems with medication and therapy makes my work much easier. Understanding the ramifications of those illnesses in my life has been at times very difficult. Sometimes the effects are very subtle and at others, rather obvious. The ADD, for example, makes it more difficult to achieve the goals I set for myself in terms of regulating my calorie intake on a consistent daily basis. When I'm not successful with this, it is easy for me to be hard on myself if I don't recognize that it is not because I'm weak or lazy. It comes down to developing strategies to help overcome this and not being ashamed to ask for help from others who understand what I'm trying to accomplish.

Without a good therapist, medication, a support system, and a spiritual connection, I would not be able to enjoy anything in my life today. I've come a long way in my ability to have meaningful interpersonal relationships with my family and friends. I've become more organized and better able to handle the conflicts and personal situations that affect my business and home life. I continue to look for ways to better myself and to figure out how I fit in this universe and what I can do to make "my" world a better place to live.

Darby's Reflections

I remember it like it was yesterday—May 1993—on a rooftop talking to my friend, Tracey, about her therapist, Eve Wood. As she talked about Eve and how she was helping her, I realized for the first time that maybe I could get help, too. At the time, I was very deep into my eating disorder, having suffered for years with both anorexia and bulimia. I always thought it was my problem and my secret, but now, married and with a baby, the suffering with the food continued and now I was having an affair with a man from work, hurting my husband and my child. I really hated myself and realized that with the help of a psychiatrist, maybe I could get help to stop being the person I had become. I had no idea where the next ten years with Eve would take me.

The day I walked into Eve's office, she asked me why I was there. I explained to her about my suffering with anorexia and bulimia and believed that my life, my family, and my world were perfect. I just had this problem of wanting to be skinny. It took weeks of talking with Eve for me to open up about the affair and when I finally did, even though I didn't tell her the whole truth initially, it was the beginning of my realization that maybe my world wasn't so perfect. Although from the outside it seemed that my world was perfect, on the inside it was anything but. I had many people around me—my friends, my family, my husband—all who said they loved me, but the honest truth is they didn't even know me. I believed that if they did, they would all leave.

Soon after starting individual therapy with Eve, I became part of a group of people all suffering from some type of addictive illness. With the help of my group and Eve, I learned who I really was and that I actually am a good person and have some self-worth. During those early years, I learned that I could actually tell people what was on my mind and they would still love and care about me. I never thought it possible that people would like me even after I told them my dark secrets.

I thought I grew up in a family where everyone was perfect and had no problems. What, in fact, I grew up in was a family that didn't talk about anything deeper than what you ate for dinner last night, and still really doesn't; parents who loved me, but in no way supported my emotional development; a family that promoted the idea of religion, but understood nothing about God or being spiritual; a family that never really accepted me for who I was. Through the last ten years, I have tried many times to talk to my parents, particularly my mom, about growing up in my family. Although she listens and at times tries to communicate with me, most of the time I leave the conversation feeling empty.

About five years ago now, I found out that my father also suffered with a sexual addiction. My husband went out with my dad one night and my father made sexual advances toward him. Dealing with that was one of the hardest things I've ever had to do. In one way, I felt validated. "Look everyone, my dad is a sex addict, too. It's not all my fault." For the most part though, I was depressed. How could my father violate my husband and, in turn, me like that? How could I ever look him in the face again?

I think this is when I learned how to really reach out to others. During my whole life, I went it alone, thinking that it was a bad thing to ask for help. Who would want to help me anyway? This time I couldn't get through this alone and realized that I didn't have to. I was in a partnership with my group members and my therapist, who all really believed in me. They helped me to do what I needed to do—confront my parents. My parents, of course, pretended that they didn't know what I was talking about. But that was okay. I had said everything I needed to. Today, although I will never forget what happened, I have forgiven my father for his actions and my mother for trying to cover up for him.

Several months later, I was in a terrible car accident and walked away with barely a bruise. The next day I got a phone call from my friend Alex. Alex had become my daily check-in partner. Imagine that, a male friend who wanted nothing more from me than my honesty and support. When I told Alex about my accident, although of course concerned about my physical well-being, he talked with me about the accident from a more spiritual place. Why was I so lucky to walk away from an accident where my car turned over several times? Was there any connection between this and the incident with my father? Was there not a greater meaning to all of this?

As I thought about the questions, I, too, wondered why. Why had my father made sexual advances toward my husband and not any of my other siblings or their spouses? Why at this time in my life had I become aware of his addiction? How could I walk away from an accident where the car looked like a sardine can? Maybe God was sending me a message.

To me, religion was a holiday meal where I could either sit around and feel empty with my family, or binge and purge. The thought that God was sending me some sort of message and that I was in a place to hear it, was never something I experienced before. I remembered sitting in on OA meetings or in my group, hearing some people talk about their "higher power." I asked Eve about it because honestly I thought a "higher power" had to be a non-Jewish thing. I certainly didn't understand the concept.

Now, after many years in therapy, I was ready to add another component to my path. I began, with the help of Eve and my friend Alex to learn through classes that the Torah, which encompasses Jewish law, is an amazing book about how to live one's life; how to be the best person you can be without ever having to be perfect. I learned that being connected to God makes me feel peaceful through and through. It is a feeling I never really understood before, but being spiritual not only helps me to grow as a person, even when I make mistakes, but enables me to be part of a community that shares my goals. Today, I am involved in my synagogue, have a personal relationship with my rabbi, and my children attend a Jewish day school.

About six months after my accident, Eve decided that it was time for my group to end. I had been involved in the group for six years, and by June of

1999, we were going to finish up our group's journey together. I had very mixed feelings. Meeting with my group every Wednesday night had become a guaranteed time for support during the week, a place where I learned I wasn't the only person in the world who struggled with life.

Over the next six months, we discussed where we had been when we entered group and where we still wanted to go. I don't remember exactly what Eve said to me, but something she said made me realize that there was one thing that I still hadn't done that I needed to do within the confines of our group. My husband didn't know that I had slept with the man from work back in 1993. I needed to tell him.

At that time, I couldn't bear the truth myself and told my husband that I had kissed the man—period. In order to really move forward in my relationship with my husband, I needed to be totally honest. I was so afraid, afraid that he would leave me and I couldn't survive alone. Once again with Eve, my group, and this time, God, I realized that I wasn't the same person that had broken my vows six years before. I was a better person, someone who had learned how to be an honest, faithful, and loving person and wife. I loved my husband very much but realized that if he couldn't get to a place where he could see that, then I could in fact not only survive on my own, but continue to go forward with my life.

After much love, care, and support, my relationship today with my husband has never been better. That's one of the things that always amazes me about Eve. She teaches me how to be a better person and has confidence that I can attain any goal I set out to achieve.

The journey with my husband has certainly had its ups and downs, as our paths toward personal growth have not always been in sync. There were definitely times where our survival as husband and wife had been in question. But each time when I can't figure out how we're going to get past a stumbling block, I pray for help, I go to Eve, I talk to my friends and, with all three components, I figure out that the world doesn't have to always be so black and white; that within the gray, there are many options; and as long as we can discuss our feelings with one another and really show our care and respect for one another, then there is a workable solution out there.

It's an amazing thing to me that today my husband is as invested as I am in really changing how we relate to one another. For years, he fought against change, in particular, change that involved getting help from a psychiatrist. Today, he not only gets help for himself, but we work together with a therapist who has really helped us to grow stronger as a couple.

Although there are many times I still wish my life was "perfect" and that the world could be "black and white," the gray is an area I've grown more accustomed to and actually like much more than having to achieve the unattainable goal of perfection. Although most days I still have to talk myself through my insecurities, I am not alone in that struggle. I can reach out to many people, including God. Although I still struggle with my eating disorder, I am now beginning to really share all my hidden secrets and shame that go along with my illness. I believe that this is the road to recovery for me.

When I started therapy with Eve, in my wildest dreams I never thought I would be with her for as long as I have. Through these ten years together, an amazing thing happened: I look in the mirror, and I really like the person I've become. Thank you, Eve, for helping me to feel good about who I am.

Sarah's Reflections

Sarah chose to share her experience of therapy by writing about it in a letter to me. She found it difficult to describe her journey without me as the conduit. Her letter is printed here as I received it. No edits or changes have been made.

Dear Eve,

I am writing to describe my experience in therapy with you over the past ten years. When I called you to make my first appointment, I was no stranger to therapy, having seen four different therapists in the preceding eighteen years, due to lifelong overwhelming anxiety and depression. I never got better during those eighteen years, and I felt like I could no longer go on with my life the way it was.

When you answered the phone, I was amazed at how much time you were willing to spend talking with me to get some preliminary facts. Because I was always in a hurry, pushing forward on a pre-set agenda, I was shocked. You asked me what my problem was, answered my question about the parking situation, and told me where to sit to wait for you when I got there. You explained everything so I would know what to expect. I would never have been able to ask for all of that.

During our first session, you asked a lot of questions, some of which seemed irrelevant; for example, the role of religion in my life. Even though I am Jewish, I had no idea how to answer. You seemed very young to me and, to this day, I remember the color of your eye shadow, which you have since abandoned. Your office was very peaceful and not fancy or pretentious. You sat with your feet up on a little needlepoint footrest, and I felt vaguely embarrassed by that. That was because of my own level of self-consciousness and self-hatred; if my feet had needed to be elevated, I would never have shown that to anybody. Instead, I would have pretended that I was comfortable.

Your office was different from those of my former therapists who had had "cookie cutter" setups, replete with diplomas, pictures of Sigmund Freud and Karl Menninger arranged like shrines, and elaborate systems of doors to get in and out of without running into the next patient. One even had a coffee bar. You didn't even have your own bathroom and had to go out in the hall to use a ladies' room—just like your patients. I felt like the invisible wall that existed between me and the others was gone and you and I were both on the same side, in the room together.

I was very mindful of how gentle and patient you were in your approach, and, yet, how painstakingly thorough you were in questioning me regarding every single criterion of depression in the DSM. That part seemed very boring to me, and I thought you could have done it a lot quicker. From my typical vantage point of detachment, I observed that you appeared to be holding my self in your hands like a most delicate, fragile, and beautiful piece of pottery. I actually was a complete nervous wreck, which I thought I covered up pretty well with intelligent, articulate responses. It blew my mind when you told me that you could tell that I was highly anxious based on what I told you about how I grew up.

One of the first things you did was recommend a book called *Women, Sex, and Addiction*. I had no idea why, as I had never mentioned sex or addiction (addiction being one of the problems I didn't have). Reading the book was an electrifying experience for me. When I got to the parts about boundaries and co-dependence, it felt like I was reading an instruction manual on how to be me. Not one of the prior four therapists had ever mentioned boundary or co-dependence issues. It certainly seemed on point, since a lot of my dreams involved insects or snakes getting into my kitchen from cracks in the wall or slithering up from the basement. Ten years later, I still refer to the twenty or so points I took from that book when I need a refresher. It seemed like magic to me that you knew that I would benefit from that book.

For the first two or three months of treatment with you, my desire to present a good image and impress you with my control took up most of my energy and helped me maintain a nice distance from you. I was filing things away about you, though, in my mind that were very different from my other therapists. You spoke like a real person, unlike my other psychiatrists who used jargon, analogies I couldn't understand, or who just sat there, waiting and nodding. When I told you that one of them told me I must be getting my period because I was dressed in red, you were so enraged that you told me to put everything that "clown" ever told me in the garbage. I point this out because I never experienced my other therapists as real human beings, and I could see that that was exactly what you were. At that time, I didn't know how to deal with a real human being. I knew only how to act in a role and treat other actors.

For many years, I used to tell you that I knew that there were two Eves—-Eve, the person, and Eve Wood, the psychiatrist. Because I fragmented "my self" into so many pieces, I naturally did that to you (and everyone else, of course). There was the lawyer, "I," and the person, "me," and they were different. By consistently showing me that you were the same person at all times, you helped me bring the parts of "my self" together.

During our work, you required me to be fully present during every minute of every session. I told you during one of our first sessions that my core belief is that "I'm nobody" and "I'm invisible." You looked at me and said, "Then who is sitting in that chair talking and who the heck am I talking to?" I didn't know that common sense and logic had any part in therapy. I realized then that talking like that wasn't going to get me anywhere. You dealt with me as though I existed and were real, even though I didn't believe I was at the time. I kept testing you, even asserting that I absolutely knew that your husband was more real to you than I. You told me that I was just as real as he was, although the relationship was different. I took comfort in knowing that and was shocked to hear it.

No one in my life, in therapy or out, had ever required or taught me to be present and to function as *me* in my own life, separate from him or her. You required that each second. Therapy with you was not something I showed up for to get sympathetic affirmations or temporary catharsis for my pain, although you were unfailingly empathetic and compassionate. Nor was therapy something you did to me or for me. It was something we did together. If I didn't participate, or opted out through detaching, you called me on it in that moment. Every detail mattered to you. You told me that when I talked about one thing, while feeling another, which I frequently did, I was wasting our time and my money and we had to deal with it. I used to talk about one thing, while looking out your window and thinking about throwing a shoe at you or screaming when you were saying something I didn't want to take in. I learned to stop and tell you exactly when I had those moments so we could address what was really going on with me.

One time I came in wearing sunglasses and didn't take them off. By the time my posterior landed in the chair, you said, "What's with the glasses?" I told you very defiantly that I didn't want to be looked at that day and you told me you couldn't work if you couldn't see my eyes. Everything you did showed me that your rules were for my benefit and that you were there to help me. Although, at the time, I was convinced you always had to have everything your way, I realize now that I was relieved to have someone else take charge, since I was used to doing that all my life, and I certainly had made a mess of almost everything. I used to take your rules and boundaries as a personal affront. I now know I couldn't have gotten better without them.

Another way in which you differed from the prior therapists was that you didn't seem to operate from any script or one point of view. Each of the others had some one thing they clung to and offered as the answer to every problem. One was into lithium, which I think he dispensed to everyone; another was a family therapy proponent who dragged my poor parents in for a horrendous session where they didn't have a clue why they were there, but thought they must have done something wrong; and another looked at himself as the father of everyone in his practice, disclosing intimate confidences of one patient with any another in his "extended family." You explained that you used whatever worked and that you didn't learn how to do this solely in medical school. You didn't have any secrets or speak in a foreign, coded language.

In my constant quest to understand how you did your work, I read every book I could find on how to be a therapist. Once I asked you, "If you could get perfect results with each patient, would we all come out exactly the same?" You said that if that were the case, we might as well sit in your office and bang our heads against the wall. Many years later, I wonder how I could have asked such a thing. What you did for me was to help me be me, not based on anyone's expectations or hopes or ideas of what I "should" be.

Another thing you taught me was that questions can be answered and that you could teach me. Up until then, I felt ashamed of anything I didn't already know. I wouldn't take a tennis lesson or try anything new because I didn't want to show anyone I couldn't do that thing perfectly from the get-go. I no longer had to hate myself for not knowing things I thought everyone else did or limp along pretending that I did.

For example, I could not tell the difference between thoughts and feelings. A lot of times I'd tell you how I felt, and you'd say, "That's a thought, not a feeling." I would get very angry at you because I thought you were splitting hairs. I had always lived in my head, by my thoughts, and kept my feelings so far underground that, except for instances of paralyzing fear and depression, I didn't know what they were. You gave me a typed list of about one hundred different feelings. Your response of giving me a specific study aid was totally foreign to me. A concrete answer to a specific problem. I also learned why it is so important to differentiate between thoughts and feelings.

I can now use my feelings to guide me and teach me, and I am no longer afraid of being overwhelmed by them. I also know that a lot of times, my thoughts are really judgments I make when I don't identify the feelings behind them. I used to be held captive by my thoughts—which were often based on all the "shoulds" and proscriptions I learned as I grew up. This was a significant contributor to my depression. To illustrate, I went through a terrible few years as the single parent of a very rebellious adolescent son. He refused to eat anything I cooked or prepared, and at 6:30, when I'd rushed home from work to make him dinner, all he would eat would be take-out Chinese food or pizza. I'd also given up going to the gym to be home in time to make him this dinner which he was refusing to eat. I did this because "you're supposed to eat dinner with your child." You said, "No you're not. Fill the freezer with pizzas and TV dinners and go to the gym." This was completely liberating and felt illicit in the beginning. No one had ever taught me to take care of my needs and to stop doing things that didn't work (like forcing him to eat my meals). Once I started doing this, he and I were both happier and every now and then he'd actually ask me to cook.

Within four months of seeing you, to my horror, I began to develop very strong feelings for you of which I was very ashamed and which I tried not to talk about. It felt like the kind of sexually driven feelings I used to get for men I was attracted to. I had never experienced this during my other treatments. I felt a consuming need to see you, to get to your office, to be your favorite and only patient, and to be the only person in your life, professionally and personally. I couldn't deal with the pictures of your family you had in your office. In fact, my anxieties around the realities of your life were so overwhelming that I looked at a picture of your two sons and saw one daughter. The first time I saw a man patient leaving your office I was devastated and felt like you betrayed me. How could you see others and be nice to them when I needed you so badly? For years, I tried everything in my power to keep out any details of your life involving times and people outside your door and our fifty minutes. When something did come in, it felt like you were taking a stick and cracking open my piñata. It took years of talking about this and living it until I could get through it, and it was the worst pain of my treatment. I became furious with you when you told me I'd learn to have a healthy relationship in our therapy, when it was an unhealthy one I craved (like all the others I'd had which were based on needs, filling up holes in each other, etc.).

I was driven to find out your home phone number, your husband's name, and your age, and I felt like I couldn't live without knowing these things. Your telling me these things would make me special to you, I thought, and if you didn't tell me, it proved you didn't care about me. In our second session, before this drive reared its head in full, I asked you how old you were, as I was literally out the door. Instead of telling me on the spot, you said that you would tell me the next time, but that I had to think about what that meant to me. I was furious. When I came in the next time, and you worked through it with me, it revealed one of my key operating mechanisms. I categorized *everything*, assigning meanings to things that were often not true. It was how I made sense of the world, since I was not aware of my feelings or who I was. Growing up, I learned to rate everything on a line with only two points—one end was A+, perfect, the other was F-, doesn't count. For example, being a doctor is better than being a nurse; being a surgeon is better than being a psychiatrist; being a rabbi is better than being a cantor; being a lawyer at a big firm is better than being a law professor or working in the government. I guess I needed to know your age so I could compare me and my accomplishments to you and yours. It was very hard for me to accept not only needing, but also getting help from someone younger than I. Years later, this seems completely bizarre to me, as I don't use rigid classifications and ranking systems to determine how I feel. I look inside.

You did refuse to tell me your husband's name or give me your home phone number. I literally couldn't accept this, and it pushed me into a state of despair. You explained your reasons thoroughly and told me that you thought my question about his name was coming from an unhealthy place and that I would use the information to hurt me. Regarding your phone number, you pointed out that I would always be able to reach you through your office number and answering machine. This was not nearly enough for me. You held fast to your position, and it was key to my learning. You showed me how I ascribed meanings to things that were completely erroneous, and I did it to hurt myself—i.e., prove you don't care and I don't matter.

Many sessions later, when I was able to talk about it, I asked you why I felt this urgency and drive to have to know everything about you. I wasn't able to come right out and say that the drive felt like it used to when I was sexually attracted to a man, because I found the feeling so shameful and I so much didn't want to have it. You told me that it seemed like I was trying to form some type of unhealthy primitive fusion with you. You said it in a totally nonjudgmental tone, with no condemnation or scorn attached to it. I reeled from the words, then and for a long time, because that was *exactly* what it felt like. It was a relief that you knew and that you had the words to explain it.

These feelings that I developed for you were very familiar to me, as they usually arose at the beginning of every sexual relationship I had with a man, and often disappeared after I got to know him (and learned that he was not a healthy choice for me). I was afraid that having that same rush of feelings for you meant that I was going to turn out to be gay, on top of everything else, and you told me that it was a pre-genital issue. In your matter-of-fact way, you asked me if I was sexually attracted to women, and I said no. You said I wasn't gay, and I could cross that off the list.

You explained that my desire to fuse stemmed from never having had a validating relationship with my mother, which would have allowed me to become a fully separate individual. You told me that if you didn't have that mother, you can't get that elsewhere. One of my biggest transformations, which took years of work, is that this drive to fuse doesn't come up and no longer affects how I relate to men. The whole issue played out in the confines of your office, where it was safe, where you did not use my vulnerability for your own needs, where you taught me what it meant, and where I learned how to take care of myself and get what I did need as an adult.

This desire to fuse was also the most painful part of therapy, not only because of the strength of the feelings, but also because I believed that this impacted you personally and would make you think less of me. You always reassured me that you never thought these things were about you personally, that you understood them, and that you didn't like me any the less for them. You also told me that the strong feelings, as painful as they were, were key to my being able to form a bond with you and get better. That is exactly what happened. The fact that it never happened with the others meant that my work couldn't and didn't get done.

I am consciously aware of three particular things you did that enabled me to rid myself of the crippling pain of depression, anxiety, and self-hatred. Early on, I told you how I never believed anyone and looked behind everything everyone said to see what they really meant. This was because my mother greatly exaggerated my abilities beyond any semblance of reality and my father thought that nothing I did was good enough. They were both very extreme, and reality had no cachet in our home. When I told you this, you said, "I will only ever tell you the truth." Your words resonate with me to this day, and when I need to pull myself out of a hole, I think of them and picture what you'd tell me. You didn't even want anything from me in return; only that I do my work and get better.

The second thing you said in the same session was "I will treat everything you say as important." You said this after I asked you how you could stand listening to me, as I hated the sound of my own voice and thought a lot of what I said was ridiculous. I thought your saying that was a bad call on your part, but I came to learn that by your taking me seriously and assigning importance to what I said, I would, too. No one had ever done that before.

The third thing that was crucial to my recovery happened sometime within the first year of my therapy. During that time, I was so deep into my depression that all I wanted to do was lie on the pretty blue rug in your office, not speak, and not ever move again. At that same time, I also found a perverse satisfaction in showing you diagrams I drew of my insides with a knife cutting around all the edges, as if I had hollowed myself out. I thought the cutting drawing was a good way to show you how bad I felt and how much pain I could take and still live. I hated myself for feeling bad all the time, which of course made me feel worse. This was my recurring cycle: get depressed, feel bad, feel worse for feeling bad and not being able to fix it, hate myself even more than usual, and accept my fate.

You told me that my feelings weren't me, and that just because I felt bad didn't mean I was bad. You also taught me that a lot of my feelings came from erroneous thoughts that I had and things I told myself. Before this, I had thought that what I felt was what I was. Since I felt bad nearly all the time, I felt I was worthless, a fraud who knew how to pretend that I was someone when I had to. You told me that I had the same value as a human being when I was that depressed as I did when I wasn't. We are created in God's image, a reflection of the divine. On the same day that I showed you the knife picture, when I left your office, I took something with me to cherish, ponder, and ultimately be able to accept and grow from. For the first time, I realized that I had enough support to hold me until I could walk on my own. I used to write voluminously in my journal after each session, to treasure what you told me and to incorporate it into me. It was all that got me through the time until I got to our next session, as a weekend separated the visits.

My work with you has led me to find myself, which has not been easy and is not done. Since I don't use the automatic categories and rigid classifications anymore, I have to go inside myself for guidance. It's harder in that way, but it's liberating. I know that only I can determine who I am, what my gifts are, and how I am going to use them. I know that when I am depressed, it's usually because I have given myself bad messages and have used the world around me as "evidence" to confirm that I am a failure, hopeless, and different than all other human beings. I am usually able to avoid going to that place, and if I feel myself skirting near it, I get out a lot faster by making better choices about what I tell myself and what I choose to do.

While I came to you with the gift of being born Jewish, the ability to read Hebrew, and the cultural identity of a Jew, religion was not a "real" part of my life. Although I had a spiritual hunger, I would never have guessed that becoming involved in my own religion would turn out to be an instrument for my well-being and a source of enormous satisfaction. In therapy, I did remember how much I cherished my college courses in Judaism and Jewish history and how that didn't inform any of my choices regarding a major, a career, or a way of life. In my late teens and early twenties, I did not know how to make life decisions based on what I liked or what resonated with me. Only after extensive therapy with you, my fifth doctor, did I come to find that for me, daily prayer and involvement in my synagogue are my most useful tools for maintaining, growing, and appreciating my emotional health and identity.

When I read my favorite passage in the Torah, I think of how much of the universe is available to me because of what I have learned from my competent therapist. I identify my task with the words Moses used in addressing the Israelites who would shortly cross into the Promised Land without him:

For the commandment that I command you this day:

It is not too extraordinary for you,
It is not too far away!
It is not in the heavens,
(For you) to say:
Who will go up for us to the heavens and get it for us

And have us hear it, that we may observe it?
And it is not across the sea
(For you) to say:
Who will cross for us, across the sea, and get it for us
And have us hear it, that we may observe it?
Rather, near to you is the word, exceedingly.
In your mouth and in your heart, to observe it!
See, I set before you today
Life and good, and death and ill...
I call-as-witness against you today the heavens
and the earth:
Life and death I place before you, blessing and curse;
Now choose life, in order that you may stay-alive, you
and your seed...

Today I can choose. I am finally in one piece and at peace.

With gratitude, respect, and appreciation,

Sarah

My Reflections on my Patients' Reflections

I am still learning...
I am still learning to appreciate the nuances of beauty in my patients' pain, the wisdom embodied in their moving renditions of challenge, and the eternal wellspring of hope that infuses their words with meaning.
I am still learning...
I am learning how to take life on life's terms, nurture my imperfect self, and develop support systems.

I am still learning...

I am learning how much more we need one another, how much pain we all share, and how anxious we all are to make a difference.

I am still learning...

I am learning to trust the voice that tells me to ask others to help me, to reach out to an expanding universe for support and to end my book to you with a blessing.

You are still learning...

You are learning to acknowledge your own pain and past history.

You are still learning...

You are learning how to approach your healing in an integrated way.

You are still learning...

You are learning to identify who you are, what you think, and why you are here.

You are still learning...

You are learning to appreciate the oneness in the universe and the importance of finding your unique place in the cosmos.

You are still learning...

You are learning to nurture hope, share pain, and reach out to the universe for greater help as you travel your blessed healing journey.

Take-Home Messages and Closing Blessing

A SUMMARY AND A CALL TO ACTION

My dear reader,

I am filled with both deep sadness and great joy as I write the closing paragraphs of this book. I am sad because when I finish this book, my current conversation with you will come to an end. I am simultaneously joyous because, in concluding this book, I have the opportunity to share it with you and make a difference in your life. Bittersweet is how I describe this experience. It is truly bittersweet.

I hope to have empowered you in your growth journey. I trust that you have learned something about how to proceed from here in visiting the tales and lessons I have shared. I pray that all of your efforts to heal will be bounteously rewarded.

I urge you to take on and stay with your journey no matter how challenging it seems to be at times. I am committed to doing my part to help you succeed. Since you are a necessary part of the universe, we are all diminished when you shrink from nurturing your wondrous being. We *need* one another.

Although I could start my next book right now by offering you a whole new set of lessons and guidance, I think it best that I stop at this point. Before offering you my closing blessing, I want to recap some of what you have learned in this healing guide. Here is a list of twelve take-home points:

1. We all have psychic blind spots and need Seeing-Eye-dog equivalents to negotiate them.
2. Even the blind can teach us how to see a little bit better.
3. How we live is ultimately a reflection of how we choose to look at life.
4. Where there is a will, there is *always* a way.
5. The healing journey is a life-long project.
6. A model that integrates body, mind, and spirit is the only real model of healing that makes sense.
7. Step One is a forever and always step.
8. Identifying and addressing diagnoses and feelings is a crucial beginning and a necessary ongoing project in the healing journey.
9. To heal and grow, we must nurture constructive messages that we learned in childhood, and rewrite the harmful ones that we simultaneously internalized.
10. We each have a spiritual self that longs to be expressed. We owe it to ourselves to cultivate that miracle piece within us.

11. The healing journey is fraught with challenge, confusion, and reward. We need to continue to travel it no matter how tough it seems to be.

12. There is help available to us for every life challenge. We have a right and a responsibility to ask for it.

I Believe in You: A Closing Blessing

May you rise to face each day with hope,
May you cherish your accomplishments however small,
May you share of your gifts however humble,
And accept your limitations however huge.

May you strive to grow and help others to do so,
May you ask for help more often than before,
May you offer assistance more freely than you used to,
And relish the pleasure that comes from shared lives.

May you cultivate your capacity to give and receive love,
And nurture the pleasure you experience in small gifts,
May you ever choose life,
And never give up growing.

May you experience fulfillment,
And live a life of peace.
Amen.

With my love and blessing,
Eve A. Wood, M.D.
Tucson, Arizona

Appendix I

DEPRESSION

Reprinted from NIH Publication No. 02-3561
Printed 2000; reprinted September 2002

In any given one-year period, 9.5 percent of the population, or about 18.8 million American adults, suffer from a depressive illness. The economic cost for this disorder is high, but the cost in human suffering cannot be estimated. Depressive illnesses often interfere with normal functioning and cause pain and suffering not only to those who have a disorder, but also to those who care about them. Serious depression can destroy family life as well as the life of the ill person. But much of this suffering is unnecessary.

Most people with a depressive illness do not seek treatment, although the great majority—even those whose depression is extremely severe—can be helped. Thanks to years of fruitful research, there are now medications and psychosocial therapies such as cognitive/behavioral "talk," or interpersonal therapy that can ease the pain of depression.

Unfortunately, many people do not recognize that depression is a treatable illness. If you feel that you or someone you care about is one of the many undiagnosed depressed people in this country, the information presented here may help you take the steps that may save your own or someone else's life.

What Is a Depressive Disorder?

A depressive disorder is an illness that involves the body, mood, and thoughts. It affects the way a person eats and sleeps, the way one feels about oneself, and the way one thinks about things. A depressive disorder is not the same as a passing blue mood. It is not a sign of personal weakness or a condition that can be willed or wished away. People with a depressive illness cannot merely "pull themselves together" and get better. Without treatment, symptoms can last for weeks, months, or years. Appropriate treatment, however, can help most people who suffer from depression.

Types of Depression

Depressive disorders come in different forms, just as is the case with other illnesses such as heart disease. This section briefly describes three of the most common types of depressive disorders. However, within these types there are variations in the number of symptoms, their severity, and persistence.

Major depression is manifested by a combination of symptoms (see symptom list to follow) that interfere with the ability to work, study, sleep, eat, and enjoy once pleasurable activities. Such a disabling episode of depression may occur only once but more commonly occurs several times in a lifetime.

A less severe type of depression, *dysthymia,* involves long-term, chronic symptoms that do not disable, but keep one from functioning well or from feeling good. Many people with dysthymia also experience major depressive episodes at some time in their lives.

Another type of depression is *bipolar disorder,* also

called manic-depressive illness. Not nearly as prevalent as other forms of depressive disorders, bipolar disorder is characterized by cycling mood changes: severe highs (mania) and lows (depression). Sometimes the mood switches are dramatic and rapid, but most often they are gradual. When in the depressed cycle, an individual can have any or all of the symptoms of a depressive disorder. When in the manic cycle, the individual may be overactive, over talkative, and have a great deal of energy. Mania often affects thinking, judgment, and social behavior in ways that cause serious problems and embarrassment. For example, the individual in a manic phase may feel elated, full of grand schemes that might range from unwise business decisions to romantic sprees. Mania, left untreated, may worsen to a psychotic state.

Symptoms of Depression and Mania

Not everyone who is depressed or manic experiences every symptom. Some people experience a few symptoms, some many. Severity of symptoms varies with individuals and also varies over time.

Depression
   * Persistent sad, anxious, or "empty" mood
   * Feelings of hopelessness, pessimism
   * Feelings of guilt, worthlessness, helplessness
   * Loss of interest or pleasure in hobbies and activities that were once enjoyed, including sex
   * Decreased energy, fatigue, being "slowed down"
   * Difficulty concentrating, remembering, making decisions
   * Insomnia, early-morning awakening, or oversleeping

* Appetite and/or weight loss or overeating and weight gain
* Thoughts of death or suicide; suicide attempts
* Restlessness, irritability
* Persistent physical symptoms that do not respond to treatment, such as headaches, digestive disorders, and chronic pain

Mania
   * Abnormal or excessive elation
   * Unusual irritability
   * Decreased need for sleep
   * Grandiose notions
   * Increased talking
   * Racing thoughts
   * Increased sexual desire
   * Markedly increased energy
   * Poor judgment
   * Inappropriate social behavior

Causes of Depression

Some types of depression run in families, suggesting that a biological vulnerability can be inherited. This seems to be the case with bipolar disorder. Studies of families in which members of each generation develop bipolar disorder found that those with the illness have a somewhat different genetic makeup than those who do not get ill. However, the reverse is not true: Not everybody with the genetic makeup that causes vulnerability to bipolar disorder will have the illness. Apparently, additional factors, possibly stresses at home, work, or school, are involved in its onset.

In some families, major depression also seems to occur generation after generation. However, it can also occur in people who have no family history of depression. Whether inherited or not, major depressive disorder is often associated with changes in brain structures or brain function.

People who have low self-esteem, who consistently view themselves and the world with pessimism or who are readily overwhelmed by stress, are prone to depression. Whether this represents a psychological predisposition or an early form of the illness is not clear.

In recent years, researchers have shown that physical changes in the body can be accompanied by mental changes as well. Medical illnesses such as stroke, a heart attack, cancer, Parkinson's disease, and hormonal disorders can cause depressive illness, making the sick person apathetic and unwilling to care for his or her physical needs, thus prolonging the recovery period. Also, a serious loss, difficult relationship, financial problem, or any stressful (unwelcome or even desired) change in life patterns can trigger a depressive episode. Very often, a combination of genetic, psychological, and environmental factors is involved in the onset of a depressive disorder. Later episodes of illness typically are precipitated by only mild stresses or none at all.

Diagnostic Evaluation and Treatment

The first step to getting appropriate treatment for depression is a physical examination by a physician. Certain medications as well as some medical conditions such as a viral infection can cause the same symptoms as depression, and the physician should rule out these possibilities through examination, interview, and lab tests. If a physical cause for the depression is ruled out, a psychological evaluation should be done, by the physician or by referral to a psychiatrist or psychologist.

A good diagnostic evaluation will include a complete history of symptoms, i.e., when they started, how long they have lasted, how severe they are, whether the patient had them before and, if so, whether the symptoms were treated and what treatment was given. The doctor should ask about alcohol and drug use, and if the patient has thoughts about death or suicide. Further, a history should include questions about whether other family members have had a depressive illness and, if treated, what treatments they may have received and which were effective.

Last, a diagnostic evaluation should include a mental status examination to determine if speech or thought patterns or memory have been affected, as sometimes happens in the case of a depressive or manic-depressive illness.

Treatment choice will depend on the outcome of the evaluation. There are a variety of antidepressant medications and psychotherapies that can be used to treat depressive disorders. Some people with milder forms may do well with psychotherapy alone. People with moderate to severe depression most often benefit from antidepressants. Most do best with combined treatment: medication to gain relatively quick symptom relief and psychotherapy to learn more effective ways to deal with life's problems, including depression. Depending on the patient's diagnosis and severity of symptoms, the therapist may prescribe medication and/or one of the several forms of psychotherapy that have proven effective for depression.

Electroconvulsive therapy (ECT) is useful, particularly for individuals whose depression is severe or life threatening or who cannot take antidepressant medication. ECT often is effective in cases where antidepressant medications do not provide sufficient relief of symptoms. In recent years, ECT has been much improved. A muscle relaxant is given before treatment, which is done under brief anesthesia. Electrodes are placed at precise locations on the head to deliver electrical impulses. The stimulation causes a brief (about 30 seconds) seizure within the brain. The person receiving ECT does not consciously experience the electrical stimulus. For full therapeutic benefit, at least several sessions of ECT, typically given at the rate of three per week, are required.

Where to Get Help

If unsure where to go for help, check the Yellow Pages under "mental health," "health," "social services," "suicide prevention," "crisis intervention services," "hotlines," "hospitals," or "physicians" for phone numbers and addresses. In times of crisis, the emergency room doctor at a hospital may be able to provide temporary help for an emotional problem, and will be able to tell you where and how to get further help.

Listed below are the types of people and places that will make a referral to, or provide, diagnostic and treatment services.

* Family doctors
* Mental health specialists, such as psychiatrists, psychologists, social workers, or mental health counselors
* Health maintenance organizations
* Community mental health centers
* Hospital psychiatry departments and outpatient clinics
* University—or medical school—affiliated programs
* State hospital outpatient clinics
* Family service, social agencies, or clergy

* Private clinics and facilities
* Employee assistance programs
* Local medical and/or psychiatric societies

Further Information:

National Institute of Mental Health
Information Resources and Inquiries Branch
6001 Executive Boulevard
Room 8184, MSC 9663
Bethesda, MD 20892-9663
Telephone: 301-443-4513
FAX: 301-443-4279
TTY: 301-443-8431
FAX4U: 301-443-5158
Website: www.nimh.nih.gov
E-mail: nimhinfo@nih.gov

National Alliance for the Mentally Ill (NAMI)
Colonial Place Three
2107 Wilson Blvd., Suite 300
Arlington, VA 22201
Phone: 800-950-NAMI (6264) or 703-524-7600
Website: www.nami.org
A support and advocacy organization of consumers, families, and friends of people with severe mental illness—over 1,200 state and local affiliates. Local affiliates often give guidance to finding treatment.

Depression & Bipolar Support Alliance (DBSA)
730 N. Franklin St., Suite #501
Chicago, IL 60610-7224
800-836-3632
312-642-0049
Fax: 312-642-7243
Website: www.DBSAlliance.org
Purpose is to educate patients, families, and the public concerning the nature of depressive illnesses. Maintains an extensive catalog of helpful books.

National Foundation for Depressive Illness, Inc.
P.O. Box 2257
New York, NY 10116
212-268-4260; 800-239-1265
Website: www.depression.org
A foundation that informs the public about depressive illness and its treatability and promotes programs of research, education, and treatment.

National Mental Health Association (NMHA)
2001 N. Beauregard Street, 12th Floor
Alexandria, VA 22311
Phone: 800-969-6642 or 703-684-7722
TTY: 800-433-6642
Website: www.nmha.org
An association that works with 340 affiliates to promote mental health through advocacy, education, research, and services.

Appendix II

BIPOLAR DISORDER

Reprinted from NIH Publication No. 02-3679
Printed 2001; reprinted September 2002

Bipolar disorder, also known as manic-depressive illness, is a brain disorder that causes unusual shifts in a person's mood, energy, and ability to function. Different from the normal ups and downs that everyone goes through, the symptoms of bipolar disorder are severe. They can result in damaged relationships, poor job or school performance, and even suicide. But there is good news: bipolar disorder can be treated, and people with this illness can lead full and productive lives.

More than two million American adults, or about 1 percent of the population age 18 and older in any given year, have bipolar disorder. Bipolar disorder typically develops in late adolescence or early adulthood. However, some people have their first symptoms during childhood, and some develop them late in life. It is often not recognized as an illness, and people may suffer for years before it is properly diagnosed and treated. Like diabetes or heart disease, bipolar disorder is a long-term illness that must be carefully managed throughout a person's life.

What Are the Symptoms of Bipolar Disorder?

Bipolar disorder causes dramatic mood swings—from overly "high" and/or irritable to sad and hopeless, and then back again, often with periods of normal mood in between. Severe changes in energy and behavior go along with these changes in mood. The periods of highs and lows are called episodes of mania and depression.

*Signs and symptoms of **mania** (or a **manic episode**) include:*
   * Increased energy, activity, and restlessness
   * Excessively "high," overly good, euphoric mood
   * Extreme irritability
   * Racing thoughts and talking very fast, jumping from one idea to another
   * Distractibility, can't concentrate well
   * Little sleep needed
   * Unrealistic beliefs in one's abilities and powers
   * Poor judgment
   * Spending sprees
   * A lasting period of behavior that is different from usual
   * Increased sexual drive
   * Abuse of drugs, particularly cocaine, alcohol, and sleeping medications
   * Provocative, intrusive, or aggressive behavior
   * Denial that anything is wrong

A manic episode is diagnosed if elevated mood occurs with three or more of the other symptoms most of the day, nearly every day, for one week or longer. If the mood is irritable, four additional symptoms must be present.

*Signs and symptoms of **depression** (or a **depressive episode**) include:*
   * Lasting sad, anxious, or empty mood
   * Feelings of hopelessness or pessimism

* Feelings of guilt, worthlessness, or helplessness
* Loss of interest or pleasure in activities once enjoyed, including sex
* Decreased energy, a feeling of fatigue or of being "slowed down"
* Difficulty concentrating, remembering, making decisions
* Restlessness or irritability
* Sleeping too much, or can't sleep
* Change in appetite and/or unintended weight loss or gain
* Chronic pain or other persistent bodily symptoms that are not caused by physical illness or injury
* Thoughts of death or suicide, or suicide attempts

A depressive episode is diagnosed if five or more of these symptoms last most of the day, nearly every day, for a period of two weeks or longer.

A mild to moderate level of mania is called *hypomania.* Hypomania may feel good to the person who experiences it and may even be associated with good functioning and enhanced productivity. Thus, even when family and friends learn to recognize the mood swings as possible bipolar disorder, the person may deny that anything is wrong. Without proper treatment, however, hypomania can become severe mania in some people or can switch into depression.

Sometimes, severe episodes of mania or depression include symptoms of *psychosis* (or psychotic symptoms). Common psychotic symptoms are hallucinations (hearing, seeing, or otherwise sensing the presence of things not actually there) and delusions (false, strongly held beliefs not influenced by logical reasoning or explained by a person's usual cultural concepts). Psychotic symptoms in bipolar disorder tend to reflect the extreme mood state at the time. For example, delusions of grandiosity, such as believing one is the President or has special powers or wealth, may occur during mania; delusions of guilt or worthlessness, such as believing that one is ruined and penniless or has committed some terrible crime, may appear during depression. People with bipolar disorder who have these symptoms are sometimes incorrectly diagnosed as having schizophrenia, another severe mental illness.

It may be helpful to think of the various mood states in bipolar disorder as a spectrum or continuous range. At one end is severe depression, above which is moderate depression and then mild low mood, which many people call "the blues" when it is short-lived but is termed "dysthymia" when it is chronic. Then there is normal or balanced mood, above which comes hypomania (mild to moderate mania), and then severe mania.

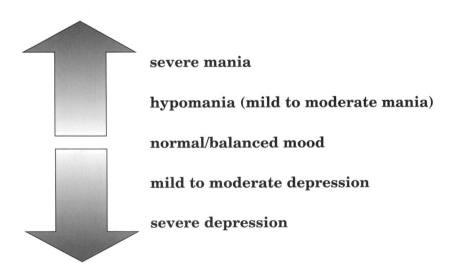

severe mania

hypomania (mild to moderate mania)

normal/balanced mood

mild to moderate depression

severe depression

In some people, however, symptoms of mania and depression may occur together in what is called a mixed bipolar state. Symptoms of a mixed state often include agitation, trouble sleeping, significant change in appetite, psychosis, and suicidal thinking. A person may have a very sad, hopeless mood while at the same time feeling extremely energized.

Bipolar disorder may appear to be a problem other than mental illness—for instance, alcohol or drug abuse, poor school or work performance, or strained interpersonal relationships. Such problems in fact may be signs of an underlying mood disorder.

Diagnosis of Bipolar Disorder

Like other mental illnesses, bipolar disorder cannot yet be identified physiologically—for example, through a blood test or a brain scan. Therefore, a diagnosis of bipolar disorder is made on the basis of symptoms, course of illness, and, when available, family history. The diagnostic criteria for bipolar disorder are described in the *Diagnostic and Statistical Manual for Mental Disorders, fourth edition (DSM-IV)*.

Descriptions offered by people with bipolar disorder give valuable insights into the various mood states associated with the illness:

Depression: *I doubt completely my ability to do anything well. It seems as though my mind has slowed down and burned out to the point of being virtually useless.... [I am] haunt[ed]... with the total,* *the desperate hopelessness of it all.... Others say, "It's only temporary, it will pass, you will get over it," but of course they haven't any idea of how I feel, although they are certain they do. If I can't feel, move, think, or care, then what on earth is the point?*

__Hypomania:__ At first when I'm high, it's tremendous... ideas are fast... like shooting stars you follow until brighter ones appear... All shyness disappears, the right words and gestures are suddenly there... uninteresting people, things become intensely interesting. Sensuality is pervasive; the desire to seduce and be seduced is irresistible. Your marrow is infused with unbelievable feelings of ease, power, well-being, omnipotence, euphoria...you can do anything...but, somewhere this changes.

__Mania:__ The fast ideas become too fast and there are far too many...overwhelming confusion replaces clarity...you stop keeping up with it—memory goes. Infectious humor ceases to amuse. Your friends become frightened...everything is now against the grain...you are irritable, angry, frightened, uncontrollable, and trapped.

Suicide

Some people with bipolar disorder become suicidal. **Anyone who is thinking about committing suicide needs immediate attention, preferably from a mental-health professional or a physician. Anyone who talks about suicide should be taken seriously**. Risk for suicide appears to be higher earlier in the course of the illness. Therefore, recognizing bipolar disorder early and learning how best to manage it may decrease the risk of death by suicide.

Signs and symptoms that may accompany suicidal feelings include:
  * Talking about feeling suicidal or wanting to die
  * Feeling hopeless, that nothing will ever change or get better
  * Feeling helpless, that nothing one does makes any difference
  * Feeling like a burden to family and friends
  * Abusing alcohol or drugs
  * Putting affairs in order (e.g., organizing finances or giving away possessions to prepare for one's death)
  * Writing a suicide note
  * Putting oneself in harm's way, or in situations where there is a danger of being killed

---

If you are feeling suicidal or know someone who is:

  * Call a doctor, emergency room, or 911 right away to get immediate help
  * Make sure you, or the suicidal person, are not left alone
  * Make sure that access is prevented to large amounts of medication, weapons, or other items that could be used for self-harm

---

While some suicide attempts are carefully planned over time, others are impulsive acts that have not been well thought out; thus, the final point in the box above may be a valuable *long-term* strategy for people with bipolar disorder. Either way, it is important to understand that suicidal feelings and actions are symptoms of an illness that can be treated. With proper treatment, suicidal feelings can be overcome.

What Is the Course of Bipolar Disorder?

Episodes of mania and depression typically recur across the life span. Between episodes, most people with bipolar disorder are free of symptoms, but as many as one-third of people have some residual symptoms. A small percentage of people experience chronic unremitting symptoms despite treatment.

The classic form of the illness, which involves recurrent episodes of mania and depression, is called bipolar I disorder. Some people, however, never develop severe mania but instead experience milder episodes of hypomania that alternate with depression; this form of the illness is called bipolar II disorder. When four or more episodes of illness occur within a 12-month period, a person is said to have rapid-cycling bipolar disorder. Some people experience multiple episodes within a single week, or even within a single day. Rapid cycling tends to develop later in the course of illness and is more common among women than among men.

People with bipolar disorder can lead healthy and productive lives when the illness is effectively treated (see next page—How Is Bipolar Disorder Treated?). Without treatment, however, the natural course of bipolar disorder tends to worsen. Over time, a person may suffer more frequent (more rapid-cycling) and more severe manic and depressive episodes than those experienced when the illness first appeared. But in most cases, proper treatment can help reduce the frequency and severity of episodes and can help people with bipolar disorder maintain good quality of life.

What Causes Bipolar Disorder?

Scientists are learning about the possible causes of bipolar disorder through several kinds of studies. Most scientists now agree that there is no single cause for bipolar disorder-rather, many factors act together to produce the illness.

How Is Bipolar Disorder Treated?

Most people with bipolar disorder—even those with the most severe forms—can achieve substantial stabilization of their mood swings and related symptoms with proper treatment. Because bipolar disorder is a recurrent illness, long-term preventive treatment is strongly recommended and almost always indicated. A strategy that combines medication and psychosocial treatment is optimal for managing the disorder over time.

In most cases, bipolar disorder is much better controlled if treatment is continual than if it is on and off. But even when there are no breaks in treatment, mood changes can occur and should be reported immediately to your doctor. The doctor may be able to prevent a full-blown episode by making adjustments to the treatment plan. Working closely with the doctor and communicating openly about treatment concerns and options can make a difference in treatment effectiveness.

In addition, keeping a chart of daily mood symptoms, treatments, sleep patterns, and life events may help people with bipolar disorder and their families to better understand the illness. This chart also can help the doctor track and treat the illness most effectively.

Medications

Medications for bipolar disorder are prescribed by psychiatrists—medical doctors (M.D.) with expertise in the diagnosis and treatment of mental disorders. While primary-care physicians who do not specialize in psychiatry also may prescribe these medications, it is recommended that people with bipolar disorder see a psychiatrist for treatment.

Medications known as "mood stabilizers" usually are prescribed to help control bipolar disorder. Several different types of mood stabilizers are available. In general, people with bipolar disorder continue treatment with mood stabilizers for extended periods of time (years). Other medications are added when necessary, typically for shorter periods, to treat episodes of mania or depression that break through despite the mood stabilizer.

A Long-Term Illness That Can Be Effectively Treated

Even though episodes of mania and depression naturally come and go, it is important to understand that bipolar disorder is a long-term illness that currently has no cure. Staying on treatment, even during well times, can help keep the disease under control and reduce the chance of having recurrent, worsening episodes.

Further Information:

National Institute of Mental Health (NIMH)
Office of Communications and Public Liaison
Information Resources and Inquiries Branch
6001 Executive Blvd., Rm. 8184, MSC 9663
Bethesda, MD 20892-9663
Phone: 301-443-4513; Fax: 301-443-4279
Fax Back System, Mental Health FAX4U: 301 443-5158
Website: www.nimh.nih.gov
E-mail: nimhinfo@nih.gov

Child & Adolescent Bipolar Foundation
1187 Wilmette Avenue, PMB #331
Wilmette, IL 60091
Phone: 847-256-8525
Website: www.bpkids.org

**Depression and Related Affective Disorders
Association (DRADA)**
2330 W. Joppa Road, Suite 100
Lutherville, MD 21093
Phone: 410-583-2919
Website: www.drada.org
E-mail: drada@jhmi.edu

National Alliance for the Mentally Ill (NAMI)
Colonial Place Three
2107 Wilson Blvd., 3rd Floor
Arlington, VA 22201-3042
Toll-Free: 800-950-NAMI (6264)
Phone: 703-524-7600; Fax: 703-524-9094
Website: www.nami.org

Depression & Bipolar Support Alliance (DBSA)
730 North Franklin Street, Suite 501
Chicago, IL 60610-7224
Toll-Free: 800-826-3632
Phone: 312-642-0049; Fax: 312-642-7243
Website: www.DBSAlliance.org

National Foundation for Depressive Illness, Inc. (NAFDI)
P.O. Box 2257
New York, NY 10116
Toll-Free: 800-239-1265
Website: www.depression.org

National Mental Health Association (NMHA)
2001 N. Beauregard Street, 12th Floor
Alexandria, VA 22314
Phone: 800-969-6642 or 703-684-7722
TTY: 800-433-5959
Website: www.nmha.org

Appendix III

PANIC DISORDER

Reprinted from NIH Publication No. 00-4679
Printed 2000 and NIH Publication No. 02-3879
Printed 1994, 1995, 2000; reprinted 2002

Does This Sound Like You?

Do you have sudden bursts of fear for no reason? Please put a check in the box next to any problems you have during these sudden bursts of fear.

- ❏ I have chest pains or a racing heart.
- ❏ I have a hard time breathing or a choking feeling.
- ❏ I feel dizzy, or I sweat a lot.
- ❏ I have stomach problems or feel like I need to throw up.
- ❏ I shake, tremble, or tingle.
- ❏ I feel out of control.
- ❏ I feel unreal.
- ❏ I am afraid I am dying or going crazy.

If you put a check in the box next to some of these problems, you may have panic disorder.

What Is Panic Disorder?

Panic disorder is a real illness. It can be treated with medicine or therapy.

If you have panic disorder, you feel suddenly terrified for no reason. These frequent bursts of terror are called panic attacks. During a panic attack, you also have scary physical feelings like a fast heartbeat, labored breathing, or dizziness.

Panic attacks can happen at any time and any place without warning. They often happen in grocery stores, malls, crowds, or while traveling.

You may live in constant fear of another attack and may stay away from places where you have had an attack. For some people, fear takes over their lives and they are unable to leave their homes.

Panic attacks don't last long, but they are so scary they feel like feel like they go on forever.

When Does Panic Disorder Start, and How Long Does It Last?

It usually starts when people are young adults, around 18 to 24 years old. Sometimes it starts when a person is already under a lot of stress, for example after the death of a loved one or after having a baby.

Anyone can have panic disorder, but more women than men have the illness. It sometimes runs in families.

Panic disorder can last for a few months or for many years.

Am I the Only One with This Illness?

No. You are not alone. In any year, 2.4 million Americans have panic disorder.

What Can I Do to Help Myself?

Talk to your doctor about your fear and panic attacks. Tell your doctor if the panic attacks keep you from doing everyday things and living your life. You may want to show your doctor this booklet. It can help you explain how you feel. Ask your doctor for a checkup to make sure you don't have some other illness.

• • •

People with panic disorder have feelings of terror that strike suddenly and repeatedly with no warning. They can't predict when an attack will occur, and many develop intense anxiety between episodes, worrying when and where the next one will strike.

If you are having a panic attack, most likely your heart will pound and you may feel sweaty, weak, faint, or dizzy. Your hands may tingle or feel numb, and you might feel flushed or chilled. You may have nausea, chest pain, or smothering sensations, a sense of unreality, or fear of impending doom or loss of control. You may genuinely believe you're having a heart attack or losing your mind, or on the verge of death.

Panic attacks can occur at any time, even during sleep. An attack generally peaks within 10 minutes, but some symptoms may last much longer.

Panic disorder affects about 2.4 million adult Americans and is twice as common in women as in men. It most often begins during late adolescence or early adulthood. Risk of developing panic disorder appears to be inherited. Not everyone who experiences panic attacks will develop panic disorder—for example, many people have one attack but never have another. For those who do have panic disorder, though, it's important to seek treatment. Untreated, the disorder can become very disabling.

Many people with panic disorder visit the hospital emergency room repeatedly or see a number of doctors before they obtain a correct diagnosis. Some people with panic disorder may go for years without learning that they have a real, treatable illness.

Panic disorder is often accompanied by other serious conditions such as depression, drug abuse, or alcoholism and may lead to a pattern of avoidance of places or situations where panic attacks have occurred. For example, if a panic attack strikes while you're riding in an elevator, you may develop a fear of elevators. If you start avoiding them, that could affect your choice of a job or apartment and greatly restrict other parts of your life.

Some people's lives become so restricted that they avoid normal, everyday activities such as grocery shopping or driving. In some cases, they become housebound. Or, they may be able to confront a feared situation only if accompanied by a spouse or other trusted person.

Basically, these people avoid any situation in which they would feel helpless if a panic attack were to occur. When people's lives become so restricted, as happens in about one-third of people with panic disorder, the condition is called *agoraphobia.* Early treatment of panic disorder can often prevent agoraphobia.

Panic disorder is one of the most treatable of the anxiety disorders, responding in most cases to medications or carefully targeted psychotherapy.

For more information on panic disorder, an anxiety disorder, see Appendix VIII.

Appendix IV

OBSESSIVE-COMPULSIVE DISORDER

Reprinted from NIH Publication No. 00-4676
Printed 2000; and NIH Publication No. 02-3879
Printed 1994, 1995, 2000; reprinted 2002

Does This Sound Like You?

Do you feel trapped in a pattern of unwanted and upsetting thoughts? Do you feel you have to do the same things over and over again for no good reason? Please put a check in the box next to any problems you have.

❏ I have upsetting thoughts or images enter my mind again and again.

❏ I feel like I can't stop these thoughts or images, even though I want to.

❏ I have a hard time stopping myself from doing things again and again, like: counting, checking on things, washing my hands, rearranging objects, doing things until it feels right, collecting useless objects.

❏ I worry a lot about terrible things that could happen if I'm not careful. I have unwanted urges to hurt someone but know I never would.

If you put a check in the box next to some of these problems, you may have obsessive-compulsive disorder (OCD).

What Is Obsessive-Compulsive Disorder (OCD)?

Obsessive-compulsive disorder (OCD) is a real illness. It can be treated with medicine and therapy.

If you have OCD, you have repeated, upsetting thoughts. You do the same thing over and over again to make the thoughts go away. You feel like you cannot control these thoughts or actions.

The upsetting thoughts and images are called "obsessions." Examples include a fear of germs, a fear of being hurt, a fear of hurting others, and disturbing religious or sexual thoughts.

The actions you take over and over again to make the thoughts go away are called "compulsions." Examples of these repeated actions include counting, cleaning, and checking on things.

Many people with OCD know that their actions are not normal, and they may try to hide their problem from family and friends. Some people with OCD may have trouble keeping their job and friends because of their actions.

When Does OCD Start, and How Long Does It Last?

For many people, OCD starts when a person is a child or teenager. If they do not get help, OCD can last for a lifetime. OCD may run in families.

Am I the Only One with This Illness?

No. You are not alone. In any year, 3.3 million Americans have OCD.

What Can I Do to Help Myself?

Talk to your doctor about your unwanted thoughts, fears, and repeated actions.

Tell your doctor if these thoughts and repeated actions keep you from doing everyday things and living your life. You may want to show your physician this booklet. It can help you explain how you feel. Ask your doctor to give you a checkup to make sure you don't have some other illness.

• • •

Obsessive-compulsive disorder, or OCD, involves anxious thoughts or rituals you feel you can't control. If you have OCD, you may be plagued by persistent, unwelcome thoughts or images, or by the urgent need to engage in certain rituals.

You may be obsessed with germs or dirt, so you wash your hands over and over. You may be filled with doubt and feel the need to check things repeatedly. You may have frequent thoughts of violence, and fear that you will harm people close to you. You may spend long periods touching things or counting; you may be preoccupied by order or symmetry; you may have persistent thoughts of performing sexual acts that are repugnant to you; or you may be troubled by thoughts that are against your religious beliefs.

The disturbing thoughts or images are called obsessions, and the rituals that are performed to try to prevent or get rid of them are called compulsions. There is no pleasure in carrying out the rituals you are drawn to, only temporary relief from the anxiety that grows when you don't perform them.

A lot of healthy people can identify with some of the

symptoms of OCD, such as checking the stove several times before leaving the house. But for people with OCD, such activities consume at least an hour a day, are very distressing, and interfere with daily life.

Most adults with this condition recognize that what they're doing is senseless, but they can't stop it. Some people, though, particularly children with OCD, may not realize that their behavior is out of the ordinary.

As mentioned previously, OCD afflicts about 3.3 million adult Americans. It strikes men and women in approximately equal numbers and usually first appears in childhood, adolescence, or early adulthood. One-third of adults with OCD report having experienced their first symptoms as children. The course of the disease is variable—symptoms may come and go, they may ease over time, or they can grow progressively worse. Research evidence suggests that OCD might run in families.

Depression or other anxiety disorders may accompany OCD, and some people with OCD also have eating disorders. In addition, people with OCD may avoid situations in which they might have to confront their obsessions, or they may try unsuccessfully to use alcohol or drugs to calm themselves. If OCD grows severe enough, it can keep someone from holding down a job or from carrying out normal responsibilities at home.

OCD generally responds well to treatment with medications or carefully targeted psychotherapy.

For more information on obsessive-compulsive disorder, an anxiety disorder, see Appendix VIII.

Appendix V

POST-TRAUMATIC STRESS DISORDER

Reprinted from NIH Publication No. 00-4675
Printed 2000 and NIH Publication No. 02-3879
Printed 1994, 1995, 2000; reprinted 2002

Does This Sound Like You?

Have you lived through a very scary and dangerous event? Please put a check in the box next to any problems you have.

- ❑ I feel like the terrible event is happening all over again. This feeling often comes without warning.
- ❑ I have nightmares and scary memories of the terrifying event.
- ❑ I stay away from places that remind me of the event.
- ❑ I jump and feel very upset when something happens without warning.
- ❑ I have a hard time trusting or feeling close to other people.
- ❑ I get mad very easily.
- ❑ I feel guilty because others died and I lived.
- ❑ I have trouble sleeping, and my muscles are tense.

If you put a check in the box next to some of these problems, you may have post-traumatic stress disorder (PTSD).

What Is Post-Traumatic Stress Disorder (PTSD)?

PTSD is a real illness. People may get PTSD after living through a terrible and scary experience. It can be treated with medicine and therapy.

You can get PTSD after you have been:
  * Raped or sexually abused
  * Hit or harmed by someone in your family
  * A victim of a violent crime
  * In an airplane or car crash
  * In a hurricane, tornado, or fire

When Does Post-Traumatic Stress Syndrome, and How Long Does It Last?

For most people, PTSD starts within about three months of the terrible event. For some people, signs of PTSD don't show up until years later. PTSD can happen to anyone at any age. Even children can have it. Some people get better within six months, while others may have the illness for much longer.

Am I the Only One with This Illness?

No. You are not alone. In any year, 5.2 million Americans have PTSD.

What Can I Do to Help Myself?

Talk to your doctor about the terrible event and your feelings. Tell your doctor if you have scary memories, depression, trouble sleeping, or anger. Tell your physician if these problems keep you from doing everyday things and living your life. You may want to show your doctor this booklet. It can help you explain how you feel. Ask your doctor for a checkup to make sure you don't have some other illness.

• • •

Post-traumatic stress disorder (PTSD) is a debilitating condition that can develop following a terrifying event. Often, people with PTSD have persistent frightening thoughts and memories of their ordeal and feel emotionally numb, especially with people they were once close to. PTSD was first brought to public attention by war veterans, but it can result from any number of traumatic incidents. These include violent attacks such as mugging, rape, or torture; being kidnapped or held captive; child abuse; serious accidents such as car or train wrecks; and natural disasters such as floods or earthquakes. The event that triggers PTSD may be something that threatened the person's life or the life of someone close to him or her. Or it could be something witnessed, such as massive death and destruction after a building is bombed or a plane crashes.

Whatever the source of the problem, some people with PTSD repeatedly relive the trauma in the form of nightmares and disturbing recollections during the day. They may also experience other sleep problems, feel detached or numb, or be easily startled. They may lose interest in things they used to enjoy and have trouble feeling affectionate. They may feel irritable, more aggressive than before, or even violent. Things that remind them of the trauma may be very distressing, which could lead them to avoid certain places or situations that bring back those memories.

Anniversaries of the traumatic event are often very difficult.

PTSD affects about 5.2 million adult Americans. Women are more likely than men to develop PTSD. It can occur at any age, including childhood, and there is some evidence that susceptibility to PTSD may run in families. The disorder is often accompanied by depression, substance abuse, or one or more other anxiety disorders. In severe cases, the person may have trouble working or socializing. In general, the symptoms seem to be worse if the event that triggered them was deliberately initiated by a person—such as a rape or kidnapping.

Ordinary events can serve as reminders of the trauma and trigger flashbacks or intrusive images. A person having a flashback, which can come in the form of images, sounds, smells, or feelings, may lose touch with reality and believe that the traumatic event is happening all over again.

Not every traumatized person gets full-blown PTSD, or experiences PTSD at all. PTSD is diagnosed only if the symptoms last more than a month. In those who do develop PTSD, symptoms usually begin within three months of the trauma, and the course of the illness varies. Some people recover within six months; others have symptoms that last much longer. In some cases, the condition may be chronic. Occasionally, the illness doesn't show up until years after the traumatic event.

People with PTSD can be helped by medications and carefully targeted psychotherapy.

For more information on post-traumatic stress disorder, an anxiety disorder, see Appendix VIII.

Appendix VI

SOCIAL PHOBIA

Reprinted from NIH Publication No. 00-4678
Printed 2000 and NIH Publication No. 02-3879
Printed 1994, 1995, 2000; reprinted 2002

Does This Sound Like You?

Do you feel afraid and uncomfortable when you are around other people? Is it hard for you to be at work or school? Please put a check in the box next to problems you have.

- ❑ I have an intense fear that I will do or say something and embarrass myself in front of other people.
- ❑ I am always very afraid of making a mistake and being watched and judged by other people.
- ❑ My fear of embarrassment makes me avoid doing things I want to do or speaking to people.
- ❑ I worry for days or weeks before I have to meet new people.
- ❑ I blush, sweat a lot, tremble, or feel like I have to throw up before and during an event where I am with new people.
- ❑ I usually stay away from social situations such as school events and making speeches.
- ❑ I often drink to try to make these fears go away.

If you put a check in the box next to some of these problems, you may have social phobia.

What Is Social Phobia?

Social phobia is a real illness. It can be treated with medicine and therapy.

If you have social phobia, you are very worried about embarrassing yourself in front of other people. Your fears may be so serious that you cannot do everyday things. You may have a very hard time talking to people at work or school. Your fear may even keep you from going to work or school on some days.

You may worry that you will blush and shake in front of other people. You may believe that people are watching you, just waiting for you to make a mistake. Even talking on the phone, signing a check at the store, or using a public restroom can make you afraid.

Many people are a little nervous before they meet new people or give a speech. But if you have social phobia, you worry for weeks before. You may do anything to stay away from the situation.

When Does Social Phobia Start, and How Long Does It Last?

Social phobia usually starts when a person is still a child or teenager. It is rare for it to start after a person reaches their mid-twenties. Anyone can have social phobia, but more women than men have the illness. It sometimes runs in families.

Without treatment, social phobia can last for many years or even a lifetime.

Am I the Only One with This Illness?

No. You are not alone. In any year, at least 5.3 million Americans have social phobia.

What Can I Do to Help Myself?

Talk to your doctor about your fears and worries. Tell your physician if these worries are keeping you from doing everyday things and living your life. You may want to show your doctor this booklet. It can help you explain how you feel.

• • •

Social phobia, also called social anxiety disorder, involves overwhelming anxiety and excessive self-consciousness in everyday social situations. People with social phobia have a persistent, intense, and chronic fear of being watched and judged by others and being embarrassed or humiliated by their own actions. Their fear may be so severe that it interferes with work or school, and other ordinary activities. While many people with social phobia recognize that their fear of being around people may be excessive or unreasonable, they are unable to overcome it. They often worry for days or weeks in advance of a dreaded situation.

Social phobia can be limited to only one type of situation-such as a fear of speaking in formal or informal situations, or eating, drinking, or writing in front of others—or, in its most severe form, may be so broad that a person experiences symptoms almost anytime they are around other people. Social phobia can be very debilitating—it may even keep people from going to work or school on some days. Many people with this illness have a hard time making and keeping friends.

Physical symptoms often accompany the intense anxiety of social phobia and include blushing, profuse sweating, trembling, nausea, and difficulty talking. If you suffer from social phobia, you may be painfully embarrassed by these symptoms and feel as though all eyes are focused on you. You may be afraid of being with people other than your family.

People with social phobia are aware that their feelings are irrational. Even if they manage to confront what they fear, they usually feel very anxious beforehand and are intensely uncomfortable throughout. Afterward, the unpleasant feelings may linger, as they worry about how they may have been judged or what others may have thought or observed about them.

Social phobia affects about 5.3 million adult Americans. Women and men are equally likely to develop social phobia. The disorder usually begins in childhood or early adolescence, and there is some evidence that genetic factors are involved. Social phobia often co-occurs with other anxiety disorders or depression. Substance abuse or dependence may develop in individuals who attempt to "self-medicate" their social phobia by drinking or using drugs. Social phobia can be treated successfully with carefully targeted psychotherapy or medications.

For more information about social phobia, an anxiety disorder, see Appendix VIII.

Appendix VII

GENERALIZED ANXIETY DISORDER

*Reprinted from NIH Publication No. 00-4677
Printed 2000 and NIH Publication No. 02-3879
Printed 1994, 1995, 2000; reprinted 2002*

Does This Sound Like You?

Do you worry all the time? Please put a check in the box next to any problems you have had often over the last six months.

- ❑ I never stop worrying about things big and small.
- ❑ I have headaches and other aches and pains for no reason.
- ❑ I am tense a lot and have trouble relaxing.
- ❑ I have trouble keeping my mind on one thing.
- ❑ I get crabby or grouchy.
- ❑ I have trouble falling asleep or staying asleep.
- ❑ I sweat and have hot flashes.
- ❑ I sometimes have a lump in my throat or feel like I need to throw up when I am worried.

If you put a check in the box next to some of these problems, you may have generalized anxiety disorder (GAD).

What Is Generalized Anxiety Disorder (GAD)?

Generalized Anxiety Disorder (GAD) is a real illness. GAD

can be treated with medicine and therapy.

If you have GAD, you worry all the time about your family, health, or work, even when there are no signs of trouble. Sometimes you aren't worried about anything special, but feel tense and worried all day long. You also have aches and pains for no reason and feel tired a lot.

Everyone gets worried sometimes, but if you have GAD, you stay worried, fear the worst will happen, and cannot relax.

When Does GAD Start, and How Long Does It Last?

Most often GAD starts when a person is still a child or teenager. It can start in an adult, too. More women than men have this illness.

People with GAD may visit their doctor many times before they find out what their real illness is. They ask their doctor to help them with the signs of GAD like headaches or trouble falling asleep, but don't get help for the illness itself.

Am I the Only One with This Illness?

No. You are not alone. In any year, four million Americans have GAD.

What Can I Do to Help Myself?

Talk to your doctor about your constant worry and tension. Tell your physician about any other signs of GAD that you may have, such as aches and pains for no reason or trouble sleeping. Tell your doctor if these problems keep you from doing everyday things and living your life. You may want to show your doctor this booklet. It can help you explain how you feel. Ask your doctor for a checkup to make sure you don't have a different illness.

• • •

Generalized anxiety disorder (GAD) is much more than the normal anxiety people experience day to day. It's chronic and fills one's day with exaggerated worry and tension, even though there is little or nothing to provoke it. Having this disorder means always anticipating disaster, often worrying excessively about health, money, family, or work. Sometimes, though, the source of the worry is hard to pinpoint. Simply the thought of getting through the day provokes anxiety.

People with GAD can't seem to shake their concerns, even though they usually realize that their anxiety is more intense than the situation warrants. Their worries are accompanied by physical symptoms, especially fatigue, headaches, muscle tension, muscle aches, difficulty swallowing, trembling, twitching, irritability, sweating, and hot flashes. People with GAD may feel lightheaded or out of breath. They also may feel nauseated or have to go to the bathroom frequently.

Individuals with GAD seem unable to relax, and they may startle more easily than other people. They tend to have difficulty concentrating, too. Often, they have trouble falling or staying asleep.

Unlike people with several other anxiety disorders, people with GAD don't characteristically avoid certain situations as a result of their disorder. When impairment associated with GAD is mild, people with the disorder may be able to function in social settings or on the job. If severe, however, GAD can be very debilitating, making it difficult to carry out even the most ordinary daily activities.

GAD affects about four million adult Americans, and about twice as many women as men. The disorder comes on gradually and can begin across the life cycle, though the risk is highest between childhood and middle age. It is diagnosed when someone spends at least six months worrying excessively about a number of everyday problems. There is evidence that genes play a modest role in GAD.

GAD is commonly treated with medications. GAD rarely occurs alone, however; it is usually accompanied by another anxiety disorder, depression, or substance abuse. These other conditions must be treated along with GAD.

For more information on generalized anxiety disorder, an anxiety disorder, see Appendix VIII.

Appendix VIII

ANXIETY DISORDERS: RESOURCES

Reprinted from NIH Publication No. 02-3879
Printed 1994, 1995, 2000; reprinted 2002

National Institute of Mental Health (NIMH)
Office of Communications and Public Liaison
6001 Executive Blvd., Room 8184, MSC 9663
Bethesda, MD 20892-9663
General inquiries: 301-443-4513
TTY: 301-443-8431
E-mail: nimhinfo@nih.gov
Website: www.nimh.nih.gov

Anxiety Disorders Association of America
8730 Georgia Ave., Suite 600
Silver Spring, MD 20910
240-485-1001
Website: www.adaa.org

Freedom from Fear
308 Seaview Avenue
Staten Island, NY 10305
718-351-1717
Website: www.freedomfromfear.com

Obsessive Compulsive (OC) Foundation
676 State Street
New Haven, CT 06511
203-401-2070
Website: www.ocfoundation.org

American Psychiatric Association
100 Wilson Blvd., Suite 1825
Arlington, VA 22209-3901
703-907-7300
Website: www.psych.org/index.cfm

American Psychological Association
750 1st Street, NE
Washington, DC 20002-4242
Phone: 800-374-2721 or 202-336-5510
Website: www.apa.org

Association for Advancement of Behavior Therapy
305 7th Avenue, 16th floor
New York, NY 10001-6008
212-647-1890
Website: www.aabt.org

National Alliance for the Mentally Ill (NAMI)
Colonial Place Three
2107 Wilson Blvd., Suite 300
Arlington, VA 22201
Phone: 800-950-NAMI (6264) or 703-524-7600
Website: www.nami.org

National Mental Health Association (NMHA)
2001 N. Beauregard Street, 12th Floor
Alexandria, VA 22311
Phone: 800-969-6642 or 703-684-7722
TTY: 800-433-6642
Website: www.nmha.org

National Center for PTSD
U.S. Department of Veterans Affairs
116D VA Medical and Regional Office Center
215 N. Main St.
White River Junction, VT 05009
802-296-6300
E-mail: ncptsd@ncptsd.org
Website: www.ncptsd.org

Appendix IX

ATTENTION DEFICIT HYPERACTIVITY DISORDER

Reprinted from NIH Publication No. 96-3572
Printed 1994; reprinted 1996

Imagine living in a fast-moving kaleidoscope, where sounds, images, and thoughts are constantly shifting. Feeling easily bored, yet helpless to keep your mind on tasks you need to complete. Distracted by unimportant sights and sounds, your mind drives you from one thought or activity to the next. Perhaps you are so wrapped up in a collage of thoughts and images that you don't notice when someone speaks to you.

For many people, this is what it's like to have attention deficit hyperactivity disorder, or ADHD. They may be unable to sit still, plan ahead, finish tasks, or be fully aware of what's going on around them. To their family, classmates or co-workers, they seem to exist in a whirlwind of disorganized or frenzied activity. Unexpectedly—on some days and in some situations—they seem fine, often leading others to think the person with ADHD can actually control these behaviors. As a result, the disorder can mar the person's relationships with others in addition to disrupting their daily life, consuming energy, and diminishing self-esteem.

ADHD, once called hyperkinesis or minimal brain dysfunction, is one of the most common mental disorders among children. It affects 3 to 5 percent of all children, perhaps as many as two million American children. Two to three times more boys than girls are affected. On the average, at least one child in every classroom in the United States needs help for the disorder. ADHD often continues into adolescence and adulthood, and can cause a lifetime of frustrated dreams and emotional pain.

But there is help...and hope. In the last decade, scientists have learned much about the course of the disorder and are now able to identify and treat children, adolescents, and adults who have it. A variety of medications, behavior-changing therapies, and educational options are already available to help people with ADHD focus their attention, build self-esteem, and function in new ways.

Understand the Problem

Mark

Mark, age 14, has more energy than most boys his age. But then, he's always been overly active. Starting at age 3, he was a human tornado, dashing around and disrupting everything in his path. At home, he darted from one activity to the next, leaving a trail of toys behind him. At meals, he upset dishes and chattered nonstop. He was reckless and impulsive, running into the street with oncoming cars, no matter how many times his mother explained the danger or scolded him. On the playground, he seemed no wilder than the other kids. But his tendency to overreact—like socking playmates simply for bumping into him—had already gotten him into trouble several times. His parents didn't know what to do. Mark's doting grandparents reassured them, "Boys will be boys. Don't worry, he'll grow out of it." But he didn't.

Lisa

At age 17, Lisa still struggles to pay attention and act appropriately. But this has always been hard for her. She still gets embarrassed thinking about that night her parents took her to a restaurant to celebrate her 10th birthday. She had gotten so distracted by the waitress's bright red hair that her father called her name three times before she remembered to order. Then before she could stop herself, she blurted, "Your hair dye looks awful!"

In elementary and junior high school, Lisa was quiet and cooperative but often seemed to be daydreaming. She was smart, yet couldn't improve her grades no matter how hard she tried. Several times, she failed exams. Even though she knew most of the answers, she couldn't keep her mind on the test. Her parents responded to her low grades by taking away privileges and scolding, "You're just lazy. You could get better grades if you only tried." One day, after Lisa had failed yet another exam, the teacher found her sobbing, "What's wrong with me?"

Henry

Although he loves puttering around in his shop, for years Henry has had dozens of unfinished carpentry projects and ideas for new ones he knew he would never complete. His garage was piled so high with wood, he and his wife joked about holding a fire sale.

Every day Henry faced the real frustration of not being able to concentrate long enough to complete a task. He was fired from his job as stock clerk because he lost inventory and carelessly filled out forms. Over the years, afraid that he might be losing his mind, he had seen psychotherapists and tried several medications, but none ever helped him concentrate. He saw the same lack of focus in his young son and worried.

What Are the Symptoms of ADHD?

The three people you've just met, Mark, Lisa, and Henry, all have a form of ADHD—attention deficit hyperactivity disorder. ADHD is not like a broken arm, or strep throat. Unlike these two disorders, ADHD does not have clear physical signs that can be seen in an x-ray or a lab test. ADHD can only be identified by looking for certain characteristic behaviors, and as with Mark, Lisa, and Henry, these behaviors vary from person to person. Scientists have not yet identified a single cause behind all the different patterns of behavior—and they may never find just one. Rather, someday scientists may find that ADHD is actually an umbrella term for several slightly different disorders.

At present, ADHD is a diagnosis applied to children and adults who consistently display certain characteristic behaviors over a period of time. The most common behaviors fall into three categories: inattention, hyperactivity, and impulsivity.

Inattention. People who are inattentive have a hard time keeping their mind on any one thing and may get bored with a task after only a few minutes. They may give effortless, automatic attention to activities and things they enjoy. But focusing deliberate, conscious attention to organizing and completing a task or learning something new is difficult.

For example, Lisa found it agonizing to do homework. Often, she forgot to plan ahead by writing down the assignment or bringing home the right books. And when trying to work, every few minutes she found her mind drifting to something else. As a result, she rarely finished and her work was full of errors.

Hyperactivity. People who are hyperactive always seem to be in motion. They can't sit still. Like Mark, they may dash around or talk incessantly. Sitting still through a lesson can be an impossible task. Hyperactive children squirm in their seat or roam around the room. Or they might wiggle their feet, touch everything, or noisily tap their pencil. Hyperactive teens and adults may feel intensely restless. They may be fidgety or, like Henry, they may try to do several things at once, bouncing around from one activity to the next.

Impulsivity. People who are overly impulsive seem unable to curb their immediate reactions or think before they act. As a result, like Lisa, they may blurt out inappropriate comments. Or like Mark, they may run into the street without looking. Their impulsivity may make it hard for them to wait for things they want or to take their turn in games. They may grab a toy from another child or hit when they're upset.

Not everyone who is overly hyperactive, inattentive, or impulsive has an attention disorder. Since most people sometimes blurt out things they didn't mean to say, bounce from one task to another, or become disorganized and forgetful, how can specialists tell if the problem is ADHD?

To assess whether a person has ADHD, specialists consider several critical questions: Are these behaviors excessive, long-term, and pervasive? That is, do they occur more often than in other people the same age? Are they a continual problem, not just a response to a temporary situation? Do the behaviors occur in several settings or only in one specific place like the playground or the office? The person's pattern of behavior is compared against a set of criteria and characteristics of the disorder. As mentioned previously, these criteria appear in a diagnostic reference book called the DSM (short for the *Diagnostic and Statistical Manual of Mental Disorders*).

According to the diagnostic manual, there are three patterns of behavior that indicate ADHD. People with ADHD may show several signs of being consistently inattentive. They may have a pattern of being hyperactive and impulsive. Or they may show all three types of behavior.

According to the DSM, signs of inattention include:
   * Becoming easily distracted by irrelevant sights and sounds
   * Failing to pay attention to details and making careless mistakes
   * Rarely following instructions carefully and completely
   * Losing or forgetting things like toys; or pencils, books, and tools needed for a task

Some signs of hyperactivity and impulsivity are:
   * Feeling restless, often fidgeting with hands or feet, or squirming
   * Running, climbing, or leaving a seat, in situations where sitting or quiet behavior is expected
   * Blurting out answers before hearing the whole question
   * Having difficulty waiting in line or for a turn

Because everyone shows some of these behaviors at times, the DSM contains very specific guidelines for determining when they indicate ADHD. The behaviors must appear early in life, before age seven, and continue for at least six months. In children, they must be more frequent or severe than in others the same age. Above all, the behaviors must create a real handicap in at least two areas of a person's life, such as school, home, work, or social settings. So, someone whose work or friendships are not impaired by these behaviors would not be diagnosed with ADHD. Nor would a child who seems overly active at school but functions well elsewhere.

What Causes ADHD?

Understandably, one of the first questions parents ask when they learn their child has an attention disorder is: "Why? What went wrong?"

Health professionals stress that since no one knows what causes ADHD, it doesn't help parents to look backward to search for possible reasons. There are too many possibilities to pin down the cause with certainty. It is far more important for the family to move forward in finding ways to get the right help.

Scientists, however, do need to study causes in an effort to identify better ways to treat, and perhaps some day, prevent ADHD. They are finding more and more evidence that ADHD does not stem from the home environment, but from biological causes. When you think about it, there is no clear relationship between home life and ADHD. Not all children from unstable or dysfunctional homes have ADHD. And not all children with ADHD come from dysfunctional families. Knowing this can remove a huge burden of guilt from parents who might blame themselves for their child's behavior.

Over the last decades, scientists have come up with possible theories about what causes ADHD. Some of these theories have led to dead ends, some to exciting new avenues of investigation.

One disappointing theory was that all attention disorders and learning disabilities were caused by minor head injuries or undetectable damage to the brain, perhaps from early infection or complications at birth. Based on this theory, for many years both disorders were called *"minimal brain damage"* or *"minimal brain dysfunction."* Although certain types of head injury can explain some cases of attention disorder, the theory was rejected because it could explain only a very small number of cases. Not everyone with ADHD or learning disabilities (LD) has a history of head trauma or birth complications.

Another theory was that refined sugar and food additives make children hyperactive and inattentive. As a result, parents were encouraged to stop serving children foods containing artificial flavorings, preservatives, and sugars. However, this theory, too, came under question. In 1982, the National Institutes of Health (NIH), the federal agency responsible for biomedical research, held a major scientific conference to discuss the issue. After studying the data, the scientists concluded that the restricted diet only seemed to help about 5 percent of children with ADHD, mostly either young children or children with food allergies.

ADHD is not usually caused by:
* Too much TV
* Food allergies
* Excess sugar
* Poor home life
* Poor schools

In recent years, as new tools and techniques for studying the brain have been developed, scientists have been able to test more theories about what causes ADHD.

Using one such technique, NIMH scientists demonstrated a link between a person's ability to pay continued attention and the level of activity in the brain. Adult subjects were asked to learn a list of words. As they did, scientists used a PET (positron emission tomography) scanner to *observe the brain at work*. The researchers measured the level of glucose used by the areas of the brain that inhibit impulses and control attention. Glucose is the brain's main source of energy, so measuring how much is used is a good indicator of the brain's activity level. The investigators found important differences between people who have ADHD and those who don't. In people with ADHD, the brain areas that control attention used less glucose, indicating that they were less active. It appears from this research that a lower level of activity in some parts of the brain may cause inattention.

The next step will be to research *why* there is less activity in these areas of the brain. Scientists at NIMH hope to compare the use of glucose and the activity level in mild and severe cases of ADHD. They will also try to discover why some medications used to treat ADHD work better than others, and if the more effective medications increase activity in certain parts of the brain.

Researchers are also searching for other differences between those who have and do not have ADHD. Research on how the brain normally develops in the fetus offers some clues about what may disrupt the process. Throughout pregnancy and continuing into the first year of life, the brain is constantly developing. It begins its growth from a few all-purpose cells and evolves into a complex organ made of billions of specialized, interconnected nerve cells. By studying brain development in animals and humans, scientists are gaining a better understanding of how the brain works when the nerve cells are connected correctly and incorrectly. Scientists at NIMH and other research institutions are tracking clues to determine what might prevent nerve cells from forming the proper connections. Some of the factors they are studying include drug use during pregnancy, toxins, and genetics.

Research shows that a mother's use of cigarettes, alcohol, or other drugs during pregnancy may have damaging effects on the unborn child. These substances may be dangerous to the fetus's developing brain. It appears that alcohol and the nicotine in cigarettes may distort developing nerve cells. For example, heavy alcohol use during pregnancy has been linked to fetal alcohol syndrome (FAS), a condition that can lead to low birth weight, intellectual impairment, and certain physical defects. Many children born with FAS show much the same hyperactivity, inattention, and impulsivity as children with ADHD.

Drugs such as cocaine—including the smokable form known as crack—seem to affect the normal development of brain receptors. These brain cell parts help to transmit incoming signals from our skin, eyes, and ears, and help control our responses to the environment. Current research suggests that drug abuse may harm these receptors. Some scientists believe that such damage may lead to ADHD.

Toxins in the environment may also disrupt brain development or brain processes, which may lead to ADHD. Lead is one such possible toxin. It is found in dust, soil, and flaking paint in areas where leaded gasoline and paint were once used. It is also present in some water pipes. Some animal studies suggest that children exposed to lead may develop symptoms associated with ADHD, but only a few cases have actually been found.

Other research shows that attention disorders tend to run in families, so there are likely to be genetic influences. Children who have ADHD usually have at least one close relative who also has ADHD. And at least one-third of all fathers who had ADHD in their youth bear children who have ADHD. Even more convincing: the majority of identical twins share the trait. At the National Institutes of Health, researchers are also on the trail of a gene that may be involved in transmitting ADHD in a small number of families with a genetic thyroid disorder.

How Is ADHD Identified and Diagnosed?

Only the paragraphs pertaining to adults are provided here.

Adults are diagnosed for ADHD based on their performance at home and at work. When possible, their parents are asked to rate the person's behavior as a child. A spouse or roommate can help rate and evaluate current behaviors. But for the most part, adults are asked to describe their own experiences. One symptom is a sense of frustration. Since people with ADHD are often bright and creative, they often report feeling frustrated that they're not living up to their potential. Many also feel restless and are easily bored. Some say they need to seek novelty and excitement to help channel the whirlwind in their minds. Although it may be impossible to document when these behaviors first started, most adults with ADHD can give examples of being inattentive, impulsive, overly active, impatient, and disorganized most of their lives.

Until recent years, adults were not thought to have ADHD, so many adults with ongoing symptoms have never been diagnosed. People like Henry go for decades knowing that something is wrong, but not knowing what it is. Psychotherapy and medication for anxiety, depression, or manic-depression fail to help much, simply because the ADHD itself is not being addressed. Yet half the children with ADHD continue to have symptoms through adulthood. The recent awareness of adult ADHD means that many people can finally be correctly diagnosed and treated.

A correct diagnosis lets people move forward in their lives. Once the disorder is known, they can begin to receive whatever combination of educational, medical, and emotional help they need.

An effective treatment plan helps people with ADHD and their families at many levels. For adults with ADHD, the treatment plan may include medication, along with practical and emotional support. For children and adolescents, it may include providing an appropriate classroom setting, the right medication, and helping parents to manage their child's behavior.

What Treatments Are Available?

For decades, medications have been used to treat the symptoms of ADHD. Three medications in the class of drugs known as stimulants seem to be the most effective in both children and adults. These are methylphenidate (Ritalin), dextroamphetamine (Dexedrine or Dextrostat), and pemoline (Cylert). For many people, these medicines dramatically reduce their hyperactivity and improve their ability to focus, work, and learn. The medications may also improve physical coordination, such as handwriting and ability in sports. Recent research by NIMH suggests that these medicines may also help children with an accompanying conduct disorder to control their impulsive, destructive behaviors.

Ritalin helped Henry focus on and complete tasks for the first time. Dexedrine helped Mark to sit quietly, focus his attention, and participate in class so he could learn. He also became less impulsive and aggressive. Along with these changes in his behavior, Mark began to make and keep friends.

Unfortunately, when people see such immediate improvement, they often think medication is all that's needed. But these medicines don't cure the disorder, they only temporarily control the symptoms. Although the drugs help people pay better attention and complete their work, they can't increase knowledge or improve academic skills. The drugs alone can't help people feel better about themselves or cope with problems. These require other kinds of treatment and support.

For lasting improvement, numerous clinicians recommend that medications should be used along with treatments that aid in these other areas. There are no quick cures. Many experts believe that the most significant, long-lasting gains appear when medication is combined with behavioral therapy, emotional counseling, and practical support. Some studies suggest that the combination of medicine and therapy may be more effective than drugs alone. NIMH is conducting a large study to check this.

Can ADHD Be Outgrown or Cured?

Even though most people don't outgrow ADHD, people do learn to adapt and live fulfilling lives. Mark, Lisa, and Henry are making good lives for themselves—not by being cured, but by developing their personal strengths. With effective combinations of medicine, new skills, and emotional support, people with ADHD can develop ways to control their attention and minimize their disruptive behaviors. Like Henry, they may find that by structuring tasks and controlling their environment, they can achieve personal goals. Like Mark, they may learn to channel their excess energy into sports and other high energy activities. And like Lisa, they can identify career options that build on their strengths and abilities.

As they grow up, with appropriate help from parents and clinicians, children with ADHD become better able to suppress their hyperactivity and to channel it into more socially acceptable behaviors, like physical exercise or fidgeting. And although we know that half of all children with ADHD will still show signs of the problem into adulthood, we also know that the medications and therapy that help children also work for adults.

All people with ADHD have natural talents and abilities that they can draw on to create fine lives and careers for themselves. In fact, many people with ADHD even feel that their patterns of behavior give them unique, often unrecognized, advantages. People with ADHD tend to be outgoing and ready for action. Because of their drive for excitement and stimulation, many become successful in business, sports, construction, and public speaking. Because of their ability to think about many things at once, many have won acclaim as artists and inventors. Many choose work that gives them freedom to move around and release excess energy. But some find ways to be effective in quieter, more sedentary careers. Sally, a computer programmer, found that she thinks best when she wears headphones to reduce distracting noises.

Like Henry, some people strive to increase their organizational skills. Others who own their own business find it useful to hire support staff to provide day-to-day management.

Support Groups and Organizations

Attention Deficit Information Network (Ad-IN)

58 Prince Street

Needhan, MA 02492

781-455-9895

Provides up-to-date information on current research, regional meetings. Offers aid in finding solutions to practical problems faced by adults and children with an attention disorder.

ADD Warehouse

300 NW 70th Avenue, Suite 102

Plantation, FL 33317

800-233-9273

Website: www.addwarehouse.com

Distributes books, tapes, videos, assessment on attention deficit hyperactivity disorders. A central location for ordering many of the books listed above. Call for catalog.

Center for Mental Health Services

Office of Consumer, Family, and Public Information

5600 Fishers Lane, Room 15-105

Rockville, MD 20857

301-443-2792

This national center, a component of the U.S. Public Health Service, provides a range of information on mental health, treatment, and support services.

Children and Adults with Attention-Deficit Hyperactivity Disorder (CHADD)

8181 Professional Place, Suite 201

Landover, MD 20785

Toll free: 800-233-4050

Phone: 301-306-7070

Fax: 301-306-7090

Website: http://www.chadd.org/index.cfm

A major advocate and key information source for people dealing with attention disorders. Sponsors support groups; and publishes two newsletters concerning attention disorders for parents and professionals.

Council for Exceptional Children

1110 N. Glebe Road, Suite 300

Arlington, VA 22201-5704

703-620-3660

888-CEC-SPED

Website: www.cec.sped.org

Provides publications for educators. Can also provide referral to ERIC (Educational Resource Information Center) Clearinghouse for Handicapped and Gifted Children.

Federation of Families for Children's Mental Health

1101 King St., Suite 420

Alexandria, VA 22314

Phone: 703-684-7710

Fax: 703-836-1040

E-mail: ffcmh@ffcmh.org

Website: www.ffcmh.org

Provides information, support, and referrals through federation chapters throughout the country. This national parent-run organization focuses on the needs of children with broad mental health problems.

HEATH Resource Center
George Washington University
Heath Resource Center
2121 K Street N.W., Suite 220
Washington, DC 20037
800-544-3284
Website: www.heath.gwu.edu
A national clearinghouse on post-high school education for people with disabilities.

Learning Disabilities Association of America
4156 Library Road
Pittsburgh, PA 15234
412-341-1515
Website: www.ida.natl.org
Provides information and referral to state chapters, parent resources, and local support groups. Publishes news briefs and a professional journal.

National Association of Private Special Education Centers
1522 K Street, NW, Suite 1032
Washington, DC 20005
202-408-3338
Provides referrals to private special-education programs.

National Center for Learning Disabilities
381 Park Avenue South, Suite 1401
New York, NY 10016
212-545-7510
Website: www.ncld.org

Provides referrals and resources. Publishes Their World *magazine describing true stories on ways children and adults cope with LD.*

National Clearinghouse for Alcohol and Drug Information
P.O. Box 2345
Rockville, MD 20847
800-729-6686
Website: www.health.org

Provides information on the risks of alcohol during pregnancy, and fetal alcohol syndrome.

National Information Center for Children and Youth with Disabilities (NICHCY)
P.O. Box 1492
Washington, DC 20013
800-695-0285
Website: www.kidsource.com/NICHCY

Publishes free, fact-filled newsletters. Arranges workshops. Advises parents on the laws entitling children with disabilities to special education and other services.

Sibling Information Network
249 Glenbrook Road
P.O. Box U64
Storrs, CT 06269
860-486-4985

Publishes a newsletter for and about siblings of children with special needs.

Tourette Syndrome Association
42-40 Bell Boulevard
Bayside, NY 11361
718-224-2999
Website: www.tsa-usa.org

State and local chapters provide national information, advocacy, research, and support.

Appendix X

EATING DISORDERS

Reprinted from NIH Publication No. 01-4901
Printed 2001

Eating is controlled by many factors, including appetite; food availability; family, peer, and cultural practices; and attempts at voluntary control. Dieting to a body weight leaner than needed for health is highly promoted by current fashion trends, sales campaigns for special foods, and in some activities and professions. *Eating disorders* involve serious disturbances in eating behavior, such as extreme and unhealthy reduction of food intake or severe overeating, as well as feelings of distress or extreme concern about body shape or weight. Researchers are investigating how and why initially voluntary behaviors, such as eating smaller or larger amounts of food than usual, at some point move beyond control in some people and develop into an eating disorder. Studies on the basic biology of appetite control and its alteration by prolonged overeating or starvation have uncovered enormous complexity, but in the long run have the potential to lead to new pharmacologic treatments for eating disorders.

Eating disorders are not due to a failure of will or behavior; rather, they are real, treatable medical illnesses in which certain maladaptive patterns of eating take on a life of their own. The main types of eating disorders are anorexia nervosa and bulimia nervosa. A third type, binge-eating disorder, has been suggested but has not yet been approved as a formal psychiatric diagnosis. Eating disorders frequently develop during adolescence or early adulthood, but some reports indicate their onset can occur during childhood or later in adulthood.

Eating disorders frequently co-occur with other psychiatric disorders such as depression, substance abuse, and anxiety disorders. In addition, people who suffer from eating disorders can experience a wide range of physical health complications, including serious heart conditions and kidney failure which may lead to death. Recognition of eating disorders as real and treatable diseases, therefore, is critically important.

Females are much more likely than males to develop an eating disorder. Only an estimated 5 to 15 percent of people with anorexia or bulimia and an estimated 35 percent of those with binge-eating disorder are male.

Anorexia Nervosa

An estimated 0.5 to 3.7 percent of females suffer from anorexia nervosa in their lifetime. Symptoms of anorexia nervosa include:

*   Resistance to maintaining body weight at or above a minimally normal weight for age and height
*   Intense fear of gaining weight or becoming fat, even though underweight
*   Disturbance in the way in which one's body weight or shape is experienced, undue influence of body weight or shape on self-evaluation, or denial of the seriousness of the current low body weight
*   Infrequent or absent menstrual periods (in females who have reached puberty)

People with this disorder see themselves as overweight even though they are dangerously thin. The process of eating becomes an obsession. Unusual eating habits develop, such as avoiding food and meals, picking out a few foods and eating these in small quantities, or carefully weighing and portioning food. People with anorexia may repeatedly check their body weight, and many engage in other techniques to control their weight, such as intense and compulsive exercise, or purging by means of vomiting and abuse of laxatives, enemas, and diuretics. Girls with anorexia often experience a delayed onset of their first menstrual period.

The course and outcome of anorexia nervosa vary across individuals: some fully recover after a single episode; some have a fluctuating pattern of weight gain and relapse; and others experience a chronically deteriorating course of illness over many years. The mortality rate among people with anorexia has been estimated at 0.56 percent per year, or approximately 5.6 percent per decade, which is about 12 times higher than the annual death rate due to all causes of death among females ages 15–24 in the general population. The most common causes of death are complications of the disorder, such as cardiac arrest or electrolyte imbalance, and suicide.

Bulimia Nervosa

An estimated 1.1 percent to 4.2 percent of females have bulimia nervosa in their lifetime. Symptoms of bulimia nervosa include:

* Recurrent episodes of binge eating, characterized by eating an excessive amount of food within a discrete period of time and by a sense of lack of control over eating during the episode

* Recurrent inappropriate compensatory behavior in order to prevent weight gain, such as self-induced vomiting or misuse of laxatives, diuretics, enemas, or other medications (purging); fasting; or excessive exercise
* The binge eating and inappropriate compensatory behaviors both occur, on average, at least twice a week for three months
* Self-evaluation is unduly influenced by body shape and weight

Because purging or other compensatory behavior follows the binge-eating episodes, people with bulimia usually weigh within the normal range for their age and height. However, like individuals with anorexia, they may fear gaining weight, desire to lose weight, and feel intensely dissatisfied with their bodies. People with bulimia often perform the behaviors in secrecy, feeling disgusted and ashamed when they binge, yet relieved once they purge.

Binge-Eating Disorder

Community surveys have estimated that between 2 percent and 5 percent of Americans experience binge-eating disorder in a six-month period. Symptoms of binge-eating disorder include:
* Recurrent episodes of binge eating, characterized by eating an excessive amount of food within a discrete period of time and by a sense of lack of control over eating during the episode
* The binge-eating episodes are associated with at least three of the following: eating much more rapidly than normal; eating until feeling uncomfortably full;

eating large amounts of food when not feeling physically hungry; eating alone because of being embarrassed by how much one is eating; feeling disgusted with oneself, depressed, or very guilty after overeating
* Marked distress about the binge-eating behavior
* The binge eating occurs, on average, at least two days a week for six months
* The binge eating is not associated with the regular use of inappropriate compensatory behaviors (e.g., purging, fasting, excessive exercise)

People with binge-eating disorder experience frequent episodes of out-of-control eating, with the same binge-eating symptoms as those with bulimia. The main difference is that individuals with binge-eating disorder do not purge their bodies of excess calories. Therefore, many with the disorder are overweight for their age and height. Feelings of self-disgust and shame associated with this illness can lead to bingeing again, creating a cycle of binge eating.

Treatment Strategies

Eating disorders can be treated and a healthy weight restored. The sooner these disorders are diagnosed and treated, the better the outcomes are likely to be. Because of their complexity, eating disorders require a comprehensive treatment plan involving medical care and monitoring, psychosocial interventions, nutritional counseling and, when appropriate, medication management. At the time of diagnosis, the clinician must determine whether the person is in immediate danger and requires hospitalization.

Treatment of anorexia calls for a specific program that involves three main phases: (1) restoring weight lost to severe dieting and purging; (2) treating psychological disturbances such as distortion of body image, low self-esteem, and interpersonal conflicts; and (3) achieving long-term remission and rehabilitation, or full recovery. Early diagnosis and treatment increases the treatment success rate. Use of psychotropic medication in people with anorexia should be considered *only* after weight gain has been established. Certain selective serotonin reuptake inhibitors (SSRIs) have been shown to be helpful for weight maintenance and for resolving mood and anxiety symptoms associated with anorexia.

The acute management of severe weight loss is usually provided in an inpatient hospital setting, where feeding plans address the person's medical and nutritional needs. In some cases, intravenous feeding is recommended. Once malnutrition has been corrected and weight gain has begun, psychotherapy (often cognitive-behavioral or interpersonal psychotherapy) can help people with anorexia overcome low self-esteem and address distorted thought and behavior patterns. Families are sometimes included in the therapeutic process.

The primary goal of treatment for bulimia is to reduce or eliminate binge eating and purging behavior. To this end, nutritional rehabilitation, psychosocial intervention, and medication management strategies are often employed. Establishment of a pattern of regular, non-binge meals, improvement of attitudes related to the eating disorder, encouragement of healthy but not excessive exercise, and resolution of co-occurring conditions such as mood or anxiety disorders are among the specific aims of these strategies. Individual psychotherapy (especially cognitive-behavioral or interpersonal psychotherapy), group psychotherapy that uses a cognitive-behavioral approach, and family or marital therapy have been reported to be effective. Psychotropic medications, primarily antidepressants such as the selective serotonin reuptake inhibitors (SSRIs), have been found helpful for people with bulimia, particularly those with significant symptoms of depression or anxiety, or those who have not responded adequately to psychosocial treatment alone. These medications also may help prevent relapse. The treatment goals and strategies for binge-eating disorder are similar to those for bulimia, and studies are currently evaluating the effectiveness of various interventions.

People with eating disorders often do not recognize or admit that they are ill. As a result, they may strongly resist getting and staying in treatment. Family members or other trusted individuals can be helpful in ensuring that the person with an eating disorder receives needed care and rehabilitation. For some people, treatment may be long term.

Further Information:

National Institute of Mental Health (NIMH)
Office of Communications and Public Liaison
6001 Executive Blvd.
Room 8184, MSC 9663
Bethesda, MD 20892
Public Inquiries: 301-443-4513
Media Inquiries: 301-443-4536
E-mail: nimhinfo@nih.gov
Website: www.nimh.nih.gov

Harvard Eating Disorders Center
c/o Massachusetts General Hospital
15 Parkman Street
Boston, MA 02114
Phone: 617-236-7766
Website: www.hedc.org

National Association of Anorexia Nervosa and Associated Disorders
P.O. Box 7
Highland Park, IL 60035
Phone: 847-831-3438
Website: www.anad.org

National Eating Disorders Association
603 Stewart Street, Suite 803
Seattle, WA 98101
Phone: 206-382-3587
Website: www.nationaleatingdisorders.org

Appendix XI

ADDICTIVE ILLNESS

Addictive illness involves a set of behaviors that are common among addicted individuals, whether or not they share an addiction to the same substance or behavioral pattern.

The addiction may involve the use of substances such as alcohol and/or drugs. It may involve compulsive use of food, sex, gambling, spending, or work. Many addicts are poly-addicted. In other words, they are addicted to more than one substance or behavior.

Characteristics of Addictive Illness include:
* Tolerance: increased amount of substance/behavior needed to achieve desired effect.
* Withdrawal: painful symptoms of emotional or physical nature when substance/behavior denied.
* Escalation in use of substance/behavior over time.
* Desire but inability to cut down or stop use of behavior or substance.
* Excessive amount of time devoted to obtaining substance/behavior and/or recovering from its effects/use.
* Important relationship activities, job functions or pleasures given up or decreased due to substance use or behavior involvement.
* Pattern continues despite the individual knowing that it is destructive to physical/psychological health.

There is help available through 12 Step recovery programs:

AA: Alcoholics Anonymous
        www.alcoholics-anonymous.org

NA: Narcotics Anonymous
        www.na.org

SLAA: Sex and Love Addictions Anonymous
        www.slaafws.org

OA: Overeaters Anonymous
        www.overeatersanonymous.org

GA: Gamblers Anonymous
        www.gamblersanonymous.org

DA: Debtors Anonymous
        www.debtorsanonymous.org

Additional information is available through:

Al-Anon Family Group Headquarters, Inc.
1600 Corporate Landing Parkway
Virginia Beach, VA 23454-5617
Phone: 757-563-1600; Fax: 757-563-1655
E-mail: WSO@al-anon.org
Website: www.al-anon.alateen.org
Makes referrals to local Al-Anon groups, which are
support groups for spouses and other significant
adults in an alcoholic person's life. Also makes refer-

rals to Alateen groups, which offer support to children of alcoholics. Free informational materials and locations of Al-Anon or Alateen meetings worldwide can be obtained by calling the toll-free number 888-425-2666 from the United States or Canada, Monday through Friday, 8 a.m.–6 p.m. (EST).

Alcoholics Anonymous (AA) World Services, Inc.
475 Riverside Drive, 11th Floor
New York, NY 10115
Phone: 212-870-3400; Fax: 212-870-3003
E-mail: via AA's Website
Website: http://www.aa.org

Makes referrals to local AA groups and provides informational materials on the AA program. Many cities and towns also have a local AA office listed in the telephone book. All communication should be directed to AA's mailing address: AA World Services, Inc., Grand Central Station, P.O. Box 459, New York, NY 10163.

National Council on Alcoholism and Drug Dependence, Inc. (NCADD)
20 Exchange Place, Suite 2902
New York, NY 10005
Phone: 212-269-7797; Fax: 212-269-7510
E-mail: national@ncadd.org
HOPE LINE: 800-NCA-CALL (24-hour Affiliate referral)
Website: http://www.ncadd.org

Offers educational materials and information on alcoholism. Provides phone numbers of local NCADD Affiliates (who can provide information on local treatment resources) via the above toll-free, 24-hour HOPE LINE.

National Institute on Alcohol Abuse and Alcoholism (NIAAA)
Scientific Communications Branch
6000 Executive Boulevard, Willco Building, Suite 409
Bethesda, MD 20892-7003
Phone: 301-443-3860; Fax: 301-480-1726
E-mail: niaaaweb-r@exchange.nih.gov
Website: http://www.niaaa.nih.gov

Makes available free informational materials on all aspects of alcoholism, including the effects of drinking during pregnancy, alcohol use and the elderly, and help for cutting down on drinking.

About the Author

Eve A. Wood, M.D., has devoted nearly two decades to the care of troubled individuals from all walks of life. Her therapeutic approach has attracted attention and acclaim from the nation's leading authorities in the fields of medicine, health, and spiritual well-being. She's the author of numerous articles for medical and professional publications, is a feature columnist for *Massage Therapy* magazine, and is a frequent speaker at national workshops and conferences. Dr. Wood is the host of a weekly call-in radio show, "Healing Your Body, Mind and Spirit," on **HayHouseRadio.com**™ and Sirius Satellite Radio Channel 114 on LIME.

She has served on the faculty of the University of Pennsylvania School of Medicine, the executive committee of The Institute of Pennsylvania Hospital, and is Clinical Associate Professor of Medicine at the University of Arizona Program in Integrative Medicine. Uniting body, mind, and spirit In One™ — in an empowering treatment model—she helps people take charge of their emotional lives. Dr. Wood lives in Tucson with her husband and four children.

For more information, please visit: **www.DrEveWood.com**.

Index

mania, 265–266, 267. *see also*
bipolar disorder; depression
manic-depressive illness. *see also*
depression
causes of, 267, 281
course of, 280–281
description, 265–266, 273
diagnosis of, 277
resources, 283–284
suicidality and, 278–280
symptoms of, 273–278
treatment of, 281–282
Mark's story, 309. *see also* attention
deficit hyperactivity disorder
Mary's story, 189–190
meaning of life. *see also spirit leg* of
the stool; spirituality
description, 13
examples of, 79–80, 190–191
search for, 169–170
spirit leg of the stool and, 20
medication
ADHD and, 319–320
bipolar disorder and, 282
depression and, 21–24, 269
eating disorders and, 332–333
examples of, 47, 71, 116–118,
129–133
panic disorder and, 106–107
meditation, 20
memory
depression and, 266
dissociative identity disorder and,
35–36
exploring internalized messages
via, 147–148
messages, internalized. *See* internalized messages
mind leg of the stool. *see also* three-
legged stool model

application of, 26, 201–202
connection to spirit and body, 16
description, 19–20, 139–140
examples of, 72–77, 149–166
major depression and, 22
Mishna Sanhedrin, 13
mixed bipolar state, 277. *see also*
bipolar disorder
mood problems, 266, 274. *see also*
bipolar disorder; depression
mountain metaphor, 194–197. *see
also* growth
multiple personality disorder,
33–37. *see also* Gillie's story
mysticism, 20

N

Nancy's story, 229–235
narcissistic personality disorder,
108–109

O

obsessions, 94–96, 291. *see also*
obsessive-compulsive disorder
obsessive-compulsive disorder. *see
also* anxiety disorders
Baxter's story, 124–135
description, 127–128, 289–292
OCD. *See* obsessive-compulsive
disorder

P

panic disorder. *see also* anxiety
disorders
description, 285–288
examples of, 91–107, 125–127

Notes

Notes

Notes

Hay House Titles of Related Interest

Books

Deep Healing: *The Essence of Mind / Body Medicine,*
by Emmett E. Miller, M.D.

Doctors Cry, Too: *Essays from the Heart of a Physician,*
by Frank H. Boehm, M.D.

Heal Your Body: *The Mental Causes for Physical Illness and the
Metaphysical Way to Overcome Them,* by Louise L. Hay

Help Me to Heal: *A Practical Guidebook for Patients, Vistiors, and
Caregivers,* by Bernie S. Siegel, M.D., and Yosaif August

The Power of the Mind to Heal: *Renewing Body, Mind, and Spirit,*
by Joan Borysenko, Ph.D., and Miroslav Borysenko, Ph.D.

The Reconnection: *Heal Others, Heal Yourself,* by Dr. Eric Pearl

The Wellness Book, by John Randolph Price

Card Decks

Healing the Mind and Spirit Cards, by Brian L. Weiss, M.D.

Healthy Body Cards, by Louise L. Hay

I Can Do It™ Cards: *Affirmations for Health,* by Louise L. Hay

Women's Bodies, Women's Wisdom Healing Cards,
by Christiane Northrup, M.D.

Wisdom for Healing Cards, by Caroline Myss

All of the above are available at your local bookstore,
or may be ordered by visiting:

Hay House USA: **www.hayhouse.com**®
Hay House Australia: **www.hayhouse.com.au**
Hay House UK: **www.hayhouse.co.uk**
Hay House South Africa: **orders@psdprom.co.za**
Hay House India: **www.hayhouseindia.co.in**

We hope you enjoyed this Hay House book.
If you'd like to receive a free catalog featuring additional
Hay House books and products, or if you'd like information about the
Hay Foundation, please contact:

Hay House, Inc.
P.O. Box 5100
Carlsbad, CA 92018-5100

(760) 431-7695 or **(800) 654-5126**
(760) 431-6948 (fax) or **(800) 650-5115 (fax)**
www.hayhouse.com® • **www.hayfoundation.org**

• • •

Published and distributed in Australia by: Hay House Australia Pty. Ltd.
18/36 Ralph St. • Alexandria NSW 2015 • *Phone:* 612-9669-4299
Fax: 612-9669-4144 • www.hayhouse.com.au

Published and distributed in the United Kingdom by: Hay House UK, Ltd.
• Unit 62, Canalot Studios • 222 Kensal Rd., London W10 5BN
Phone: 44-20-8962-1230 • *Fax:* 44-20-8962-1239 • www.hayhouse.co.uk

Published and distributed in the Republic of South Africa by: Hay House SA
(Pty), Ltd., P.O. Box 990, Witkoppen 2068 • *Phone/Fax:* 27-11-706-6612
orders@psdprom.co.za

Published in India by: Hay House Publications (India) Pvt. Ltd., 3 Hampton
Court, A-Wing, 123 Wodehouse Rd., Colaba, Mumbai 400005 • *Phone:* 91 (22)
22150557 or 22180533 • *Fax:* 91 (22) 22839619 • www.hayhouseindia.co.in

Distributed in India by: Media Star, 7 Vaswani Mansion, 120 Dinshaw Vachha
Rd., Churchgate, Mumbai 400020 • *Phone:* 91 (22) 22815538-39-40
Fax: 91 (22) 22839619 • booksdivision@mediastar.co.in

Distributed in Canada by: Raincoast • 9050 Shaughnessy St., Vancouver, B.C.
V6P 6E5 • *Phone:* (604) 323-7100 • *Fax:* (604) 323-2600 • www.raincoast.com

• • •

Tune in to **HayHouseRadio.com**™ for the best in
inspirational talk radio featuring top Hay House authors!
And, sign up via the Hay House USA Website to receive the Hay House
online newsletter and stay informed about what's going on with your
favorite authors. You'll receive bimonthly announcements about:
Discounts and Offers, Special Events, Product Highlights, Free
Excerpts, Giveaways, and more!
www.hayhouse.com®